COMPETING FOR CONTROL

COMPETING FOR CONTROL
America's Stake in Microelectronics

MICHAEL G. BORRUS

Ballinger Publishing Company • Cambridge, Massachusetts
A Subsidiary of Harper & Row, Publishers, Inc.

International Standard Book Number: 0-88730-306-4

Library of Congress Catalog Card Number: 88-11965

Printed in the United States of America

Library of Congress Cataloging-in-Publication Data

Borrus, Michael G.
    Competing for control: America's stake in microelectronics /
Michael G. Borrus.
    p.   cm.

Includes bibliographies and index.

    ISBN 0-88730-306-4
    1. Microelectronics industry—United States. 2. Microelectronics
industry. 3. Competition, International.   I. Title.
HD9696.A3U528   1988   338.4′76213817′0—dc19   88-11965

To A.S. for your courage, strength and sense of humor

CONTENTS

LIST OF FIGURES

LIST OF TABLES

ACKNOWLEDGMENTS

I owe much to many, but have only the space to acknowledge a few. Many of the ideas and the interpretation set out here were developed directly in collaboration with James Millstein in more conversations and jointly authored papers than can be recounted here. Suffice it to say that my own understanding would have been immeasurably less rich, and the effort much less fun, without our collaboration. To my colleagues at BRIE, Steven Cohen, Laura Tyson, and John Zysman, I owe the depth of thought, nuance, texture, and patience that can only be developed through the easy collegial interaction that they have made such a critical part of BRIE's work life. My ongoing conversations with Alberto SanGiovanni Vincentelli helped to shape my understanding and account of the evolution of chip technology. My thanks go as well to the rest of BRIE's participants, particularly Julie Herendeen and Jay Tharp, who saw me through, in various ways, the often tortured production of this manuscript.

Financial support for this work was provided by several public and nonprofit sources over several years, but largely by the Ford Foundation and by the Carnegie Corporation of New York in conjunction with its Forum on Education and the Economy. Early versions of Chapters 4 and 5 first appeared in Michael Borrus, James Millstein, and John Zysman, "U.S.-Japanese Competition in the Semiconductor Industry: A Study in International Trade and Technological Development," *Policy*

Papers in International Affairs, #17 (Berkeley: Institute of International Studies, 1982); parts of Chapter 6 first surfaced in Michael Borrus, "Responses to the Japanese Challenge in High Technology: Innovation, Maturity and U.S.-Japanese Competition in Microelectronics," *BRIE Working Papers,* #6 (Berkeley: Berkeley Roundtable on the International Economy, July 1983); and an early version of Chapter 8 first appeared in "Reversing Attrition: A Strategic Response to the Erosion of U.S. Leadership in Microelectronics," *BRIE Working Papers,* #13 (Berkeley: BRIE, March 1985).

An enormous number of others in and around the semiconductor industry were instrumental in this book's progress. Regis McKenna has been the source of enormous insight and support. Joe Bower, Warren Davis, Jeff Hart, Daryl Hatano, Dick Heimlich, Jim McGrotty, Bob Noyce, Jim Peterman, George Scalise, Charlie Sporck and Alan Wolff all made extremely useful suggestions about the manuscript and my interpretation at various stages of progress. My thanks, respect, and appreciation go to all of these fine folk and to many others who participated along the way, including the talented people at Ballinger.

Thanks, finally, to Kathy Borrus without whom this book would still lack a title.

INTRODUCTION
Autonomy and Growth at Stake

Over the next decade, the United States faces an adjustment of unusual size and unique significance. At the end of 1987, U.S. foreign indebtedness passed the $400-billion mark, and for the second consecutive year the deficit on current account reached toward the palatial terrain of $140 billion. The United States must bring its debt and deficits back into balance without sacrificing its cherished standard of living. If it fails to do so, America may well become too weak economically to carry its adopted burden of free world political leadership. American capacities to act autonomously in the world will be severely damaged, and prospects for economic growth will surely suffer. As three years of a declining dollar without improvement in the trade figures suggests, the macroadjustment problem cannot be solved by simple fixes. U.S. adjustment must occur at the industry level: U.S.-produced goods must be of low enough cost and high enough quality to sell abroad and displace imports at home.

That sounds easy, but consider the size of the problem. The United States must increase exports or decrease imports not by ten or twenty or even fifty billions of dollars, but by hundreds of billions of dollars. And the sad fact is that very little of the required growth in exports can be accomplished because the foreign markets simply are not there. The enormous levels of Third World debt preclude the countries there from more than marginally increasing their purchases from the United States.

1

The wealthier among the developing countries, Taiwan, Singapore, Hong Kong, and Korea, do not together comprise a market of sufficient size to absorb the needed increase in U.S. exports. Europe already purchases 40 percent of total U.S. exports; given its economic problems, particularly its high unemployment, Europe can be expected to resist massively increasing its purchases of U.S. goods. Japan—the only national market with sufficient wealth and size to buy in the quantities required—simply will not dramatically increase its purchases, principally because the domestic political and economic adjustment required to do so will be actively resisted.

U.S. adjustment must therefore occur on the import side, and there our choices are two: recession or import substitution. To effect the kind of numbers required, any recession must be long, enduring, and bitterly painful. While the most likely scenario, enduring recession is also the ugliest mode of adjustment. If the U.S. economy remains in recession for long, it will drag down the rest of the world economy. The only tolerable adjustment scenario, therefore, is to substitute domestic production for imports. Under whose ownership and control will the required increase in domestic production occur, and does it matter?

This book argues that the success of America's adjustment and the maintenance of autonomy and growth, will depend upon having leading-edge, U.S.-owned and -controlled domestic production capability in a range of crucial industries, and especially in microelectronics. It is for that reason that the loss of U.S. leadership in microelectronics is so distressing.

HIGH NOON FOR AMERICAN MICROELECTRONICS

As a succession of once dominant U.S. industries fell victim to Japanese competition during the 1960s and 1970s, U.S. hopes for continued industrial supremacy lodged more and more in the high-technology industries American risk-taking had pioneered. Nowhere were risk-taking and technological innovation joined to more successful effect than in microelectronics. Silicon chip technology was developed in the United States, and for three decades, successive waves of new semiconductor merchants radically increased the technology's capabilities while decreasing its cost. By the late 1970s, the room-sized, 30-ton, multimillion dollar ENIAC of 1946, the world's first electronic digital computer, had been reduced to a sliver of silicon, a few centimeters square, 200 times more powerful, weighing almost nothing, and costing 30,000 times less.[1]

Chips became the heart of products ranging from computers, telecommunications systems, and industrial robots, to medical instruments, videocassette recorders, even automobiles and dishwashers. More than any other product, microelectronic circuits formed the core of American high technology, though the tiny silicon chips were produced far less in the heartland than at the country's perimeter, in California, Texas, and New York.

The vibrant, venture-capital-backed merchant chip makers were the very embodiment of two very American dreams—the entrepreneurial spirit and the perfectly competitive industry. American semiconductor firms were too fast on their feet, too sure of their technological prowess, too used to intense competition to suffer the fate of their slower, lazier brethren in steel, televisions, and automobiles. Or so it seemed when U.S. firms still controlled over 60 percent of the world market for chips.

Just ten years later U.S. supremacy has waned in both the market for microelectronics and the technology. In 1986 Japanese producers surpassed the merchant U.S. industry to garner a greater share of the world market, roughly 46 percent versus 43 percent.[2] Three U.S. government studies concluded that the nation was falling behind Japan in most of the key process and manufacturing technologies necessary to the production of future generations of semiconductor technology.[3] Indeed, for over five years Japanese producers have been first to market with new memory chips that represent the next advance in miniaturization. Six Japanese firms are likely to hold up to 95 percent of the market for the latest generation of such devices, capable of storing 1 million bits of information on chip, almost a complete reversal of their 5 percent market share for the 4,000 bit memories that were the state of the art little over a decade before.

The stunning deterioration of the U.S. position in microelectronics threatens far more than the loss of just another $11 billion U.S. industry to Japanese competition. Silicon chips are critical intermediate inputs to an ever growing list of products like computers that compose an enormous chunk of the domestic U.S. economy. For electronics-based final product industries, incorporation of the latest chips delivering the best possible performance at the lowest possible cost is key to market competition. With a few exceptions, notably IBM and AT&T, these U.S.

final product makers rely upon the purchase of chips on the open market. As independent U.S. producers of semiconductor chips are beaten in market competition, U.S. final product makers come to rely more and more on Japanese chip producers.

The problem for American manufacturers of final products is that the vertically integrated Japanese chip makers derive their principal business revenues by competing in the very same electronics-based final product markets: Japanese chip producers also are sellers of computer and telecommunications equipment, electronic instruments, robots, industrial process controls, audio and video equipment, to name but a few final products, and are also often directly tied through cross-ownership and investment to other Japanese final product producers of antiskid braking systems, electrical equipment, machine tools, and the like. Simple business strategy dictates that Japanese chip producers will not sell their best chip technology on the open market to the American computer firms against which they compete in computer markets. At stake for the U.S. economy is not simply the $25 billion market for semiconductors, but the current $0.5 trillion market for the final products that incorporate semiconductors, soon to be a $1 trillion market.[4]

But the potential loss of $1 trillion worth of market opportunities is merely the expression of an even more fundamental threat. Over 30 years, the U.S. has massively lost position to Japan in industries that span the U.S. industrial base. These include industries with high labor costs like textile manufacture, standard technology sectors like steel and shipbuilding, and complex manufactured goods like automobiles, consumer electronics, and machine tools. So long as the competitive problems were confined to these sectors, it was possible to argue that U.S. problems were due chiefly to lower labor costs abroad and to the rapid international spread of standard production technologies. Inevitably, the United States would slough off these older industries and move into the sunrise high technologies where the nation's technological lead and superior expertise would guarantee success.[5]

The loss to Japanese competition of high-technology sectors suggests that the old excuses no longer wash. The losses of the past 25 years are too widespread, cover too many industries, form too sharp a pattern. The once isolated instances now sum to a systemwide failure. Bluntly put, no part of the U.S. industrial structure is immune from the competitive challenge Japan represents.

As this book demonstrates, Japanese advantage on world markets has been attained by the concerted efforts of Japanese government and industry, coupled with real failures to respond competitively by U.S.

firms and U.S. policy. In industry after industry, the Japanese challenge has been systemic: Domestic Japanese policies and the structure of domestic Japanese industry have shaped the environment within which Japanese firms developed their competitive strengths and strategies. Together, domestic policies and structure paved the way for the international competitive success of Japanese firms by removing constraints and creating opportunities associated with pursuing and overcoming American technical and market leadership.

In semiconductors, government policy and later market and industry structure closed the domestic market to reserve it as a stable demand base for Japanese producers. Policy orchestrated the import, and later through cooperative R&D programs, the development of generic chip process technology. Policy and industry structure helped to diffuse the technology throughout Japanese industry. Policy and structure also made available a plentiful supply of cheap capital that permitted Japanese firms to invest even during economic downturns. Critically, policy also subsidized the diffusion of final market products like computers, thereby helping to create the initial market demand for the most advanced chips. With the costs of technology development and application shared, and plentiful investment capital available, Japanese firms could concentrate resources on honing manufacturing efficiencies. With the closed and controlled market providing a stable base of demand on which to build volumes and efficient marginal-cost export capacity, Japanese firms entered world markets with substantial advantages.

As a second illustration, consider how and why Japanese producers are using policy and structure to foster domestic supply of the tooling (equipment like photolithographic systems) for semiconductor manufacturing.[6] The technology for semiconductor tooling was diffused to Japanese producers in a cooperative R&D program orchestrated and subsidized by the Japanese government. Subsequent development of equipment by the smaller tooling producers, linked to the larger electronics chip companies and their industrial group, is often financed by an affiliated bank, on the chip company's balance sheet. If development is too risky, government policy subsidizes it through cooperative programs or through partly public institutions like the national telecommunications giant, Nippon Telegraph and Telephone. In either case, policy or structure solves for Japanese firms the problem of limited capital that plagues competing U.S. tooling producers.

The Japanese chip producer's technical resources are shared closely with the tooling producer, and the production engineers responsible for chip manufacture help to define and develop equipment. The chip producer's development and production lines become a laboratory for solving the tooling producer's technical and systems integration problems. Sharing development costs means that the risk to the Japanese tooling producer is reduced compared to American competitors'. The Japanese chip producer and public procurement guarantee an internal market that enables the Japanese tooling producer to attain production experience in the domestic market before entering international competition.

There are several strategic results. First, Japanese chip producers get much earlier access to next-generation tooling, permitting them to be first to market with the latest semiconductor devices, and of course, with the final products like computers that contain them. Second, given the risk-sharing, the resulting Japanese tooling can be priced more competitively on world markets than can competing U.S. tooling. Over time, U.S. tooling producers will be driven out of business. Indeed, recent data suggests that the U.S. semiconductor tooling industry has lost market share to Japan faster than the U.S. chip industry, falling from over 85 percent of the world market in 1978 to 50 percent in 1987.

Third, as U.S. tooling producers exit, U.S. chip producers—including captive producers like IBM and AT&T—are forced to rely on their Japanese competitors' affiliated tooling firms to supply the latest technology. Needless to say, dependence on their Japanese competitors leaves U.S. producers of both chips and the final products that use them extremely vulnerable in international competition. The final result is likely to be that Japanese firms win in the $5 billion world tooling market, the $25 billion world semiconductor market, *and* the $0.5 trillion world market for final electronic products.

As the semiconductor chip and tooling cases suggest, the Japanese challenge rests on a highly orchestrated economic system for promoting domestic economic growth and development.[7] The system also fosters characteristic business tactics like excessive investment in production capacity that leads to dumping, sales of product at prices that non-Japanese competitors find very difficult to match. Almost as a by-product, the system delivers substantial advantages for Japanese firms operating in international markets.

Most often the principal Japanese advantage is clear manufacturing superiority, the ability to deliver high quality at lowest cost. American chip producers have discovered that loss of the manufacturing game eventually deprives them of the know-how and revenues necessary to sustain design and technology superiority. Failing to understand the systemic nature of the competition they faced, American producers went abroad in search of cheap labor rather than attempting to match Japanese innovation in domestic manufacturing. Domestic skills were thereby eroded, leaving U.S. producers helpless once they recognized that Japanese advantage was not the result of cheap labor. The microelectronics story thus demonstrates that, as in other industries, you cannot control over time what you do not continue to produce competitively.[8]

Initial American technology advantages have eroded in the semiconductor competition. Japanese producers now lead in many areas of process R&D, they have eliminated U.S. design advantages, and they can now match U.S. strengths in most products.

Since their own domestic chip market is now the world's largest and fastest growing, Japanese producers' dominance of the world chip market threatens to be more or less assured, *even if U.S. producers were to recapture parity in process R&D and manufacturing.* That will remain true unless the Japanese market can be forced open to U.S. producers while they still have some product and market advantages.

The microelectronics story is thus a perfect case study of how the Japanese system of policy and domestic market structure and the business practices they helped create gives real advantage to Japanese producers in international competition. The results over the past several decades have been thorough routs of once competitive U.S. industries. Most damaging to the U.S. economy, there are no examples of U.S. industries that have recovered dominant world market position once lost to Japanese producers. If the challenge is systemic, so too is the American failure to recover.

Perhaps the most distressing systemic failure in high-technology industries lies in the inability of the American economy to support the growth to sustainable scale of the entrepreneurial firms that successfully commercialized new technology like semiconductors, once they enter international competition against the large, domestically supported Japanese producers. The business tactics that the Japanese economic system fosters and the real competitive advantage it helps to produce combine to deny smaller U.S. firms the capital they need to reinvest and grow to a scale that would permit them to respond to Japanese practice more effectively.

By contrast, a Digital Equipment Corporation (DEC) could grow to sustainable size during the 1970s in part because it only had to worry about domestic U.S. competitors who were operating in the United States under roughly similar systemic constraints: There were few entrenched international competitors operating according to a different set of business constraints. The space that afforded DEC to grow is no longer available for U.S. entrepreneurs in those industries where the Japanese are entrenched. This is a systemic failure within the domestic U.S. economy, which lacks the financial, structural, and policy supports necessary to enable the transition from innovative small firm to sustainable international competitor.

The erosion of U.S. leadership in microelectronics and the larger, systemwide, competitive failures it exposes come at a crucial time for the American economy. U.S. producers have been adjusting to interational competition and to the loss of the unchallenged technological supremacy that fueled postwar growth.[9] Postwar production was premised on a limited vision of the possibilities of production innovation.[10] When they encountered international competition at home or abroad, American firms did not attempt to innovate to remain low-cost producers. Production costs mattered less then, because American products sold on the basis of superior quality and performance.[11]

Eventually, innovation in the technology and organization of production abroad, particularly in Japan, began to deliver high quality and unique performance in products at costs that substantially undercut those of American producers. America's dwindling technological lead could no longer compensate for relative manufacturing weakness. As a result, America's adjustment to increased competition has been severely troubled.[12] Restoring long-term growth at current or increasing standards of living is going to require systemwide changes in American business and policy practices, including a more rapid application of new technologies to the reorganized production of traditional goods and services.[13]

It is for this reason that the United States needs to respond to the Japanese challenge in microelectronics. Losing the microelectronics industry would impair the ability of the U.S. economy to adjust to the dramatic changes occurring in international markets. Chip technology's widespread economic impacts on the users, suppliers, and the broad R&D activities in physics, chemistry, and materials sciences will be important agents of a successful U.S. adjustment. Japanese supply of microelectronics technology is an imperfect and inadequate substitute for a leading-edge domestic U.S. industry.

The microelectronics story of this book, then, matters for two compelling reasons. First, it will be impossible for the U.S. economy to adjust competitively and restore domestic economic growth without a world-class domestic microelectronics industry. Any successful economywide effort will rely on the technical capabilities the application of micro-electronics makes possible and on a secure domestic chip industry making that technology available in timely fashion. Second, and just as critical, the American microelectronics dilemma offers broad lessons for the domestic U.S. economy which, if applied, can help to restore growth and nurture competitiveness overall. The central issues raised by U.S.-Japanese competition in microelectronics, then, are issues at the heart of our modern, democratic nation-state: Autonomy and domestic economic growth.

Competitive and comparative advantage in microelectronics and in the technology's application to production in the economy does not rely upon an immutable resource endowment, static technology, and perfectly competitive markets. Indeed, none of those conditions hold in international competition in microelectronics or in the international race to apply the technology for national economic benefit. Advantage is created by government policy, domestic market strucutres, industrial investment, and business strategies.

Viewed in static terms, Japanese producers simply seem to be better, more competent, more aggressive competitors. Conventional prescription would counsel that America accept the benefits of being outcompeted, shift resources to more economic uses, and absorb the direct losses of high-value-added employment and income which result from losing a formerly competitive industry. But viewed dynamically, over time, three things become clear.

First, it is obvious that Japanese advantage was the product of domestic Japanese choices and American responses. Second, the direct economic losses of a competitively troubled U.S. chip industry are insignificant compared to the potential loss over time of the economywide economic benefits that leadership in microelectronics fosters. Third, therefore, decisions made by U.S. firms and policymakers will largely determine whether or not the United States regains the advantage in microelectronics. (What the U.S. industry can do and what role policy needs to play are the subject of Chapters 8–10.)

The bottom line is this: Restoring U.S. leadership in microelectronics and restoring domestic U.S. economic growth and competitiveness are really matters of choice. American decisions will determine whether or not the U.S. economy continues to earn the resources necessary to sustain our political and military commitments in the world. And if we do not decide, the choices of others will determine the outcomes for us.

NOTES

1. See the description in Allen A. Boriako, "The Chip," *National Geographic,* October 1982, p. 421.
2. Estimates based on data collected by the World Semiconductor Trade Statistics program (hereafter: WSTS). Yen appreciation against the dollar is partly responsible for the relative dollar–denominated market share figures, but the current valuation is probably closer to a true purchasing power parity estimate.
3. These include Defense Science Board to the U.S. Department of Defense (hereafter DSB), "Report of the Defense Science Board Task Force on Defense Semiconductor Dependency," Office of the Under Secretary of Defense for Acquisition, Washington, D.C., February 1987; National Materials Advisory Board to the National Science Foundation (hereafter: NSF), *Advanced Processing of Electronic Materials in the United States and Japan* (Washington, D.C.: National Academy Press, 1986); and "JTECH: Panel Report on Opto- and Microelectronics," Science Applications International Corporation, La Jolla, Calif., May 1985 (hereafter: JTECH).
4. The dollar value estimate comes from DSB, "Report on Defense Semiconductor Dependency," as modified by estimates derived from data provided by the U.S. and Japanese electronics industry associations, and the *Mackintosh Yearbook on European Electronics,* various issues. If anything, the estimate is likely to be conservative.
5. The sunrise/sunset scenario is most cogently put forth by Robert Laurence in *Can America Compete?* (New York: Praeger, 1981).
6. This story is drawn partly from ongoing work on international competition in the semiconductor equipment and materials industries by Jay Stowsky of the Berkeley Roundtable on the International Economy (BRIE) in "The Weakest Link: Semiconductor Production Equipment, Linkages, and the Limits to International Trade," BRIE Working Paper 27, 1987.
7. The developmental system is best described in Chalmers Johnson, *MITI and the Japanese Miracle* (Stanford, Calif.: Stanford University Press, 1985), who does not, however, draw the conclusion about the international competitive impacts of domestic Japanese policies and structures.
8. This is the central insight in Stephen Cohen and John Zysman, *Manufacturing Matters: The Myth of The Post Industrial Economy* (New York: Basic Books, 1987).
9. Edward Denison, *Trends in American Economic Growth 1929–1982* (Washington, D.C.: Brookings Institution, 1985).
10. This is treated best in William Abernathy, *The Productivity Dilemma: Roadblock to Innovation in the Automobile Industry* (Baltimore: Johns Hopkins University Press, 1978).

11. Business theorists and economists will recognize this as a statement of product cycle theory. To operate as a theory accounting for the trade and investment actions of domestic firms, product cycle theory implicitly presumes a constant stream of new product innovations in the domestic economy.

12. Steve Cohen, David Teece, Laura D'Andrea Tyson, and John Zysman, *Competitiveness*. Vol. III, *Global Competition: The New Reality* The Report of the President's Commission on Industrial Competitiveness (Washington, D.C.: U.S. Government Printing Office, 1985).

13. Cohen and Zysman, *Manufacturing Matters;* Charles F. Sabel and Michael J. Piore, *The Second Industrial Divide: Possibilities for Prosperity* (New York: Basic Books, 1984).

I THE CHALLENGE TO U.S. AUTONOMY AND GROWTH

1 AMERICA'S MICROELECTRONICS DILEMMA

U.S. producers of semiconductors face three problems in competition with the Japanese: a market problem, a technology problem, and a structural problem. Having lost dominance of the world market, the U.S. industry is simultaneously being beaten technologically and, though undergoing change, its own structure leaves U.S. firms continuously vulnerable to Japanese competition.

THE MARKET PROBLEM

Since the late 1970s, the world market share of merchant U.S. producers of semiconductor components has been steadily eroded, and finally overtaken, by Japanese competition. The world market share of U.S. firms fell from about 60 percent in 1978 to about 43 percent by the end of 1986, while the market share held by Japanese producers rose from about 24 to 46 percent.[1] Evidently Japanese gains have come at the expense of the U.S. industry.

In 1978 U.S. firms dominated every major category of semiconductor product: simple commodity memory (dynamic and static random access memory, RAM), more complex nonvolatile memory, commodity bipolar logic, linear circuits, microprocessors, microcomputers, and peripherals. By 1986, Japanese firms had established an overwhelming leadership position in state-of-the-art commodity memory (both dynamic and static RAM) and in high-speed logic; parity had been achieved in complex commodity nonvolatile memory and semicustom gate arrays. U.S. dominance of microprocessors, microcomputers, and peripherals was being directly challenged, and a clear U.S. lead extended only to industrial linear circuits, older families of bipolar logic and cell-based semicustom circuits. Even in those categories, Japanese firms had begun to compete impressively.

Despite renewing their focus on the entrepreneurial strategies and strengths in product design, innovation, and market development, U.S. merchant firms have been unable to reverse Japanese gains. Secure in the relatively closed and rapidly growing domestic Japanese market, now the world's largest for microelectronics, backed by state policy and massive structural resources, Japanese firms seized the competitive initiative from their U.S. rivals. (The structural resources include investment capital loaned from affiliated banks at low cost and derived from sales of the final systems products that comprise the bulk of the business of these large, diversified equipment producers.)

Table 1–1 portrays the seemingly unstoppable Japanese drive toward preeminence in semiconductor competition, examining the shuffle of

Table 1–1. Rankings of Ten Leading Merchant Chip Firms ($millions).

Firm	1978	Firm	1986
Texas Instruments	990	NEC[a]	2,638
Motorola	720	Hitachi[a]	2,305
NEC[a]	520	Toshiba[a]	2,261
Philips[b,c]	520	Motorola	2,025
National	500	Texas Instruments	1,820
Fairchild	500	Philips[b,c]	1,356
Hitachi[a]	460	Fujitsu[a]	1,310
Toshiba[a]	400	Matsushita[a]	1,233
Intel	360	Mitsubishi[a]	1,177
Siemens[b]	270	Intel	991

[a]Japanese firm.
[b]European firm.
[c]Philips includes Signetics.

Source: 1986 figures from Dataquest; 1978 Japanese figures from Hambrecht and Quist; other 1978 figures from data supplied by the European Economic Community.

position among the world's 10 leading merchant semiconductor producers between 1978 and 1986.

As the table shows, by 1987 Japanese firms commanded the top three spots and six of the top ten spots. Japanese firms prospered by achieving real manufacturing advantage in production of the highest volume segments of the semiconductor market, in particular, commodity RAM chips. They were able to deliver chips in high volume at the lowest cost with superior quality. In high-volume commodity memory production, Japanese firms typically achieve higher yields of good, working chips out of each wafer processed.[2] Since wafer processing costs are more or less fixed, higher numbers of good chips per wafer result in lower per-chip costs and a cost advantage for the most efficient producers of high-volume products. Although U.S. firms made continuous efforts to improve their manufacturing yields and quality during the decade, with few exceptions they could not catch up to the moving target of continuous improvement in best Japanese practice.[3]

Japanese dominance of the commodity memory market placed severe pressure on U.S. merchant producers for several reasons. RAMs have historically been the highest volume product that can be moved most rapidly into production in successive chip generations. As such, dRAMs of a given generation represent the initial leading edge in process implementation and manufacture; experience gained in their production has heretofore provided U.S. merchant firms with the know-how to fabricate ever more complex devices.[4] In addition, as usually the largest market, RAMs used to generate sufficient margins for U.S. merchant firms to invest to capture the necessary advanced process experience, and to attract capital for R&D and growth.

The Japanese industry was able to shift the terms of competition in the industry largely because, by the early 1980s, it was outspending its U.S. counterpart in capital investment, and reaching parity in R&D spending (Tables 1–2 and 1–3).[5] The leap in Japanese spending suggests that Japanese firms simply spent their way into a leadership position.

Such leaps, even in the face of recessionary downturns in the highly cyclical semiconductor industry, characterized the Japanese push toward leadership in the industry. During each major industry recession over the last decade, Japanese firms have gained market share through capital investment higher than most merchant U.S. firms can afford during a downturn. Their investments in 1974–1976 permitted them to enter the U.S. market in the late 1970s. Their spending in 1980–1983 permitted them to seize leadership in commodity memory.

Table 1–2.   Comparison of U.S. and Japanese Capital Spending for Semiconductor Production Facilities ($millions).

	1981	1982	1983	1984	1985	1986
U.S. merchants	1,330	1,300	1,350	2,340	1,700	1,000
Japanese	830	1,100	1,450	3,500	2,750	1,600

Source: Extrapolated from data from Hambrecht and Quist and Morgan Stanley, *Japan Economic Journal*, and SIA.

The latest burst of Japanese investment is very well timed for Japan's world market position. As Table 1–4 hints, the early U.S. lead in design-intensive chips and associated market development stemmed from the nature of the final systems markets in which the United States then retained a lead: complex, design-intensive chips were precisely what the final U.S. computing, telecommunications, and industrial systems markets demanded from U.S. chip producers. By contrast, Japanese market demand was driven by consumer electronics applications requiring far less sophisticated chips. In addition to high-end consumer products with large memory requirements like digital TV, recent development in Japan of electronics systems products capable of processing *kanji*, the symbols used for written Japanese, has required memory chips with much greater storage capacity. That situation has pushed Japanese chip producers to emphasize and attain leadership in commodity memory development.

During the 1980s, the type of components required by the U.S. and Japanese final systems markets converged. As Table 1–5 shows, the importance to Japanese chip producers of final consumer electronics system applications declined dramatically by 1984. The shift described in

Table 1–3.   Comparison of Semiconductor R&D Spending ($millions).

	1981	1982	1983	1984	1985	1986
U.S. merchants	480	540	675	990	720	700
Japanese	260	320	550	880	750	900

Source: Extrapolated from data from Hambrecht and Quist and Morgan Stanley, *Japan Economic Journal*, and SIA.

Table 1–4. Comparison of U.S. and Japanese Final Product Markets, by Percentage of Domestic Semiconductor Consumption, 1980.

Market	United States	Japan
Consumer	15	55
Computer	39	25
Industrial	18	14
Communictions	17	6
Government	11	—

Source: EEC and BRIE estimates based on European Electronics Components Manufacturers Association (EACEM) and Japanese Electronics Industry Association (EIAJ) data.

Table 1–5 has pushed Japanese producers into the production of complex nonvolatile memory like erasable programmable read-only memory (EPROM), and underlies their emerging capabilities in microprocessor, microcomputer, and peripheral chips.

Japanese market leadership now poses a greater problem for U.S. firms because the domestic Japanese chip market is larger than the U.S. market. Even without the revaluation of the yen, the Japanese market for chips would have surpassed the U.S. market in value by the mid–late 1980s. Indeed, the Japanese and other Asian markets for electronics are growing faster than the North American and European markets, the mainstays of the U.S. chip and electronics industries' world market share. The U.S. electrical connector industry, for example, shipped more product within and to Asia than to North America and Europe in

Table 1–5. Shifts in End Uses of Integrated Circuits, by Percentage of Domestic Japanese IC Shipments.

Product Market	1980	1984
Consumer products	55	40.9
Industrial products	45	59.1
Computers	25	34.4
Telecommunications	6	10.5
Industrial	14	14.2

Source: Electronics Industry Association of Japan.

Figure 1-1. Average Semiconductor Market Share, 1982–1986.

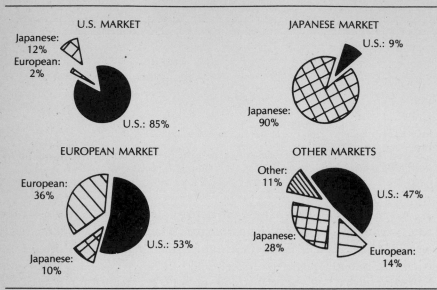

Source: "The Challenge of a Competitive World: Leveraging through Semiconductors," Semiconductor Industry Association, March 1987, p. 3.

1986.[6] Figure 1–1 shows the respective market shares for the U.S., Japanese, and European chip markets.

Japan's emerging strength in the computer, telecommunications, industrial, and automotive electronics markets is driving the growth of consumption of chips and connectors in Japan. Similarly, the rapid growth of other Asian nations' demand is a result of the rise of Asian newly industrializing countries (NICs) like Korea as major producers of consumer electronics, IBM PC "clones," and computer peripherals, as well as of the shift of other advanced countries' electronics production to Asian export platforms.

The growth of Asian chip demand has sparked a surge of new Asian entrants into the already overcrowded field of chip production. These include several Japanese and Korean giants and smaller producers in Taiwan and other industrializing countries. Table 1–6 lists some of these new entrants. Virtually all of the strongest new Asian entrants, and their governments have attempted to replicate aspects of the industrial structure or policies that fostered the Japanese industry's rise to prominence. Although they may not become forces in international market

Table 1–6. Pacific Rim Start-up Companies and Location, by Region.

Company	Location	Date Formed
Canada		
Calmos Systems	Kanata, Ontario	1983
Spectrum Semiconductor	Toronto, Ontario	1985
Korea		
Daewoo	Korea	1980s
Goldstar	Korea	1979
Hyundai	Korea	1980s
Samsung	Korea	1977
Japan		
A&D Company		1977
Kyoto Semiconductor	Japan	1980
Nihon Information Center	Japan	1977
NMBS	Japan	1984
Nihon Semiconductor	Japan	1986
Kawasaki Steel	Japan	1986
Nippon Steel	Japan	1986
Taiwan		
Opto Tech	Taiwan	1983
United Microelectornics	Taiwan	1979
UMC	Taiwan	1984
Mosel	Taiwan	(not available)
Quasel	Taiwan	1985
Other		
Austek Microsystems	Australia	1984
SID Microelectronics	Brazil	1984

Source: © 1986 Dataquest, *IC Start-ups 1987.*

competition for several years, these new entrants will nevertheless change market dynamics.

Without an entrenched position in Asia, the U.S. chip industry will continue to lose world market share to Japanese firms even if it achieves complete technological parity. It is for this reason that opening the domestic Japanese market to U.S. producers is so critical. But the market access problems are becoming intractable because the erosion of U.S. market leadership has also eroded the once unchallenged U.S. technical supremacy.

THE TECHNOLOGY PROBLEM

Once technical expertise is developed, progress in chip development is directly related to resources spent on design, process development, fabrication (including assembly and test), and to the experience accumulated in implementing the advancing technology in actual production. Since feedback from production repetition guides the implementation of the next technical goals, state-of-the-art chip R&D can best be maintained when investment in new production facilities is continuous.

That environment of rapid growth and continuous new investment precisely describes the Japanese chip industry's recent experience. Rapid increases in spending on both R&D and capital investment provided ideal feedback for learning. Each new production facility became a laboratory for implementing the latest developments in process and fabrication. In turn, the know-how gained from successful production helped to refine and guide R&D. It is estimated that some Japanese fabrication equipment is already two to three revisions (3 to 5 years) ahead of the U.S. industry.[7] Similarly, it is not surprising that cumulative spending and production experience have placed the Japanese in a leadership position in process technology.[8]

As Table 1–7 suggests, the central technology problem, then, is that the U.S. industry is, or is in danger of, falling behind the Japanese industry in most of the key process and manufacturing technologies needed for the development of future generations of chip technology. Indeed, whether or not it currently holds a lead in any of the categories, the U.S industry is losing ground almost everywhere. Process and manufacturing inferiority has forced U.S. producers to cede product leadership to Japan in several of the most important chip market segments. Given the strong linkages between process, manufacturing, and product, it appears that the U.S. industry cannot, on the basis of strengths in software and design, successfully hold product leadership in any category if it fails to maintain a leading position in process and manufacturing technology.

U.S. leadership in chip technology is likely to erode further for two reasons. First, the most advanced R&D facilities in Japan are almost without peer in the U.S. chip industry. All of the major Japanese producers, and several of the smaller, new entrants have brought R&D facilities on-line capable of implementing a 64 megabit generation of devices (or three generations beyond the current state of the art).[9]

Second, and directly related, the riskiness of future development has encouraged the Japanese government to initiate a series of cooperative technology development programs without equal in the United States. The aims of these programs are developed in close consultation with the chip producers, directly mirror their priorities for spending, and reflect their judgments about R&D areas where long-term public initiative can leverage long-term private returns.[10] There are at least three cooperative programs—aimed at the development of superspeed chip, opto-electronic chip, and sub-half-micron fabrication technologies. A large number of similar efforts are carried on under the auspices of Japan's publicly controlled telecommunications monopoly, NTT.

The NTT and government projects aim at the development of generic technologies.[11] A generic technology is one with broad application to product and processes. Generic technologies would include work on superlattice and heterostructures, compound materials development and purification, and optical transistors, to name several new technologies.

Cooperation on generic R&D reduces the risks of private firms' technology investment. Through direct and indirect subsidies, the government or NTT covers a substantial portion of the cooperative R&D budgets. Investment in new R&D facilities is given very preferential tax treatment. And experimental laboratory and process equipment is often loaned very cheaply, even free of charge, by the government to the companies for use in their "private" R&D labs.[12] Indeed, the next-generation private R&D labs are as much a creature of government policy as of private expenditure.

Even more critical, however, cooperative generic R&D eliminates the duplication of research characteristic of the fragmented U.S. industry's approach. The elimination of duplication reduces per-firm costs, frees additional private resources, and permits their focus on attaining advantage in products or processes that embody the generic technologies. Thus, the Japanese chip industry's R&D program appears to be more efficient than the U.S. industry's.[13] Tight links between Japan's chip producers and their tooling suppliers also tend to create more efficient R&D spending since the resulting sharing of personnel and R&D efforts tend to reduce transactions costs associated with tooling development and integration into the actual production environment.

Absent some degree of cooperation on both generic R&D and tooling integration, then, it appears that the U.S. industry would have trouble keeping abreast of the Japanese technological effort. This is, of course, the principal argument in favor of the U.S. industry's proposed

Table 1-7. Status and Trends of U.S. Semiconductor Technology Relative to Japan.

	U.S. Lag			Parity with Japan	U.S. Lead		
	Substantial	Clear	Slight		Slight	Clear	Substantial
Silicon products							
dRAM		▼					
sRAM		▼					
EPROM				●			
Microprocessors						▼	
Custom, semicustom logic					▼		
Bipolar		▼					
Nonsilicon products							
Memory			▼				
Logic			▼				
Linear					●		
Optoelectronics	▼						
Heterostructures		▼					
Materials							
Silicon			▼				
Gallium arsenide		▼					

Processing equipment
Lithography
  Optical
  E-beam
  X-ray
Ion implantation technology
Chemical vapor deposition
Deposition, diffusion, other
Energy-assisted processing
Assembly
Packaging
Test
CAE
CAM

▲ U.S. position improving
● U.S. position maintaining
▼ U.S. position declining

Source: U.S. Government, Interagency Working Group on Semiconductor Technology.

cooperative venture to develop next generation semiconductor manufacturing technology, Sematech. In these terms, the U.S industry's troubles are fundamentally a problem of structure, to which we now turn.

THE STRUCTURAL PROBLEM

The foundation for the earlier advances of the U.S. chip industry was its constant development of new applications and markets through improved price and performance. For our analysis, the main components of that structure, developed over nearly 40 years, are

1. The independent, merchant chip producers
2. The electronics systems producers who incorporate the merchants' products
3. The largest systems houses, led by IBM and AT&T, who, though they buy from the merchants, also have substantial, captive chip production and consequently engage in broad-based, sometimes widely shared chip R&D
4. The infrastructure—suppliers of the tooling and materials that go into the semiconductor design and manufacturing processes

The central advantage of the merchant firms over larger scale systems producers has been in continuously advancing component technologies and introducing them into new uses. The stream of component innovations has in turn forced final systems producers to incorporate component innovations into their final products quickly and inventively.

IBM and AT&T have played a special role in the chip industry's dynamism as they strove to preserve their final product advantages through in-house chip R&D and production. Their advances in microelectronic products and processes have diffused to the other segments of the electronics industry in various ways. Antitrust constraints on AT&T–Bell Laboratories originally forced the licensing of chip-related patents. Diffusion has also occurred through technology exchanges, cross-licenses, and investments (such as IBM–Intel), and, more recently, close working arrangements with tooling producers (such as IBM–Perkin-Elmer) in the development of next generation chip production equipment in which much advanced process know-how is embedded.

As demands on the process equipment and materials necessary to continued advance in chip miniaturization became ever more rigorous and expensive to achieve, in the 1970s, independent firms specializing in tooling and materials spun off from the chip and systems producers.[14] By focusing their limited resources on specific parts of the production steps of design, fabrication, assembly, and testing, the tooling and materials suppliers advanced processing technology and diffused it broadly to both the merchants and systems producers.

Fragmentation and specialization have characterized the U.S. industry structure. The development of the specialized segment of tooling and materials suppliers permitted the increasing costs of process development to be spread across the purchases of several merchant producers, thus reducing the cost to any individual merchant. In turn, merchant firms were freed to define new chip product innovations. The independent merchant chip segment had itself spun off from electronics systems manufacturers early in the industry's history. The merchants spread the costs of new chip development among several system company buyers, permitting the systems producers to concentrate their resources on systems development, and, where they continued to produce chips as well, on specialized captive chip production of custom chips.

This pattern continues at an even faster pace. In the integrated circuit (IC) segment alone, there have been at least 150 new entrants (counting both merchant start-ups and captive producers) in the last decade alone, all aimed at least in part at developing new niches and technologies.[15] Further fragmentation is obvious in the proliferation of specialty engineering design houses that do no manufacturing, foundries that only manufacture, process specialists that offer a limited but highly flexible range of design and manufacturing capabilities, semi-custom houses that offer no commodity chip products at all, and vertically integrated captive producers that sell chips on the merchant market. Table 1–8 sketches this evolving structure of the merchant IC industry, including a representative sample of both domestic and foreign producers. Commodity IC producers currently represent the majority of the domestic U.S. merchant industry, accounting in 1986 for at least 75 percent of total U.S. merchant chip production by value.[16] That segment is undergoing an obvious major structural change.

The advantage of commodity chip merchants historically depended upon three distinctive capabilities: circuit design, process implementation, and low-cost, high-volume manufacture. But U.S. producers are losing all three.

Circuit design is now embodied in computer-aided-design (CAD) tools, available on the open market, which are very cheap relative to

Table 1-8. The New Shape of the Merchant IC Industry.

Standard IC Makers	Design Houses	
	Digital	*Linear*
Advanced Micro Devices	Altera	Anadigics
Cherry Semiconductor	Brooktree	Analog Devices
Intel	Dallas Semiconductor	Burr-Brown
Eurosil Electronic	Lattice Semiconductor	Crystal Semiconductor
Exar	Chips & Technologies	Linear Technology
Fairchild Semiconductor	Cirrus Logic	Maxim
General Instrument	Faraday	Micro Linear
Inmos	Integrated Device Technology	Precision Monolithics
International Rectifier	Logic Devices	Silicon Systems
Matra-Harris	MOS Electronics	
Micron Technology	Vitelic	
Monolithic Memories	Weitek	
Motorola Semiconductor	Xilinx	
Products Sector	Zoran	
National Semiconductor		
SGS Microelettronica	*Process Specialists*	
Siliconix		
Sprague	Bipolar Integrated Technology	Orbit Semiconductor
Standard Microsystems	Catalyst Semiconductor	Performance Semiconductor
Texas Instruments	Cypress Semiconductor	Seeq Technology
Western Digital	Exel Microelectronics	Sierra Semiconductor
Zilog	Gazelle Microcircutis	TriQuint

Vertically Integrated Companies

AT&T
Ford Microelectronics
GE/RCA/Intersil
GM/Hughes Electronics
Gould
GTE Microcircuits
Harris
Honeywell
ITT Semiconductor
Mitel
NCR
Philips/Signetics
Plessey
Raytheon
Rockwell International
Siemens
Telefunken Electronic
Thompson Components-Mostek
TRW
All major Japanese and Korean semiconductor producers

GigaBit Logic
Hypres
Inova Microelectronics
International Microelectronic Products
Micro Power Systems
Mosaic Systems

Vitesse Electronics
Xicor

Semicustom Houses

Actel
Applied Microcircuits
California Devices
Ferraqti
Integrated Logic Systems
International Microcircuits
LSI Logic
Mican Associates

Micro Linear
Solid State Scientific
VLSI Technology
Waferscale
Zymos

Note: In this representative listing, a number of companies fit in more than one category. They are placed under the heading of their most important business.

Sources: Clifford Barney, "Winds of Change Sweep the Industry," *Electronics* April 12, 1987, p. xx.
Reprinted from *Electronics*, April 2, 1987 issue. Copyright © 1987, VNU Business Publications, Inc. All rights reserved.

their power to generate custom designs for specific applications, and particularly in permitting systems engineers with different skills to design custom chips. As a result, chip design is migrating toward the system customer. Semiconductor process know-how is increasingly embodied in the tooling and thus is also available to the systems customer and no longer the proprietary source of advantage it once represented. Meanwhile, the U.S. merchants have been surpassed by the Japanese as efficient high-volume manufacturers. In response, current fragmentation represents an attempt to find special areas of expertise—whether in aspects of design, process technology, flexible fabrication, medium-volume production, customer service, or the leveraging of internal demand—which can provide competitive advantage in the market.

There are still great strengths in the U.S. structure. The characteristic fragmentation and specialization have led to stellar advances by permitting smaller producers to bring innovations to market (whether in chips, tooling, or systems) and larger producers to concentrate their resources in their areas of greatest strength. The weaknesses of the fragmented structure—duplication of R&D and lack of sustained investment—were only recently exposed to the light of competition against a differently organized industry. The advantages of greater integration can best be seen in the success of Japanese firms, both technologically and in the market, in seizing the chip industry's leadership position, thereby positioning themselves for success in final systems markets.

Quite apart from Japanese efforts, some of the costs of fragmentation began to appear to U.S. systems producers during the 1970s when the evolution of chips began to permit more of the electronics system design to be embedded directly in silicon chips. For systems producers, it became a strategic and technical necessity to regain some control over chip development and production since essential system performance characteristics were increasingly embedded on the chips rather than in the broader system design alone. As a result, they began their move toward captive chip production.

To be certain, this move was facilitated by the very industry fragmentation that had occasioned its need. The existence of specialized tooling and materials producers meant that suppliers existed to support the backward integration by systems firms into captive chip production. The existence of merchant chip firms meant that systems producers could tailor captive chip production to special internal needs. But some degree of reintegration was nonetheless a necessity for systems firms, where it could be afforded.

By the mid-1970s, then, tentative moves in the direction of consolidation of the electronics industry structure began to occur. Complementary moves include proliferation of technology exchange and licensing agreements, equity investments, joint technology development, and cooperative R&D arrangements. Longer term, closer customer relations between chip, tooling, and systems producers have also begun to occur. These moves suggest that the U.S. industry structure is evolving.

By contrast the Japanese electronics-chip industry is dominated by several vertically integrated, multibillion dollar producers. Each is also a part of a tightly knit industrial group composed of suppliers, other producers of goods incorporating chips, users of the final electronic products, and financiers. Given this structure, it is easy to understand how Japanese firms are devoting at least 50 percent of semiconductor revenues to combined capital and R&D spending in their push for technical and market supremacy.[17]

Such a high rate of investment, especially over the past several years of billion dollar losses, could not be sustained without cross-subsidizing semiconductor investment from revenues generated by other divisions of the large, diversified Japanese firms—in particular, consumer electronics and industrial equipment. The investment would not be as efficient without the ties to affiliated suppliers. It would likely be too risky without stable, guaranteed demand of internal and affiliated consumers. And, such high levels of investment could not be sustained for long without the patience of affiliated financial institutions with a stake in the long-term market position of the Japanese electronics firm.

Needless to say, cross-subsidies, sharing of development risk, guaranteed stable demand, and financial tolerance of heavy expenditures, even losses over time, are all unavailable to most merchant U.S. producers. After all, their primary business is semiconductors, they are tied to suppliers mostly through arms-length market relations, they have few affiliated consumers, and they operate under shorter term U.S. capital market constraints. What the integrated Japanese industry structure permits and encourages, the fragmented U.S. structure discourages.

The industries' respective structures also account for the character of the respective domestic chip markets—Japan's relatively closed to foreign suppliers, the U.S. market relatively open. The integrated Japanese structure permits Japanese producers to close off their market, to use it strategically as a competitive weapon in market competition. The relatively open U.S. market, a result of the fragmented U.S. structure in which systems producers largely buy chips from unaffiliated sellers in open market competition, cannot be used in a corresponding fashion to competitive advantage.

To be sure, the integrated Japanese structure also creates competitive vulnerabilities. These include a tendency toward substantial overbuilding of capacity, slowness in developing new technological approaches and in responding to new or special market needs, and high visibility, hence, susceptibility to trade disputes. Perhaps most critical is the problem of competing in systems markets with the chip affiliate's customers, and in systems and chip markets with the tooling/materials affiliate's customers.

Despite these vulnerabilities, the integrated structure permits Japanese producers to view progress in microelectronics as strategically critical to the long-term success of the companies' other divisions, their affiliated suppliers and customers, and the larger groups as a whole. The Japanese industry can act strategically, in concert with Japanese government policy, to ensure long-term position in microelectronics. By contrast, the fragmented U.S. industry structure undercuts the ability of the U.S. industry to act strategically. This was manifest, for example, in the difficulty of gaining consensus among U.S. tooling, chip, and final electronic systems firms for a commitment to Sematech, even though the merchant U.S. industry's survival was plainly in the best interests of all three industry segments.

In the end, both the U.S. industry's market and technology problems are partly a product of the competitive vulnerability of the fragmented U.S. industry structure. So long as the structure stays fragmented, the market and technology problems are likely to repeat over time even if they are temporarily solved by short-term actions like Sematech or targeted trade and defense policies. The American microelectronics dilemma lies in permitting partial consolidation of the industry's structure to achieve a defensible long-term resolution of the market and technology problems, without sacrificing the advantages in rapid commercialization of new ideas by diverse specialty chip and systems producers.

The market alone will not solve this structural dilemma. This is partly because Japanese competition and the shifts in markets and technology create an enormously high level of adjustment costs and investment requirements that the U.S. industry is not organized to meet on its own. But it is also because the outcomes of international competition in electronics are also the product of government policies. Before turning to the question of state intervention, it is necessary to make clear why state action is necessary. That is the subject of the next chapter.

NOTES

1. These figures are based on data provided by the World Semiconductor
    Trade Statistics Program (hereafter: WSTS), Dataquest, and Integrated
    Circuit Engineering Corporation. They are somewhat misleading
    because captive Japanese production is included in the Japanese industry's
    "merchant" market share. As Chapter 5 describes, some 20–25 percent
    of total Japanese production is consumed internally, a figure that has
    been relatively constant over the last decade. Eliminating Japanese cap-
    tive production from overall figures would improve the merchant U.S.
    share, but market share trends would still remain unchanged. Similarly,
    if captive U.S. production (particularly that of IBM, AT&T, GM-Delco,
    DEC, and Hewlett-Packard) is included in world market share figures,
    the U.S. share improves, but there is no substantive change in overall
    market share trends. The Defense Science Board estimates that, including
    U.S. captive production, the U.S. world market share has fallen over
    the last decade from 67 percent to 50 percent, and the Japanese share
    has risen from under 25 percent to 39 percent.
2. Silicon chip manufacturing involves the batch processing of fixed-
    diameter (currently 4–6 inch) wafers of silicon on which the chips are
    built. Chip dimensions vary, but obviously the smaller the chip, the more
    that can be squeezed into the wafer's fixed area. For a variety of reasons,
    microscopic impurities, for example, many of the chips inscribed on a
    wafer fail to work properly. As a result, manufacturing yield is normally
    measured as the number of "good" chips per processed wafer. Yield is
    thus a function of (1) wafer size and chip size, and (2) manufacturing
    precision, including cleanliness. There are strong learning effects in the
    manufacturing process so that yields typically rise with each iteration
    from under 5 percent for initial runs of new chips to 30–70 percent,
    and occasionally upward of 90 percent in the case of highly automated
    production of mature RAM chips.
3. At the final test phase of chip manufacture, usable chips are typically
    sorted into several holding bins based on the range of performance
    specifications they meet. For example, memory chips that fall outside
    tolerable limits for computer applications—where each data bit must
    be accurate—can be downgraded to consumer electronics applications—
    where a malfunctioning data bit that translates into a missing pixel will
    not be noticed on a TV screen. Japan's broad consumer electronics
    industry thus permits Japanese chip firms to achieve higher yields.
4. At issue is the so-called technology driver (see Chapter 6). While view-
    ing RAM chips as technology drivers is appropriate, there are at least
    two limitations to the argument. First, RAMs drive most aspects of
    metal oxide on silicon (MOS) fabrication process technology used in

the production of other chips but have much less impact on bipolar processing or on the design, assembly, and test technologies used with nonmemory MOS and bipolar chips. Second, other products, like erasable programmable read-only memory (EPROM) and logic products, have driven processing technology forward.

5. There is strong anecdotal and observational evidence (based on field visits to Japanese producers and rough estimates of the value of observed new plant and equipment) that published figures grossly understate actual Japanese capital and R&D spending. It is possible that actual spending is up to 30 percent higher than the figures presented here, according to U.S. industry sources.

6. Based on conversation with Morgan Stanley's electronics industry analyst, John J. Lazlo, Jr.

7. See "Japanese Government and Industry Efforts to Improve Semiconductor Manufacturing Capabilities," MCC Technical Report, ILO-007-86, (Microelectronics and Computer Technology Corporation, 1986), p. 2.24.5.

8. David Teece, "Profiting from Technological Innovation: Implications of Interaction, Collaboration, Licensing and Public Policy," *Research Policy 15,* no. 6 (December 1986): 285–305.

9. Ibid., p. 289 and p. 290.

10. On the development and organization of the government-sponsored programs, see Ronald Dore, "A Case Study of Technology Forecasting in Japan" (London: The Technical Change Center, October, 1983).

11. For a discussion of Japanese cooperative R&D programs in this context of generic technology development, see Ken-ichi Imai, "Japan's Industrial Policy for High Tech Industries," paper given to conference on Japan's Industrial Policy in Comparative Perspective, New York, March 17–19, 1984.

12. Industry sources revealed this point.

13. This point is argued in Defense Science Board to the U.S. Department of Defense, "Report of the Defense Science Board Task Force on Defense Semiconductor Dependency," Office of the Undersecretary of Defense for Acquisition, Washington, D.C., February 1987.

14. See the work of Jay Stowsky, "The Weakest Link: Semiconductor Production Equipment, Linkages, and the Limits to International Trade," BRIE Working Paper 27, 1987.

15. For merchant start-ups see, "IC Start-Ups 1987," Dataquest, 1986. For captives, see *Integrated Circuit Engineering,* yearly "Status" reports for the years 1977–1987.

16. *Integrated Circuit Engineering,* "Status," 1986.

17. Figures from DSB, "Report on Defense Semiconductor Dependency."

2 THE NATIONAL SIGNIFICANCE OF THE ERODING POSITION IN MICROELECTRONICS

Leaving aside questions of national defense, does America's eroding position in microelectroncis really matter?[1] Conventional economic analysis would answer no to this question: The loss of position in one intermediate input industry does not matter to and may in fact help the domestic economy. This chapter argues that the conventional view is wrong. Far more than most industries, microelectronics is the source of economic and technological benefits that spur the economy and provide enormous social gains. The United States cannot fully capture those gains without an advanced domestic industry providing sufficient, timely access to the technology and the know-how to exploit it.

In the conventional view the composition of domestic production does not matter—a semiconductor is just a ball bearing. If foreign suppliers can supply chips more cheaply than American producers, then American consumers and the American economy can only benefit—presuming, of course, that the market for semiconductors is perfectly competitive, that foreign suppliers are willing to supply American chip users with what they need. This view's admonition to government is, "Hand's off." Government intervention to support a failing chip industry would only serve to raise costs to consumers, would lead only to suboptimum resource allocation, would fail to maximize domestic welfare. In the absence of other information, such analysis and prescription might well be correct.

But suppose that semiconductors are more than ball bearings. Suppose that they are a leading industry, one with broad application to the production of goods and services.[2] Suppose that chips are closely linked in positive ways to other economic activities, that they provide dramatic pervasive spillover benefits to the national economy. Indeed, imagine that chips are the leading edge of an industrial transformation that will reshuffle national leadership in trillions of dollars worth of world markets.

Imagine, too, that semiconductors are strategic—that having a leading national production capacity is necessary to capture linkage and spillover gains. Suppose that holding national position in chip production will partly determine whether the U.S. increases or loses its share of the lucrative, linked world markets, whether the domestic standard of living rises or declines. If these suppositions are correct, then the erosion of U.S. leadership in microelectronics matters mightily to the future economic well-being of the United States. Not only would this prescription demand government intervention to support a domestic chip industry, it would justify intervention by reference to free market measures: Appropriate government intervention could help to optimize resource allocation and maximize welfare.

The case for the latter interpretation of the microelectronics industry is compelling. Chips are certainly a leading industry and, given the current organization of the Japanese industry, they are necessarily strategic for the U.S. economy. Let us deal with each claim in turn.

Chips are a leading industry largely because of their widespread economic impacts on users, suppliers, and the broad R&D activities in physics, chemistry, and materials sciences associated with advancing chip technology. These external economies fall into three categories: linkage impacts, technical spillovers, and systemic transformation.[3] Linkage impacts are those that generate increasing positive benefits to economic activities tied to chip production, for example, the production and use of products that incorporate chips.[4] Technical spillovers are pervasive, benefit-creating impacts on science and technology activities more loosely associated with chip development and production, for example R&D in physics or superconduction.[5] Systemic transformation is the synergistic consequence of the impacts associated with linkages and spillovers—the sum that is greater than the parts, an industrial economy based on the processing of information rather than raw materials.

Linkage impacts, sustained economic benefits in linked activities, arise because chip production generates a cycle in which increased investment in R&D and capacity leads to increasing chip performance at decreasing costs. The improved price/performance characteristics in turn deliver improved price/performance in downstream products like computers, and also generate new markets as in antiskid braking systems. The applications generate broad societal returns. As downstream markets expand, substantially increased demand for chips is generated. Increased user demand occasions expanding investment in chip development and production, which leads to another round of improved price/performance. The cycle is repeated. Such has been the history of the microelectronics industry for over three decades.

Thus, in concrete terms, the price of an electronic function has fallen greatly from the 1950s to the mid-1980s. With that change has come expanding markets for chips, from several million dollars in the early 1960s to $25 billion by 1986. The social gains—accidents prevented by antiskid braking systems, or lives and property saved through better weather forecasting permitted by more powerful computers, or resources saved through more efficient digital telecommunications networks—far outweigh the simple private returns associated with chip development and production.

Although somewhat imprecise by contrast to linkage impacts, technical spillovers generally result from the interdependence that characterizes precursor and complementary technological activities.[6] This is most obvious in the relationship between chips and the systems that incorporate them. Increasingly, the chips embody the systems functions and performance characteristics of the products that incorporate them: Advanced chips are systems, and innovation in systems occurs at the level of the chip. This is the cleanest type of technical spillover, but there are other, broader spillovers as well.

Advances in chip technology depend upon and contribute to continued technical exploration in physics, chemistry, and materials sciences. For example, it is no coincidence that recent advances in superconducting materials originated partly at IBM Research and Bell Laboratories, where the search for superfast microelectronic switching devices for computer and telecommunications applications motivated experimentation with superconduction. The gains from superconduction will not be confined to chips but will pervasively influence activities ranging from electricity generation to high-speed transportation.

For the past 30 years, such interdependence of technology development has been the rule rather than the exception with microelectronics. Advances in materials processing and device physics have had pervasive impacts on solar energy research, new materials, optical switching and processing, and medical imaging, to name just a few examples. In turn, advances in these and other fields have spurred technical progress in chips. The spillover interrelationships range across the technical fields related to microelectronics and are economywide. They extend down into the scientific communities in industry, government, and academia, largely responsible for the transfer of technical know-how. They are a critical part of the cumulative advance in knowledge that defines current progress in science and technology. In these terms too, the national economic gains from microelectronics substantially outweigh investment in the technology.

It is probably because the consequences of linkages and spillovers sum to more than the individual impacts, that broad technical advance and economic development tend to concentrate in those countries with a strong position in leading industries like microelectronics.[7] The invention of the transistor in 1947 helped to create the modern computer, telecommunications, instrument, aerospace, and consumer electronics industries. In turn, these industries have generated remarkable changes in work and leisure, society, polity, and economy—changes unimagined and unimaginable 40 years ago.

An industrial economy based on the exchange, processing, and interpretation of information, made possible by the synergy of advances in microelectronics and related fields, is going to look vastly different from the industrial economies we have known. The application of microelectronics-based technologies is already automating both primary commodity and goods production, revamping the spatial location and transforming the activities of service work, resulting in much more rapid technological change. New markets will be created: old ones will die. My point is not to describe the transformation; it is rather to admit the likelihood that spillovers and linkages from the microelectronics industry create the possibility for systemic transformation featuring broad national economic gains.

If semiconductors may, then, properly be considered a leading industry, why are they also strategic? In the simplest terms, semiconductors are strategic because, at this moment, only the most advanced domestic development and production capacity is likely to be sufficient to capture the cumulative national economic gains described. The explanation for this stems from two sources. First, current practices and industry structure in Japan militate against the provision of leading-edge semiconductor technology to U.S. users. Thus, loss of a domestic leading-edge chip capacity risks eliminating the benefits associated with linkage effects.

Second, even if Japanese practice and structure were not an obstacle to U.S. users, access to imported chips probably cannot duplicate the dense technology diffusion interconnections characteristic of technical spillover from a domestic industry. Indeed, since chips are becoming systems, losing the capacity to control the newest advances in their design and production can threaten, quite as fully as can Japanese practice, all of the domestic industries that incorporate them and the scientific activities that spillover to and from them. In short, loss of technological superiority in chips would risk unraveling the dense network of interconnections, particularly the manpower and technical resource infrastructure, responsible for capture of benefits from technical spillovers attributed to microelectronics.

For Japan's industry, as for U.S. final product competitors, international success in computers, telecommunications equipment, electronic instruments, industrial process controls, military systems, and consumer electronics—to name roughly $500 billion worth of markets—depends at least in part upon timely access to and competitive application of semiconductor technology. It is not in the strategic business interests of Japanese producers to make available to U.S. users the chip technology that advantages the Japanese industry's own final products. If the U.S. chip industry loses its edge, Japanese producers will control the development and diffusion of chip technology, apply it first internally, create final products with unique performance advantages, and win in the half-trillion dollar final product markets. Their capture of the systemwide linkage and spillover benefits will directly follow.

The diversity of the U.S. chip industry has been a great strength for the U.S. economy. With no stake in keeping chip technology proprietary, merchant U.S. chip firms developed and diffused the technology widely throughout the U.S. industrial base. This not only spurred spillover technical and scientific activity, but also helped to broaden old industries and create entirely new ones. The industry was the source of semiconductor technology that permitted companies like DEC, Apple Computer, and SUN Microsystems to challenge giants like IBM and the Japanese.

SUN and Apple and DEC have been mightily effective mechanisms for commercializing new market innovation. Without an independent chip industry, the myriad activities that the application of their products has made possible would have been less likely to emerge or would have emerged far more slowly.

Even if such firms could purchase advanced technology from Japanese companies, something would be lost despite the flow of technical information across national boundaries embodied in the sale and purchase of Japanese-made chips.[8] The know-how associated with the technology's development and the ways it can be used or changed is embodied in the network of people who developed and apply it. It is not unusual for users of new chip technology to require knowledge of products in development months or years before such products are available on the market. Indeed, know-how is usually acquired through participation in the related research and scientific communities, and through close working relations with chip producers who can be counted on not to divulge the user's proprietary final product specifications. The current experience of American firms in Japan makes it safe to say that an Apple or Sun can neither participate in the related Japanese technical communities as effectively as their Japanese competitors nor sufficiently protect proprietary product information.

The United States risks much if it loses a substantial portion of its superiority in semiconductors to foreign competition. It risks losing the superiority of the domestic scientific community on which the ability to innovate in chips and related electronics technologies depends. It is unlikely that the international exchange of technical and scientific know-how can substitute for interconnections between business and science that constitute the domestic research base.

Japanese scientific and business communities in electronics are quite closed compared with the United States and Western Europe. This is partly cultural and partly the result of the interlinked industry and market structure. It is also clearly the result of the degree to which Japanese firms view scientific and technical resources as capable of being exploited for competitive advantage. Technological know-how, especially the kind of information that does not flow simply through product market channels, is likely to move much more rapidly within Japan than from Japan to the rest of the world.

A similar problem would remain even were Japanese producers to set up chip design and production facilities in the United States to replace those of independent U.S. merchant firms. As experience with the consumer electronics and automobiles industries suggests they would be tempted to keep their U.S. facilities a generation behind the Japanese state of the art. Economists might answer that such practice by the Japanese would simply invite new U.S. entry in microelectronics, but the costs of reestablishing state-of-the-art domestic U.S. chip capacities that had atrophied would probably daunt most private efforts. Remember that no new consumer electronic entrants emerged to produce videocassette recorders in the United States after the domestic technical infrastructure and know-how had atrophied.

Indeed, in the real world all of the linkage and spillover impacts associated with microelectronics being a leading industry are also potential sources of competitive leverage on world markets for the firms organized to capture them. As a vertically integrated set of producers who are horizontally affiliated into broader industrial groups, Japanese firms are ideally organized to exploit downstream linkages to competitive advantage. To the extent external communities are open but Japanese industry structure and policy make penetration into Japanese scientific and technical communities difficult for outsiders, Japanese firms are also ideally organized to exploit technical spillovers to competitive advantage. To recognize the consequences, simply recall the ability of Japanese producers to exploit their resources and structure to competitive advantage in the development and production of the tooling that goes into the semiconductor manufacturing process.

This analysis suggests that the potential cumulative effects across the spectrum of connected economic activities of an erosion of the U.S. semiconductor industry are substantial. A slowdown relative to Japan is likely in the pace of innovation in electronics and in the application of electronic technologies to production throughout the U.S. economy.

Such a situation invites government intervention to secure a leading-edge domestic chip industry in the United States. Moreover, government policy can be justified on the conventional market terms of optimum resource allocation and welfare gains. As currently organized, the microelectronics industry exhibits all of the characteristics—imperfect competition, increasing returns to scale and dynamic learning economies, the possibility of substantial product differentiation, linkage externalities, and concentration spillovers—that modern economic theory identifies as necessary to justify the possibility that government intervention could optimize resource allocation and maximize welfare.[9] Made coherently and judiciously, government policy will deliver a win-win situation. U.S. advantage in semiconductors could be recreated, and resource allocation and welfare could be maximized. But, as the next chapter makes clear, for government policy to succeed, it must help to create a business environment in which U.S. chip firms can choose to remain competitive at the state of the art.

NOTES

1. Defense Science Board to the U.S. Department of Defense, "Report of the Defense Science Board Task Force on Defense Semiconductor Dependency," Office of the Under Secretary of Defense for Acquisition, Washington, D.C., February 1987, argues that the eroding position in semiconductors matters mightily to the current U.S. national defense posture, premised as it is on securing a qualitative technological lead over the Soviet Union in defense weaponry. It is not the purpose of this book to support or refute the defense argument. Suffice it to say that were modern U.S. weapons systems to incorporate state-of-the-art components, the Task Force would certainly have a strong case. See also Richard van Atta and Harold Bertram, "Defense Dependency upon Foreign Sources of Semiconductors," Arlington, Va.: Institute for Defense Analysis, May 14, 1986.
2. The "leading" and "strategic" industry distinctions in this paragraph are drawn from Richard Nelson, *High Technology Policies: A Five Nation Comparison* (Washington, D.C.: American Institute for Public Policy Research, 1984).
3. The following discussion, particularly of externalities and spillovers, is drawn from Laura Tyson, "Creating Advantage: Strategic Policy for National Competitiveness," BRIE Working Paper 23, 1987. Professor Tyson bears no responsibility for my recasting, recategorization, and interpretation.
4. I have in mind here what economists would call linkage externalities. See the discussion in Elhanan Helpman and Paul R. Krugman, *Market Structure and Foreign Trade: Increasing Returns, Imperfect Competition, and the International Economy* (Cambridge, Mass.: MIT Press, 1985).
5. I have in mind here what economists would call concentration spillovers, as well as the more traditional spillovers associated with the public goods nature of R&D. See the discussion in Laura Tyson, "Creating Advantage."
6. See the discussions in Nelson, *High Technology Policies,* and Nathan Rosenberg, *Technology and the Black Box: Technology and Economics* (New York: Cambridge University Press, 1982).
7. For an incisive historical interpretation along these lines see Taizo Yakushiji, "The Dynamics of Techno-Industrial Emulation," BRIE Working Paper 15, 1985.
8. The following paragraphs draw on the discussion in Michael Borrus, Laura Tyson, and John Zysman, "How Government Policies Shape High Technology Trade," BRIE Working Paper 3, 1984; Chapter 5 in Paul R. Krugman, ed., *Strategic Trade Policy and the New International Economics* (Cambridge, Mass.: MIT Press, 1986).
9. See Tyson, "Creating Advantage," and Krugman, *Market Structure and Foreign Trade.*

3 STRUCTURE AND POLICY AS CONSTRAINTS: THE ANALYTIC APPROACH

What accounts for the loss of U.S. leadership in microelectronics? How did an industry conceived and dominated by the United States end up in danger of playing second fiddle in a Japanese orchestra? From one perspective the answer is easy. American firms were outinvested, outinnovated in manufacturing, outmanuevered (and underpriced) in world markets, outsmarted in adhering to old strategies when the rules of the game had been changed. But these explanations are really second-order effects. Each of them—the ability to invest heavily, the ability to innovate in manufacturing, the ability to underprice on world markets, and the abilities to change the rules of the game and to think more strategically—were choices that were available to Japanese firms because those firms were facing systematically different constraints and opportunities than their American competitors. The different patterns of constraint and opportunity can be traced to a set of common variables in domestic government policy and domestic industry structure.[1]

Different domestic policies and industry structures alter the pattern of constraints and opportunities facing firms as they choose strategies. Different strategies change the dynamics of competition when firms interact in international markets and shape the outcomes of the interaction. Who wins and who loses in market competition can be fundamentally altered as a consequence.

Consider, for example, just a few of the ways that government policy shaped the business environment within which Japanese electronics firms operated. Policies that made capital abundant and cheap for investment in electronics production created opportunities for Japanese firms in the continual improvement of facilities through new investment. Technology development and diffusion policies cut costs and risks associated with new market development and lifted the massive constraints that faced Japanese producers in attempts to catch up with U.S. R&D. Closed market policies created business opportunities for Japanese producers despite relative technological backwardness, by ensuring domestic launch markets and the eventual attainment of international scale.

The vertical integration and multidivisionality of Japan's domestic industry structure created the opportunity for Japanese firms to regard chip technology as a key element of a larger strategy built around electronic systems products. The structure thereby lifted for them the funding and profitability constraints that plagued U.S. firms. The horizontal family affiliations to both customers and financiers lifted the constraint of instability in financial supply and product demand, enabling Japanese producers to expand capacity even during market downturns. Once the consumer electronics industry was added to Japan's domestic structure, it provided the experience in high-volume production that permitted Japanese firms to forge a lead in manufacturing systems integration.

Structural and policy attributes permitted Japanese firms to engage in tactics that disrupted the way U.S. merchant firms did business. The pricing and dumping tactics that resulted from high investment in chip capacity could be carried on with a minimum of harm to the Japanese industry. Lacking policy and structural supports, U.S. producers could not respond successfully. Japanese strategies shifted the terms of competition in microelectronics, and with the shift came market dominance.

THE APPROACH IN CONTEXT

The use of domestic structure and policy as explanatory variables shaping the strategy choices facing firms, and through them altering the outcomes of international competition, differentiates this analysis from other work in the field of international industrial competition and the performance of national industries. Comparable work tends to fall within three related traditions of discourse within the academic bounds of disciplines normally relegated to the literature of business schools, political science, and economics.[2] The three traditions are: (1) the analysis of firm strategy and behavior (accomplished largely within the business schools)[3]; (2) the analysis of the competitive performance of national economic sectors through elucidation of either factor endowments and product cycles, or state policies, institutions, and the interaction of domestic interests[4]; and (3) the analysis of how the international system affects national performance.[5]

The firm-level approach is useful for describing the panoply of tactics firms may adopt to differentiate themselves in market competition. Indeed, most of this literature (Porter is highly representative) presents a matrix of variables ranging from the management of production systems to marketing strategy to account for relatively successful firm performance in the market.

While this approach provides guidance in accounting for why similarly positioned firms succeed or fail in the market, it cannot account for the relative performance of national industries nor for characteristic national strategies in international competition. It cannot explain why some of the business strategies and tactics presented work for some national industries and firms but fail for others; Abegglan and Stalk are representative when they presume, without examination, that American firms can simply adopt the tactics of Japanese companies.

By contrast, the international system's approach views international interaction as subject to systemic parameters, and is thus particularly useful for defining the channels of possible actions of national and industry actors. By defining permissible behavioral pathways (the work of Keohane and the game theorists is indicative) this approach can account for the range of possible outcomes of international interactions. The literature is also useful for elucidating the consequences of a failure to adhere to the system's defined parameters; Kindleberger's work on the Great Depression is exemplary in this regard.

The international approach is relatively silent, however, in differentiating the relative performance of similarly situated actors, of accounting for why some nations and firms, subject to the same international systemic parameters, win and others lose in competition. The approach fails to elucidate the variations in tactics and characteristic strategies open to the system's actors within the broad systemic constraints.

Analysis at the national level explains strategies and outcomes with domestic variables like factor and technology endowments, domestic policy and institutions, and the interaction of domestic interests. This approach attempts to account for relative national industrial performance and outcomes. More often than not, the focus is on a principal domestic explanatory variable—for example, factor endowments (as in Hecksher-Ohlin), policy as conducted by an independent policymaking bureaucracy (as in Chalmers Johnson's work), or domestic interests as implemented in the process of government (as in the interest group pluralism versus corporatist work).

The approach of this book is to focus jointly on domestic policy and industry structure as variables that interact to shape the environment within which firm level choices are made, opening up some opportunities while foreclosing others. This approach builds on the national level analysis by wedding it to implications in the firm-level analysis, particularly Alfred Chandler's two great works, *Strategy and Structure* and *The Visible Hand*. Chandler showed that corporate structures evolved in response to strategic dilemmas facing businesses that existing corporate structures could not solve. By implication, the evolved corporate structure created a new set of opportunities and lifted constraints that the old structure had placed on the firm. By extrapolating this insight to the level of the industry, we can examine the ways that different industry structures create different sets of opportunities and risks for firms situated in different national economies.

This approach permits us to examine the consequences of a different pattern of constraint and opportunity facing Japanese firms than faced America's large corporations in international competition during this century. The U.S. structure can be characterized as oligopolistically organized industries, multidivisional firms with vertically integrated production in each division, integrated financial and industrial capital across the enterprise as a whole, companywide and systematic research and development, all managed through a hierarchical bureaucracy. A systemic pattern of constraint and opportunity can be derived from this structure: The bureaucracy provides central guidance. R&D is harnessed in the service of competitive product advantage. Integrated capital within the enterprise permits resources to be utilized to maximize returns among divisions. Vertical integration provides scale economies and, along with multidivisionality, control over instability in upstream and downstream markets. Oligopolistic organization provides both advantages of scale and market control. The result, as a competitive organizational model, is substantial competitive advantage over differently structured industries.

By contrast, the Japanese economy provides a new set of competitive structural characteristics partly accounting for the success of Japanese firms. We find oligopolistic competition rather than simple oligopoly, loose vertical integration and multidivisionality with strong horizontal linkages to industrial groups of affiliated suppliers and customers, strong integration of financial and industrial capital across the industrial group rather than the enterprise, systematic R&D and engineering in process as well as product, and stripped managerial hierarchy with managerial functions—not power—devolved downward through the hierarchy.

The stripped managerial hierarchy removes overhead cost, places responsibility for decisionmaking closer to the point of implementation and thus encourages managerial responsiveness and problem solving. Systematic process R&D permits production reorganization itself to be exploited continuously to competitive advantage. Groupwide integration of capital encourages longer time horizons and more strategic use of available resources among a wider choice of uses. Looser integration with strong horizontal links alters the older model's emphasis on strict profit maximization in each division since costs can be shunted to independent affiliates and profits taken within the enterprise. The horizontal links provide broader market stability and the possibility for insulated economies of scale. They also encourage a focus on strong strategic interconnections among the group's companies. Oligopolistic competition ensures the traditional benefits of competitive markets while eliminating the anticompetitive market-sharing incentives inherent in oligopoly. The overall result is a set of industry strategies framed against the possibilities created by the structure, which have strong advantages in international competition against firms facing different constraints.

A different set of domestic policies is necessary for the new structure to be sustained and for the strategies it permits to be effected successfully in international competition. Here we draw on the literature suggesting that policy matters to sectoral economic performance. Most of that literature is lodged within the comparative political science field. With respect to Japan, the works of Chalmers Johnson and Ezra Vogel are seminal. Both implicitly adopt a Gershenkron (state-as-late-developer) approach in which a strong government bureaucracy, the legacy of central state guidance necessary for forced industrialization, continues to guide industrial planning and shape market outcomes.

This book's analysis views the Japanese government as a mediator of elite disputes—that is what the state's consensus-formation function amounts to in national perspective—and as an industrial institution with its own resources shaping strategies and affecting outcomes.[6] Indeed, the government's very role as mediator is what gives it the autonomy to act independently of any set of domestic elites. The tools and resources at its disposal broadly constrain the impacts state policy can have.

Government policy need not be the subject of extreme rationality it is portrayed to be in the industrial policy or industrial targetting literature. Once set into motion, policy defines parameters of the industrial competition it shapes. Once those parameters are recognized, the players in that competition can act in undetermined ways to gain advantage—even, as so many have remarked with respect to the Japanese automotive industry's refusal to consolidate under government direction, by acting against specific parts of the thrust of policy rather than bowing to all of it. (That is, while consolidation was resisted, capital, technology and closed market policies were critical to Japanese automotive success.)

Indeed, our approach suggests that where policy and domestic structure have complementary effects in lifting constraints and framing opportunities, they lead to remarkably powerful strategies in international competition. In Japan's case, government policies were never sufficient by themselves to eliminate constraints on Japanese microelectronics competitiveness, although they did guarantee that the Japanese industry would not be eliminated in its own market. It was only after comparative market structure was altered in a complementary fashion that new opportunities for Japanese success in microelectronics emerged and could be taken advantage of. Particularly key was the capture of the consumer electronics industry as a base of demand permitting domestic production to serve as a launch market, permitting experience with high-volume manufacturing to be accrued.

Policy and structure reinforced each other in similar fashion for the merchant U.S. industry during the 1950s and 1960s. Then, government defense and antitrust policies subsidized technology development and diffusion, and provided initial, premium-price launch markets for smaller producers. The resulting merchant structure was competitively superior to the vertically integrated one it replaced but eventually was vulnerable in the 1970s to Japanese strategies premised on a quite different set of constraints. Then, existing structure and policies so constrained the choices of U.S. firms that it took almost a decade to respond in ways that are still relatively ineffective.

A final caveat is appropriate here. Although domestic policy and industry structures indirectly affect the outcomes of international competition by altering constraints facing firms in ways that enable some kinds of strategies while foreclosing others, one-way causality should not be presumed. Structure and policy evolve in response to changes in strategy and outcomes. In that sense they are less independent variables in a formal analytic then systemic constraints tending to channel strategies and outcomes in particular directions but without determining them. A social science analytic must be open at least this much, since the outcomes of economics and politics are the product of flexible interactions and are therefore contingent on what other actors do—outcomes, like strategies, are not natural phenomena subject to discoverable laws of behavior.[7]

NOTES

1. Domestic industry structure is the way in which suppliers, producers, and customers, and the relationships between them, are organized within a domestic industry. Thus, as described earlier, in microelectronics, the U.S. industry structure is composed of two tiers of producers, merchants, and captives, with arms-length market relationships to many diffuse small suppliers and, in the case of the merchants, with similar arms-length relations to more concentrated buyers—lodged largely in computing, telecom, industrial, and defense markets—and direct vertical integration ties to a single parent in the case of the captives. In Japan, the structure is composed of large quasi-vertically integrated producers with partial ownership ties to suppliers and part-ownership, part-market, part-family-group ties to buyers that include a large consumer electronics industry.

2. On the concept of traditions of discourse, see Sheldon S. Wolin, *Politics and Vision; Continuity and Innovation in Western Political Thought* (Boston: Little, Brown, 1960).

3. Representative studies include the work of Alfred Chandler, *Strategy and Structure: Chapters in the History of Industrial Enterprise* (Cambridge, Mass.: MIT Press, 1962); *The Visible Hand: The Managerial Revolution in American Business* (Cambridge, Mass.: Belknap Press, 1977); Michael Porter, *Competitive Strategy: Techniques for Analyzing Industries and Competitors* (New York: Free Press, 1980); Robert Reich and Ira Magaziner, *Minding America's Business: The Decline and Rise of the American Economy* (New York: Harcourt Brace Jovanovich: Law and Business, 1982); James C. Abegglen and George Stalk, Jr., *Kaisha: The*

Japanese Corporation (New York: Basic Books, 1985); Steven Wheelwright and Robert M. Hayes, *Restoring Our Competitive Edge: Competing through Manufacturing* (New York: Wiley, 1984); William J. Abernathy, Kim B. Clark and Alan M. Kantrow, *Industrial Renaissance: Producing a Competitive Future for America* (New York: Basic Books, 1983).

4. Representative work in the economics literature includes, on factor endowments, Hecksher-Ohlin and modern variants including those who admit the impact of imperfect markets like Krugman and Helpman, *Market Structure and Foreign Trade;* and on product cycle theory, Ray Vernon and Louis Wells, Jr., *The Economic Environment of International Business* (Englewood Cliffs, N.J.: Prentice-Hall 1986).

Representative work within political science includes that of the corporatists and interest group pluralists. See Phillipe Schmitter and Gerhard Lehmbruch, *Patterns of Corporatist Policy-Making* (London: Sage Publications, 1982); Peter A. Gourevitch, *Politics in Hard Times: Comparative Responses to International Economic Crises* (Ithaca, N.Y.: Cornell University Press, 1986); John Zysman, *Political Strategies for Industrial Order: State, Market, and Industry in France* (Berkeley: University of California Press, 1977); John Zysman and Laura Tyson, eds., *American Industry in International Competition: Government Policies and Corporate Strategies* (Ithaca, N.Y.: Cornell University Press, 1983); Daniel I. Okimoto et al. *Competitive Edge: the Semiconductor Industry in the U.S. and Japan* (Stanford, Calif.: Stanford University Press, 1984); Alan Altschuler et al., *The Future of the Automobile: The Report of MIT's International Automobile Program* (Cambridge, Mass.: MIT Press, 1984); Peter J. Katzenstein, *Corporatism and Change: Austria, Switzerland, and the Politics of Industry* (Ithaca, N.Y.: Cornell University Press, 1984); Chalmers Johnson, *MITI and the Japanese Miracle* (Stanford, Calif.: Stanford University Press, 1982); Andrew Shonfield, *Modern Capitalism: the Changing Balance of Public and Private Power* (London: Oxford University Press, 1969).

5. On the international dimension, see Robert O. Keohane and Joseph S. Nye, *Power and Interdependence: World Politics in Transition* (Boston: Little, Brown, 1977); Stephen D. Krasner, *Structural Conflict: the Third World against Global Liberalism* (Berkeley: University of California Press, 1973); Charles P. Kindleberger, *World in Depression, 1929–1939* (Berkeley: University of California Press, 1973); Alexander Gershenkron, *Economic Backwardness in Historical Perspective, a Book of Essays* (Cambridge, Mass.: Belknap Press, 1962); Immanuel Wallerstein, *The Modern World-System* (New York: Academic Press 1974).

6. In essence, this weds the view in Chalmers Johnson's *MITI* of an activist state bureaucracy, with Richard Samuel's view of the state as a creator

of bargains among competing interests, in *The Business of the Japanese State: Energy Markets in Comparative and Historical Perspective* (Ithaca, N.Y.: Cornell University Press, 1987).

7. This is manifest in the work of Roberto Unger, *Knowledge and Politics* (New York: Free Press, 1975).

II HISTORICAL DEVELOPMENT AND COMPETITIVE INTERACTION

4 THE AMERICAN ASCENT[1]

From the invention of the transistor at Bell Laboratories in 1948 and of the integrated circuit at Texas Instruments and Fairchild in 1958, through the late 1970s, the U.S. chip industry enjoyed a position of unchallenged technological preeminence and international market dominance. Innovation in circuit design and production processes kept U.S. firms the leaders of the world market. As late as 1980, U.S. firms still accounted for well over 60 percent of the world's production of integrated circuits, the most advanced semiconductors.

In the earliest period of U.S. microelectronics, U.S. policy fostered the industry's development. Policy helped to ensure availability of technological know-how and personnel via Bell Labs. Military R&D programs, emphasizing miniaturization, high performance, and reliability, set the direction for early product design, and military and space agency procurement provided a lucrative launch market for circuits. The existence of strong government demand contributed to the entry of new firms and accelerated the pace of diffusion of the new technology into nonmilitary markets.

While early defense and space demand for the integrated circuit was the most direct stimulus to industrial growth, other structural factors unique to the U.S. domestic market shaped the impact of early government support. Ready availability of venture capital, high mobility of technical personnel between firms, liberal licensing of transistor and

IC technology by the U.S. firms that had pioneered their development, as well as antitrust constraints on potential AT&T and IBM entry into the open market for microelectronics, all contributed to the creation of a domestic environment in which new entry and competition were fostered by the initial demands of the defense and space programs.

The second stage of the industry's development rested upon the U.S. microelectronics industry's synergistic relationship to the domestic computer industry. Advanced IC design moved from the implementation of basic logic circuits to entire computer subsystems on a single chip of silicon. In turn, the growth of the mainframe and minicomputer markets was both fueled by and contributed to the rapid expansion of domestic digital IC production. Demand from the computer and industrial markets spawned a new wave of merchant entrants into the production of ICs. Between 1966 and 1972, over 30 new IC firms entered the domestic market.

The third stage of the industry's development saw changed market dynamics occasioned by the shift from bipolar to metal oxide on silicon (MOS) technology, the emergence of large-scale IC designs, and the appearance of the microprocessor. Large-scale integration involved a change in the character of the product produced by IC firms; as device geometries were reduced and packing densities increased, components began to incorporate basic features of what were previously regarded as entire electronic "systems." The most salient example of this was the introduction by Intel of the microprocessor in 1971.

This stage saw a wave of new merchant entries and a vast broadening of the final systems markets served by the IC producer. Large-scale integration brought with it new markets in semiconductor memories, in consumer products, in telecommunications, and most important, in the wide variety of applications markets for the microprocessor and microcomputer. In turn, the strategies of firms changed as the markets for the more complex large-scale integration (LSI) ICs became more segmented, and as the microprocessor, the third generation of computation equipment, offered new market development opportunities and challenges. In this period, too, the industry's characteristic specialization and fragmentation fully blossomed, while moves toward reconsolidation, especially integration forward by merchant firms and backward by system producers, began to accelerate.

As the industry moved through large-scale integration, the nature of the products it produced has changed and so did its status as a components industry. In the early years, semiconductors were simply replacements for vacuum tubes. They performed the same functions more effectively but they did not fundamentally change the products into which they were incorporated. In the second stage of the industry's development, advances in semiconductor technology made possible the substitution of electronic circuits for many types of electrical mechanical functions. In the third phase of the industry's development, the advent of the microprocessor opened up new market opportunities beyond those substitution uses for which semiconductor technologies had proven cost-effective and performance-enhancing. In essence, the microprocessor and the growing range of complex large-scale integrated circuits opened the development phase of the industry.

To focus simply on the demand-pull effects of the military and newer computer markets on innovation and sales growth in the U.S. industry is to lose sight of the dynamics of competition among chip manufacturers, and particularly among the merchant firms that set the pace of technological advance. Product and process innovation and competitive interaction among the merchant firms fostered a progressive reduction in the cost and enhancement of the performance of an electronic function. As competition on cost and performance drove the price of an electronic function downward, demand for integrated circuits became greater and greater; by achieving commodity positions as market demand for the latest in IC device technology expanded, the merchants earned a sufficient return on their risk-taking to help finance the next round of product innovation and market development. Thus, competitive rivalry between the merchant firms themselves, as well as between the merchants and the more established vertically integrated electronic systems companies such as RCA, Westinghouse, and General Electric, accelerated the pace of both innovation in and diffusion of IC technology. As an independent, low-cost source of advanced IC technology, this unique merchant segment had the dynamic effect of introducing new competitive risks into the environments of established component and systems producers. By lowering technological barriers to entry in systems markets and creating the potential of new cost and product performance competition in those markets, the merchants altered the technological and competitive environment of even such dominant electronic systems manufacturers as IBM and Western Electric, creating greater uncertainty and greater competitive rivalry in the market for electronic systems. The presence of the merchants had the dynamic effect of enhancing the pace of IC innovation and diffusion across the domestic economy as a whole.

BELL LABS, MILITARY MARKETS, AND
MERCHANT PRODUCERS, 1948–1963

In the history of U.S. technology, no institution has played as important a role as the Bell Telephone Laboratories. The United States' preeminence in high-technology industries like semiconductors, lasers, and computers has been built, in large measure, on the base of research and personnel coming out of Bell Laboratories.

Government policy on competition and government funds helped shape the impact that Bell Laboratories had on technological and industrial development. During World War II, Bell Labs undertook approximately 2,000 research and development projects for the army, the navy, and the National Defense Research Council.[2] With the funding the Labs' pioneered radar and electronic communications systems. In the 10-year period 1949–1959, the U.S. government funded approximately $609 million (48 percent) of research at Western Electric and Bell Labs. Antitrust policy during the postwar period directly shaped the commercialization of the technologies developed at Bell Labs.[3] The Department of Justice initiated an antitrust suit against AT&T in 1949 which, during the period 1949–1956, "influenced the company's policy of swiftly disseminating its new technology."[4] By terms of the 1956 consent decree,[5] ending the Justice Department suit, Western Electric was required to license all existing Western Electric patents to domestic firms royalty free, and to provide licenses under future patents at reasonable rates. AT&T was permitted to retain its vertically integrated structure but was prohibited from entering into any product markets other than basic common carrier communications and defense and aerospace. The decree thereby restrained AT&T from leveraging its monopoly position in telecommunications into a dominant position in related commercial markets and from monopolizing, over the life of its patents, the commercial potential of the research and development work of Bell Labs. In short, Bell Labs was transformed into a national industrial research facility. This was a policy consciously duplicated, as we shall see, in Japan with respect to research at NTT's laboratories.

In the development of the U.S. semiconductor industry, the role of research and development at Bell Labs was crucial. It developed the original transistor in 1947 and gave rise to a series of process and product innovations of major importance in the commercialization process during the 1950s and early 1960s. During the incubation period between the invention of the transistor in 1947 and the development of the integrated circuit in 1959, Bell Labs received over 339 patents in the semiconductor field, or more than 25 percent of all semiconductor patents issued in the United States during the period.[6]

Between 1946 and 1964, Bell Laboratories' expenditures for semiconductor research and development rose from less than $1 million to almost $22 million annually. In 1959 Bell Labs accounted for about 30 percent of all privately funded semiconductor R&D in the United States.[7]

Perhaps of equal importance in Bell Labs' ability to sustain its leadership in the development of semiconductor technology were its links to Western Electric, the manufacturing arm of AT&T. Product performance objectives and feedback from Western Electric helped to focus and keep basic research at the Labs oriented to the product and process engineering problems attending commercial development and production. Indeed, during the 1950s, Bell Labs most important innovations were process innovations that greatly improved the manufacturability and thereby dramatically reduced the production costs of semiconductor devices. (See Table 4–1.)

Bell Labs' rapid dissemination of research results helped develop the semiconductor industry in the United States. The policy of dissemination was a product of the corporate culture of public service that AT&T as a regulated monopoly strove to cultivate. At the same time, with the Justice Department's 1949 antitrust complaint hanging on the horizon, the company could not afford even the appearance of monopoly. Thus, the consent decree formalized in 1956 a liberal license policy established in 1952 with regard to semiconductors. In the development of semiconductor technology, antitrust policy had the impact of widely diffusing Bell's basic technology, thereby diversifying the domestic research base and creating competitive pressures and market incentives for the technology's further refinement, development, and application.

As Western Electric moved the germanium transistor into initial commercial production, Bell Labs conducted the first of a number of symposia it would offer during the 1950s on its more important semiconductor developments. The first, held in early 1951, was strictly for military and government officials. (The Department of Defense, soon after the invention of the transistor in 1947, initiated a joint research program with the Labs to explore possible military applications of the transistor.)[8] The second, attended by representatives from government agencies, universities, and more than 80 industrial firms, was held later in the same year. It described transistor properties and applications but little of the physics and technology involved. The latter were covered

Table 4–1.   Bell Labs: Major Semiconductor Innovations.

Innovation	Date of Development	Importance
Point contact transistor	1947	First solid state amplifier. More efficient in power consumption, more reliable and eventually less costly than an electron tube.
Single crystal growing	1950, Germanium 1952, Silicon	Method of growing and doping germanium and silicon crystals.
Zone refining	1950	Produced extremely pure germanium and silicon crystals. Improved doing process.
Silicon diffusion and oxide masking	1954–1955	Improved method for forming junctions. Made batch production possible, reducing production costs. Also improved quality control and increased power and frequency capabilities of semiconductor devices.
Epitaxial process forming	1960	Technique for junction whereby one type of crystal structure is grown on another. Used with planar process, it reduces production costs and enhances performance characteristics of semiconductor devices.
Beam lead	1964	Reduces encapsulation costs for highly reliable devices. Facilitates mixing of semiconductor and thin-film technologies in hybrid ICs.

Source: John Tilton, *International Diffusion of Technology: The Case of Semiconductors* (Washington, D.C.: The Brookings Institution, 1971), Table 4–2.

in an eight-day symposium, held in April 1952 for Western Electric licensees. Western Electric by 1952 had licensed 35 companies under its original transistor patents.[9] Thus at a point when Western Electric itself was only in the early stages of junction transistor production for trial use in equipment for AT&T's long distance system, Long Lines,[10] Bell Labs was transferring transistor technology and know-how to a wide number of domestic and foreign firms. As its own technologies advanced, it held symposiums to keep its licensees current. Perhaps most important was the symposium held in 1956 attended by 65 of Western Electric's licensees that dealt with silicon diffusion, oxide masking, and other major innovations that the Labs had pioneered since 1952. With the development of silicon diffusion and oxide masking techniques, batch production of semiconductor components became possible; production costs fell, component performance and reliability improved, and the industry moved into a period of rapid growth. Diffusion by Bell of its basic patents and know-how in these areas underwrote the dramatic and widespread growth of the semiconductor industry in the later half of the decade.[11]

Mobility of Bell Labs personnel in the early 1950s underwrote the ability of many new firms to enter the semiconductor market during the decade. The mobility was encouraged by AT&T policy, given that Western Electric was limited to commercial semiconductor applications in the telecommunications market, a result of the 1956 consent decree. It also reflected the greater potential rewards to semiconductor development in a small firm context.

With basic product and process patents readily available from Western Electric and Bell Labs willing to part with key personnel (that is, not threatening suit for theft of trade secrets), many private companies formerly with no direct role in the elecronic component business entered into semiconductor development. Most notably William Shockley, one of the inventors of the transistor at Bell, received backing from Beckman Instruments in 1955, setting up the Shockley Transistor Corporation near Stanford University, where he also became a part-time member of the engineering faculty. Shockley Transistor never became the successful commercial venture that Beckman envisioned; however, Shockley had assembled some of the fledgling industry's best and brightest. With the backing of Fairchild Camera and Instrument, eight of Shockley's former employees left to found Fairchild Semiconductor in 1957. By 1960 Fairchild had become Texas Instrument's major rival in the silicon transistor and IC markets. Fairchild itself became a source of new spin-offs; the more successful include Signetics, Intel, and Advanced Micro Devices. Texas Instruments itself as well as Motorola and a host of other companies and university semiconductor departments also hired former Bell Labs personnel.

The diffusion of Bell Labs' semiconductor technology through licenses, symposiums, and personnel mobility greatly accelerated the pace of industrial development in the United States. Between 1952 and 1959, the value of annual domestic semiconductor production increased from about $20 million to over $390 million, almost doubling in value each year.[12] Moreover, the number of firms producing semiconductors in the United States increased from five in 1952 to 34 in 1959,[13] each producing under one Western Electric license or another. Of equal note, by 1959 63 percent of domestic semiconductor production was accounted for by firms that either were founded in the 1950s or had not engaged in electronic component (tube) production prior to 1952.[14] Thus, while the first companies to jump into semiconductor production were the dominant electron tube manufacturers (RCA, General Electric, and Raytheon; Westinghouse, Sylvania, Philco, Tung-Sol and CBS were all in production by 1954) by 1960, new entrants as a group dominated the market and individual companies such as Texas Instruments, Transitron, Motorola, Hughes, and Fairchild were among the industry leaders in both sales and product and process patents.[15]

Many factors, of course, contributed to the entry of new firms and to the dynamics of their growth during the 1950s and 1960s, not least among which was the impact of defense research, development, and procurement programs during the period. However, as a result of Bell Labs' impact, technological and structural barriers to entry in the markets for application of semiconductor technology were low. Cross-licensing became standard industry practice and patent infringement suits were few. With basic product and process technology so widely diffused, the subsequent pace of innovation rendered patent protection for proprietary technology relatively unimportant in market competition. Rather, developing a market for a new device or entering an existing market with a lower cost production process was its own reward. Innovative risk was thereby compensated in the market rather than in the courts, and the dynamics of market development and competition kept the pace of the innovation rapid.

Military Markets and Merchants

The direction of semiconductor technology was largely influenced by the U.S. chip industry's early relationship with the U.S. military. The demand of the defense and aerospace markets boosted industry along a specific technological trajectory and into a position of market dominance and technological leadership. During the 1950s, while Europe and Japan pursued the development and mass production of germanium transistor-based consumer electronic systems, the U.S. industry, prodded by U.S. military demands for miniaturization and devices of higher performance and reliability, became preeminent in silicon-based technology.[16]

Perhaps the most important consequence of early defense sponsorship of silicon-based devices was its impact upon the structure of the microelectronics industry. In the era of the electron tube, component production was dominated by large multidivisional electronic systems producers. In the shift to the transistor and then the integrated circuit few of the leading producers of the electron tube managed to retain their component market positions.[17] In the reshuffle, defense and aerospace R&D and procurement created a market incentive for entrepreneurial risk-taking, helping to spawn an independent sector of semiconductor component manufacturers.

During the 1950s and early 1960s, each of the branches of the armed forces developed programs of semiconductor R&D. Table 4–2 lists the most important of these laboratories. The impact of defense research was wider ranging than its few direct contributions might suggest. The defense laboratories served important technical liaison functions on the vast number of semiconductor R&D contracts let by the armed services to private industry. Defense scientists helped to frame the requirements of Defense Department contract work, participated in R&D, and provided continuous feedback and evaluation of industry efforts. The defense laboratories could venture into research areas without concern about commercial payoff. Untried theories and ideas, once proven, were turned over to civilian industry for development, and Defense scientists moved from the armed services laboratories into private industry, providing essential knowledge to industry development efforts at some critical moments.

Defense funding of research at universities also contributed directly to the U.S. industry's growth. In the early 1950s university electrical

Table 4–2. Semiconductor Research at Defense Laboratories, 1950–61.

Operation Center	Location	Nature of Semiconductor Related Research
Air Force		
Wright Air Development Division	Wright-Patterson Air Force Board, Ohio	Materials; electronic components and systems; manufacturing methods; molecular electronic and basic sciences.
Air Force Cambridge Research Center	L. G. Hanscom Field, Mass.	Electronic materials; solid state sciences; components and systems; process development (e.g., crystal growth).
Rome Air Development Center	Griffiss AFB, N.Y.	Device electronics, primarily for communication and intelligence systems.
Army		
Diamond Ordnance Fuse Laboratory	Washington, D.C.	Device electronics; materials; components and systems; process technologies (e.g., photoresist, etching, diffusion); miniaturization.
Signal Corps Res. Laboratory	Fort Mammouth, N.J.	Basic electronic research; components and systems; materials; miniaturization approaches; process technology and testing.
Navy		
U.S. Navy Electronic Laboratory	San Diego	Basic electronics research components and systems; materials.
U.S. Naval Research Laboratory	Washington, D.C.	Basic electronic science; materials.
U.S. Naval Ordnance Laboratory	White Oak, MD	Basic electronics science; components and systems; materials.

Source: U.S. Congress, Senate Committee on the Judiciary, Subcommittee on Patents, Trademarks and Copyrights, ''Patent Practices of the Department of Defense,'' 87th Congress, 1st Session, 1961, pp. 9–17; *Electronic News*, various issues, November 1957–March, 1961.

engineering departments and laboratories (with the exception of the Massachusetts Institute of Technology's Lincoln Laboratories) lagged behind military and industrial semiconductor development by a considerable margin. Much of government funding was meant to reduce this lag and lay the groundwork for the industry's anticipated expansion. During this period the Department of Defense allocated between $1 million and $2 million annually to over 100 doctoral candidates for basic research in solid-state electronics. By the late 1950s the infusion of federal funds had begun to pay important dividends. Solid state electronics labs were prospering with federal contract research funds at the major research universities. The semiconductor industry had become concentrated around the major university recipients of federal research monies, in the Boston area near Massachusetts Institute of Technology and Harvard and south and east of San Francisco near Stanford and the University of California at Berkeley.

By far the most government R&D funding of semiconductor development was in the form of R&D contracts to private industry. The transistor had obvious and important implications for defense electronics, and the Defense Department immediately supported its development.

> Competition developed among the various defense agencies to support the best idea and the best teams in the various industrial laboratories. . . . Moreover, the commonality of interest among the contractors to the federal government promoted the high diffusion rate of new information in semiconductor electronics.[18]

As with research at defense laboratories, very few of the major innovations in semiconductors were a direct result of projects sponsored by the Department of Defense.

> It is probable, that government-sponsored R&D in the industry itself was not as productive as the R&D which the industry chose to support itself. The reason for this is simply motivation. Government-sponsored R&D usually demands production of final devices that might or might not be considered useful (that is, profitable) for the company involved. If the company chooses to sponsor R&D itself, then it is highly motivated to direct this R&D effort into products that it feels will be profitable to the company.[19]

Nevertheless, the knowledge gained from defense-sponsored R&D was easily transferable to the commercial projects largely credited with achieving major innovations. Most important, direct defense development funding in the form of industrial preparedness contracts, first in

1952–1953 and again in 1956–1957, stimulated production knowledge and process refinement in the industry.

In 1952 and 1953 the Army Signal Corps provided roughly $11 million to build pilot transistor production lines at five sites, operated by Western Electric, General Electric, Raytheon, RCA, and Sylvania. These contracts encouraged the early development of production capability and cut the risk of production investment to the companies involved. Perhaps the most crucial government boost to production technology came in 1956 with the Defense Department's decision to channel $40 million in transistor production contracts to 12 semiconductor firms, including two of the most important new entrants, Motorola and Texas Instruments (TI). The government covered engineering design and development costs (some $14 million in 1956) while the companies paid for plant and facilities. In return for guaranteed government purchases at premium prices of a part of the resulting output, the companies agreed to build production capacity capable of manufacturing 10–12 times the number of devices the government wanted.

> By their action, the Federal Government created a semiconductor production capacity of about 1 million units per year; since production yields were very low, these contracts actually resulted in the creation of potential semiconductor production capacity of more than 10 million units.[20]

Since total industry production output was about 14 million units at the time, defense spending stimulated the search for new commercial markets for the potential capacity. Learning economies in turn helped to bring down costs, forging the way into new markets.

From 1955 to 1961, direct government financing of discrete semiconductor R&D and production refinement totaled at least $66 million (exclusive of integrated circuit R&D—see Table 4–3). This figure understates the amount of support, however, because indirect funds were subcontracted to semiconductor firms by weapons systems prime contractors. An internal Defense Department survey in 1960 calculated that direct and indirect government support to semiconductor development in 1958 and 1959 alone totaled $30.1 million or some 23–25 percent of total semiconductor industry R&D in these years.

From the beginning of the 1950s, the Defense Department had pushed the need for miniaturization and high reliability for the next generation of defense weaponry (missile systems). It spread much of its funding among several competing technological approaches to miniaturization

Table 4-3. U.S. Government Funds Allocated to Firms for Semiconductors for Research, Development, and Production Preparedness, 1955–65 ($millions).

	Discrete SC R&D[a]	Production Refinement/Preparedness[b]		Indirect SC R&D[a]	Direct and Indirect IC/Microelectronics R&D/Preparedness[b]
		Transistors	Diodes/Rectifiers		
1955	3.2	2.7	2.2	NA	—
1956	4.1	14.0	0.8	NA	—
1957	3.8	NA	0.5	NA	—
1958	4.0	1.9	0.2	(7.8)	NA
1959	6.3	1.0	0.0	(8.9)	10
1960	6.8	NA	1.1	NA	10
1961	11.0	1.7	0.8	NA	80
1962	NA	NA	NA	NA	NA
1965	NA	NA	NA	NA	NA

Note: Indirect funds are those subcontracted to semiconductors firms by weapons systems prime contractors.

[a]Department of Defense, Special Survey, 1960, quoted in John Tilton, *International Diffusion of Technology: The Case of Semiconductors* (Washington, D.C.: The Brookings Institution, 1971), pp. 92–93.

[b]Organization for Economic Cooperation and Development, *Gaps in Technology* (Paris: OECD, 1970), p. 58.

NA = Not available.

Source: U.S. Department of Commerce, Business and Defense Service Administration, "Semiconductors: U.S. Production and Trade," 1961, Table 8.

Table 4–4.   Summary of Miniaturization Methods and Projects.

Method Number	Techniques of Obtaining Circuit Function	Typical Identification	Sponsor
1	Integration of conventional miniature parts	Printed Wiring	
2	Integration of separate, uniform 2-D parts into 3-D modules	"Tinker Toy" Micro-Module	Navy RCA–Navy General Electric Hughes
3	Deposition and/or attachment of individual parts on common substrate	Printed Circuits Micro-Circuitry Micro-Circuit Microelectronics Micro-Systems DOFL-2D	Centralab Varo–Navy Int. Resistance Sylvania Lockheed Army Stanford Res.- Army–USAF IBM–Army Servomechanisms Bell Labs Sprague Philco Hughes
4	Solid circuits, employing semiconductor and other physical phenomena	Molecular Electronics Microelectronics	Westinghouse USAF Motorola Texas Instruments– Army–USAF IBM–Army General Electric RCA Labs

Source: *Electronic News*, March 28, 1960, p. 3.

pursued by private industry. Table 4–4 summarizes the most important of those projects.

The first integrated circuit was demonstrated by Texas Instruments in 1958 and occasioned a marked shift and major increase in defense funding channeled to IC development. While the Texas Instruments circuit was developed without direct research and development funding from the U.S. government, in mid-1959 the air force awarded the company a $1.15 million, two-and-a-half-year contract to develop various integrated circuit devices. In December 1960 the air force followed its original award with a $2.1 million contract for the development of production processes and special equipment needed for the fabrication of integrated circuits in bulk quantities.[21] Indeed, from 1959 to 1962, TI, Westinghouse, and Motorola received direct defense contracts totaling some $9 million to advance the state of the art of ICs. One important demonstration project was a small digital IC computer by TI, funded by the air force. As Asher and Strom reported, as late as 1961 the industrial and scientific communities still voiced doubts as to the worth of ICs from the viewpoint of equipment and systems. To alleviate these doubts, the air force proposed the building of a representative piece of electronic equipment using ICs. Under air force sponsorship the building of a digital computer was introduced into the TI production program. Two identical computers were built: one with 9,000 components and one containing only 587 ICs.[22] Meanwhile at Fairchild, the development of the planar process moved the IC out of the laboratory and into production. Though Fairchild used its own funds in the development, it earned the money by selling high-priced prototypes to the government for research purposes.

Government support having directed the pace of technological advance and lowered barriers to entry during the incubation period of semiconductor development, military procurement at premium prices created incentive and gave semiconductor firms the initial production experience that enabled them to enter and develop markets for commercial applications of their state-of-the-art components. The Defense Department did not require commercial market volumes, but it compensated by paying premium unit prices for its more limited demand. As Table 4–5 demonstrates, transistor sales to the military earned significantly higher unit prices than could be earned in the commercial market. Government military and aerospace procurement consistently represented over one-third of all semiconductor sales as measured by value. The substantial difference in unit prices between military and nonmilitary transistor sales created a strong market incentive encouraging technological innovation to meet military demands for more reliable and better performing semiconductor devices.

The impact of military demand on the fledgling semiconductor industry transcended the actual dollar value of procurement, although as Table 4–6 shows, defense and aerospace demand was quite substantial. As

Table 4-5. Transistor Unit Prices, 1955–59.

Year	Military Unit Price / Quantity (millions)		Commercial Unit Price / Quantity (millions)	
1955	$11.75	0.4	$2.47	3.5
1956	11.10	1.1	2.04	13.6
1957	8.10	2.6	1.86	25.2
1958	7.90	4.7	1.81	41.4
1959	7.33	14.4	1.78	69.1

Source: U.S. Department of Commerce, Business and Defense Service Administration, "Semiconductors: U.S. Production and Trade," 1961.

production for the military proceeded, learning occurred and unit costs typically fell, and within a few years the price of a given device was low enough to penetrate the industrial market and eventually the consumer market. Table 4–7 illustrates this typical shifting market and price pattern.

The most important consequence of early defense demand for silicon transistors and ICs was its impact upon the structure of the industry. By 1959, new entrants accounted for 63 percent of all semiconductor sales and 69 percent of military sales. For individual firms such as Transitron, TI, and Fairchild, military sales were critical to their early product development efforts and market survival. Between 1963 and 1965, 14 major defense and NASA procurement contracts were let, calling for the incorporation of monolithic ICs, most notably in the Minuteman II missile guidance system and the Apollo spacecraft guidance computer. Texas Instruments (Minuteman II) and Fairchild (Apollo), the two new firms that had pioneered IC development, each became major subcontractors. The surge forward in military and aerospace utilization of IC technology also enabled emergent contenders such as Motorola and Signetics to lift their IC production volumes. Moreover, defense and aerospace procurement allowed Westinghouse and RCA to gain experience in IC production (each, under defense contracts, had been pursuing alternative approaches to miniaturization ultimately inferior to the IC).

Military development and procurement programs facilitated intercompany diffusion of technology. Where Department of Defense funds contributed to the development of patentable products or processes used by a private defense contractor in production for defense procurement, such as with the development of the transistor and IC, the Defense

Table 4-6. U.S. Production of Semiconductors and Integrated Circuits for Defense Requirements, 1955–1968 ($millions).

Year (1)	Total (2)	Space and Defense (3)	(3) as a Percentage of (2) (4)	Total (5)	Space and Defense (6)	(6) as a Percentage of (5) (7)	Total (8)	Space and Defense (9)	(9) as a Percentage of (8) (10)
1955	$ 40	15	38%				$ 40	15	38%
1956	90	32	36				90	32	36
1957	151	54	36				151	54	36
1958	210	81	39				210	81	39
1959	396	180	45				396	180	45
1960	542	258	39				542	258	48
1961	565	222	39				565	222	39
1962	571	219	38	$ 4	$ 4	100%	575	223	39
1963	594	196	33	16	15	94	610	211	35
1964	635	157	25	41	35	85	676	192	28
1965	805	190	24	79	57	72	884	247	28
1966	975	219	22	228	98	43	1,123	298	27
1967	879	295	23	228	98	43	1,107	303	27
1968	847	179	21	312	115	37	1,159	294	25

Sources: Eli Ginzberg, Thierry Noyelle, and Thomas Starback, *Economic Impact of Large Public Programs: The NASA Experience* (Boulder, Colo.: Westview Press, 1986), p. 58.

Table 4–7.   U.S. IC Production and Prices, 1962–1968.

Year	Total Production ($millions)	Average Price per Integrated Circuit	Defense Production as a Percentage of Total Production
1962	$ 4	50.00	100
1963	16	31.00	94
1964	41	18.50	85
1965	79	8.33	72
1966	148	5.05	53
1967	228	3.32	43
1968	312	2.33	37

Source: John Tilton, *The International Diffusion of Technology: The Case of Semiconductors* (Washington, D.C.: The Brookings Institution, 1971), p. 91, Table 4–8.

Department would generally obtain a comprehensive license of free use. The comprehensive license included provisions permitting "any use of the invention by the Government itself and any use by a Government contractor or subcontractor in connection with performance of a Government contract, and any use by anyone in connection with projects funded by the Government." In tandem with the broad cross-licensing agreements generally entered into by U.S. semiconductor firms, these conditions assured rapid intercompany diffusion of technological advances. Defense procurement programs operated like a patent pooling agreement among all defense contractors. As Table 4–7 illustrates, in 1963 government procurement constituted 94 percent of the market for monolithic ICs, which had an average selling price of $31. In 1965 government procurement constituted only 72 percent of demand, but the price per IC had dropped below $9. Over the three-year period, total IC production grew rapidly, from $4 million in 1963 to $80 million in 1965,[23] and new companies such as Signetics, Siliconix, General Microelectronics, and Molectro were founded primarily to manufacture ICs. Older electronics systems producers such as RCA, Sylvania, Motorola, Westinghouse, and Raytheon began to move more slowly into volume production.

The support of the Department of Defense and the National Aeronautics and Space Administration (NASA) had two effects: The first was the intended effect of encouraging and accelerating the pace of technological advance; the second was the unintended effect of fostering the development of unique segment of merchant producers. The latter result could not have been predicted, but was perhaps the more significant. The merchant producers kept the pace of technological innovation and diffusion alive and thriving in commercial markets long after the strategic objectives of the military had been realized.

DOMESTIC SYNERGY: THE COMPUTER MARKET AND MERCHANT COMPETITION, 1966–1972

U.S. production of integrated circuits more than doubled between 1966 and 1972.[24] The rapid growth in IC production reflected accelerating demand from computer and industrial equipment manufacturers. Whereas in 1965 military sales still constituted more than 55 percent of the total value of domestic IC sales, by 1972 some 65 percent of all IC sales in the United States went to the computer and industrial markets, and military sales fell to less than 25 percent of the market[25] (Table 4–8). The age of data processing had arrived, and the IC industry broke away from military tutelage to supply the more prodigious demands of commercial markets.

Table 4–8. Changing Distribution of Integrated Circuit Devices in U.S. Markets, 1962–1978.

U.S. Markets for ICs by End Use	1962[a]	1965[b]	1969[b]	1974[b]	1978[c]
Government	100%	55%	36%	20%	10%
Computer	0	35	44	36	37.5
Industrial	0	9	16	30	37.5
Consumer	0	1	4	15	15
Total U.S. domestic shipment ($millions)	$ 4	39	413	1,204	2,080

[a]Figures for 1962 are derived from John Tilton, International Diffusion of Technology: The Case of Semiconductors (Washington, D.C.: The Brookings Institution, 1971).

[b]Figures for 1962, 1969, and 1974 come from the U.S. Department of Commerce, Report on the U.S. Semiconductor Industry (Washington, D.C.: Government Printing Office, 1979), p. 102.

[c]These figures are rough estimates based on figures found in U.S. International Trade Commission, "Competitive Factors Influencing World Trade in Integrated Circuits," USITC Publication 1013, 1979, p. 102; Business Week, December 3, 1979, p. 68; and "1980 Semiconductor Forum," Rosen Electronics Letter (Rosen Research Inc., New York), July 14, 1980, p. 15.

The relationship between the IC and computer industries has been characterized by Ian Mackintosh as a classic example of "industrial synergism":

> Just as the American computer industry growth has been critically dependent on the availability of ever-increasing numbers of improved ICs, so has the spectacular growth of the American IC industry depended to a very high degree on having a large, innovative and "local" computer market avid to make use of its rapidly developing semiconductor capabilities.[26]

Indeed, during the 1960s the computer industry's spectacular growth was due mainly to its ability to produce equipment that would compute at ever-increasing speeds and reliability, with ever-decreasing costs and size, and most of these attributes stemmed from advances in silicon technology.[27]

The infant computer industry in the 1950s had been an early market for discrete semiconductor devices. Because of the relative unreliability of electron tubes, transistors were rapidly assimilated into computer hardware design. In 1960 a large computer could easily contain over 100,000 diodes and 25,000 transistors.[28] While the shift to discrete semiconductor devices offered the advantage of greater reliability and speed, it also entailed high assembly and connection costs.

In 1964 IBM introduced the first computer line not based on discrete semiconductor technology. The IBM System 360 packaged together several transistors and other devices to form an operating circuit. The hybrid design helped to reduce the cost of producing a computer, further reduced its power consumption, and increased its speed and capacity. With the introduction of user software that could be used on all models within the 360 line, the commercial computer market began to expand rapidly.

IBM's competitors reacted to the System 360 with computer hardware based on the integrated circuit. The IC allowed for the design and production of an entire logic circuit on a monolithic chip of silicon. With 50 or more transistors packed on a single chip of silicon, transistor interconnection distances were dramatically reduced. The result was vastly improved speed, power consumption, and reliability. The IC eliminated much of the assembly cost associated with discrete and hybrid devices. As IC prices declined rapidly during the late 1960s and the functional complexity of the IC increased (both an outcome of merchant competition), companies such as RCA and Burroughs turned to IC designs to lower their computer prices in the battle against IBM. With lower prices, the domestic computer market entered a period of rapid sales growth.

The availability in volume of advanced ICs helped to spawn a new segment in the computer market. In 1965 Digital Equipment Corporation introduced the world's first minicomputer, the PDP-8. Relatively low-cost IC logic chips from companies such as Texas Instruments and Fairchild helped to lower the capital and technological barriers to entry in the computer manufacturing industry. As a consequence, by the early 1970s minicomputers had become a high-growth and fiercely competitive market. The merchant IC industry also became fiercely competitive, as the firms strove through cost reduction and product innovation to preempt their competitors in the race for minicomputer designs that used their respective "families" of IC devices.

In the 1960s early digital IC designs incorporated fewer than 50 transistors per silicon chip. The early digital ICs, individual chips, needed to be connected to one another to perform computing functions. As a consequence, to sell digital ICs, semiconductor houses had to provide computer equipment makers with a complete "kit" of electrically compatible parts that could be interconnected into a computer configuration. Digital IC products came to be grouped into families characterized by resistor-transistor logic (RTL), diode transistor logic (DTL), or the durable transistor-transistor logic (TTL).[29] The early computer market was dominated by competition among these design families.

The first proprietary ICs were introduced by Fairchild and Texas Instruments: Fairchild offered circuits based on resistor capacitor transistor logic (RCTL) and TI offered circuits based on direct coupled transistor logic (DCTL). These early product families, while used in the Apollo guidance computer and the Minuteman II missile system, had design weaknesses and were quickly supplanted by DTL and RTL. Fairchild's 930 series DTL emerged as the industry leader in the period from 1965 to 1967. Its share of the then emerging commerical IC market, with demand from computer manufacturers the driving force, grew quickly from 18 percent in 1964 to 24 percent in 1967.[30] Texas Instruments, which had been the industry's leading producer of ICs with more than 32 percent of the market in 1964, watched its market share drop almost by half by 1967 during a period in which total industry sales of integrated circuits almost doubled.[31] Innovative circuit design and aggressive price cutting enabled Fairchild to grow rapidly and to lead an increasing number of new IC merchant producers into the computer and industrial markets.

Texas Instruments soon regained its market momentum with the introduction of a family of proprietary TTL circuits whose fast switching speeds proved to be more appealing to the computer market than Fairchild's earlier family of DTL circuits. TI's advance was built on innovation in IC design, the introduction by TI of a set of TTL chips that individually implemented complete computer functions (adders, coders, decoders, and four-bit serial memories), and on aggressive price-cutting by TI's second source—National Semiconductors, a new entry in the merchant market. (A "second source" refers to a firm that produces a product originally introduced by someone else. Most users of components require a second source to assure a stable supply. Second source thus refers to a specific role in the market.) Together, innovation and price cutting enabled TI's TTL bipolar logic family to regain a dominant position in computer hardware design by 1969. In 1970 TI introduced Schottky TTL, which greatly improved the speed and packing density of its earlier TTL family and sustained TI's leadership in the merchant bipolar logic market through the early 1970s.

TI's introduction of single-chip adders, coders, decoders, and memories in the late 1960s illustrates the technical trajectory of component-system evolution. Increasingly components are technically able to implement basic features of what previously had been regarded as an electronic system. By designing computer hardware subsystems on single component chips, TI reduced the cost of these subsystems to the computer market and put itself in a dominant market position. Component manufacturers could not, however, develop a chip version of every electronic subsystem in existence for two reasons. First, the costs of designing chip subsystem families were very large; second, large production runs were necessary to amortize high design costs and attain low per-chip production costs. Large production runs were simply not possible for the smaller markets of most electronic system products.

As the industry approached the era of large-scale integration, these economic considerations influenced the strategic planning of IC manufacturers and came to be characterized as the custom-versus-standard debate. As neatly summarized by Charles River Associates:

> Although not universally held, the general semiconductor industry consensus in the late 1960s was that the future of digital integrated circuits lay in custom LSI. The need for standard parts was expected to be small (*Electronics,* 2/20/67). The principal reason LSI was expected to be dominated by custom rather than standard products was that most semiconductor experts believed that the innovating equipment maker would not want to find that the complex integrated circuits, which determined the performance of its product, were readily available to its competitors. With early bipolar logic the

equipment maker could differentiate itself from competitors by cleverly inter-connecting standard ICs. In a design where LSI was to be used, most of the logic needed was now packed into a few ICs and therefore much fewer performance differentiating options were open to the equipment manufacturer, unless the LSIs used were circuits custom designed.[32]

A number of strategies were developed to meet the expected demand for custom circuits. Both TI and Fairchild foreshadowed the later emergence of gate arrays by planning to build wafers for inventory containing different standard logic gate designs. The wafers could then be pulled and processed through final masking to connect the logic gates on the wafer into the customer's unique circuit requirements. TI called its approach "Discretionary Wiring" and Fairchild called its system "Micromatrix."[33]

The custom market, however, never really emerged as conventional wisdom in the mid-1960s had anticipated. The pull of newly emerging mass markets in special calculator chips and semiconductor memories and the push of a newly developed technology—metal oxide on silicon (MOS)—conjoined to render the custom versus standard debate relatively moot and served to smooth the industry's entry into the era of large-scale integration (LSI). Two choices then came to dominate the competitive strategies of IC manufacturers: on the one hand, LSI products were designed that implemented widely used components; on the other, LSI products were designed with sufficient flexibility that they could be used to implement a variety of system functions.

The calculator market posed the custom-versus-standard LSI conflict most starkly. Mostek, founded in 1969, was the first company to produce a single-chip calculator—a chip that included four functions: add, subtract, multiply, and divide. Intel, founded in 1969, working with the same calculator manufacturer as Mostek, was faced with the task of having to design a custom chip for a family of calculators. The key issue the company faced was whether the custom circuit could command a sufficient market to justify the investment in design and production costs, and to get far enough down the learning curve in production to permit low prices. Intel's solution, the microprocessor, was a pioneering advance in flexible product design which gave the industry a new way out of the custom-versus-standard battle: by programming the on-chip memory, the microprocessor could be customized for each application.

Note here the importance of final product demand in generating and sustaining component innovation. It was not until later in the 1970s that Japanese calculator manufacturers took control of the industry;

only then did leadership in production of chips used in calculators pass to Japan. Had the United States lacked a strong domestic consumer electronics base in the early 1970s, it is conceivable that U.S. leadership in microprocessors never would have emerged.

The custom-versus-standard conflict therefore was resolved from two directions. On the one hand, what appeared to be custom markets rapidly proved to be mass markets for relatively low-cost MOS integrated circuits in calculators, wristwatches, and semiconductor memories. On the other had, the microprocessor, a standard single-chip central processing unit whose add-on memory could be programmed for customized functions, allowed IC manufacturers to break out of the vicious circle of greater complexity leading to higher costs leading to smaller markets and enter a wide field of new applications markets.

Exploiting these new market opportunities, 30 new merchant companies entered the U.S. industry between 1966 and 1972. As Table 4–9 indicates, most of the new entrants were founded by management and technical personnel from existing companies. The mobility of technical personnel in the industry derived from two factors. First, at least until the 1969 changes in the capital gains tax, the venture capital market was a ready source for start-up capital. Second, the domestic IC market was growing so rapidly and the number of potential product technologies becoming so diverse, that none of the major merchant companies could exploit and develop the full potential of its existing technological resources. The capital constraints that rapid growth placed on company resources meant that firms often had to choose between expanding capacity and developing new products. Frustration with the pace of product development as well as a market growth environment favoring entreprenuerial risk thus contributed to the emergence during the period of numerous new entrants.

By the early 1970s, then, the wave of new entrants was creating a highly competitive industry structure. In 1965 the four largest merchant firms accounted for 69 percent of the industry's total shipments, but by 1972 their share had dropped to 53 percent. Likewise, the largest eight firms in 1965 accounted for 91 percent of the total, but by 1972 their share had dropped dramatically to 67 percent.[34] Similarly, increased price competition characterized the merchant sector as a whole:

From 1966 through 1971, a period of rapid expansion in both output and the number of firms entering the industry, net earnings as a percent of sales declined from 5.3 percent to 2.7 percent. In each of these years, they were well below the all-manufacturing industries average. Due primarily to vigorous price competition, profits per unit of sales decreased even though sales volume increased.[35]

Such razor-thin margins could sustain competitive advance only so long as the U.S. industry's major firms operated under the same capital market constraints. Given the industry's domestic structure and government antitrust policies, dumping of product could not be sustained for long nor, critically, could overbuilding of capacity. Only with the entry, in the late 1970s, of Japanese firms did such tactics occur systematically, and only at that point was the competitive vulnerability of the U.S. industry structure exposed.

In 1967 the leading firms were, in descending order, Fairchild, Texas Instruments, Motorola, Signetics, Sylvania, RCA, and Westinghouse. By 1973 the entire order had been reshuffled, with Texas Instruments regaining its early leadership followed by Motorola, National Semiconductor, Fairchild, Signetics, Intel, American Microsystems, and Mostek.[36]

THE ERA OF LARGE-SCALE INTEGRATION: STRATEGY AND STRUCTURE, 1972–1978

The third stage of the industry's development rested upon a succession of technological advances that allowed ever greater numbers of transistors to be built into a single silicon chip. The generic technology—metal oxide on silicon—proved to have technical advantages in cost and density over the bipolar techniques that had dominated early IC design and fabrication. Bipolar devices offered enhanced speed of circuit operation, but the fewer masking steps and higher yields associated with MOS design and fabrication offered the advantage of lower cost per electronic function. Thus, in tandem with enhanced circuit complexity, MOS facilitated progressive reductions in the cost of complex electronic functions and thereby opened new growth opportunities in old and new markets.

As noted earlier, between 1966 and 1972 30 new companies entered the U.S. industry. These new companies made their entry on the back of MOS technology. By 1973 approximately 85 percent of the sales of these newly established IC firms were concentrated in MOS technology, whereas among those firms established before 1966 only 35 percent of sales were in MOS devices.[37] Spurred by the products' use in

Table 4–9. U.S. Semiconductor Companies Founded between 1966 and 1976.

Company Name/Date Founded	City	Previous Employment/ Number of Founders
American Microsystems (1966)	Cupertino	Philco-Ford (4)
National Semiconductor	Santa Clara	Fairchild (3)
Electronic Arrays (1967)	Mountain View	Philco-Ford (4), Bunker-Ramo (2)
Intersil (1968)	Sunnyvale	Union Carbide (3)
Avantek (1968)	Santa Clara	Applied Technology (4)
Integrated Systems Technology (1968)	Santa Clara	Philco-Ford (3)
Nortec Electronics Corp. (1968)	Santa Clara	Philco-Ford (2)
Intel (1968)	Santa Clara	Fairchild (3)
Precision Monolothic (1969)	Santa Clara	Fairchild (3)
Computer Microtechnology (1968)		Fairchild (3)
Qualidyne (1968)	Sunnyvale	Fairchild (1), IBM (2), Motorola (1), Collins
Communications Transistor Corp. (1969)	San Carlos	National Semiconductor (3)
Monolithic Memories (1969)	Santa Clara	IBM (1)
Advanced LSI Systems (1969)		Nortec (1)
Mostek (1969)	Carrollton, TX	TI
Signetics Memory Systems (1969)	Sunnyvale	Signetics (2), IBM (2), HP (1)
Advanced Micro Devices (1969)	Sunnyvale	Fairchild (8)
Spectronics (1969)	Richardson, TX	TI
Four Phase (1969)	Cupertino	Fairchild (6), General Instruments (2), Mellonics (1)

Company	Location	Source (number of personnel)
Litronix (1970)	Cupertino	Monsanto (1)
Integrated Electronics (1970)	Mountain View	Fairchild (2)
Varadyne (1970)		
Caltex (1971)	Sunnyvale	TI (2), Nortec (4)
Exar (1971)	Santa Clara	Signetics (3)
Micropower (1971)		Intersil (2)
Standrd Microsystems (1971)	Hauppage, NY	Four Phase (1), Electro-Nuclear Labs (1), Nitron (1)
Antex (1971)	Cupertino	Caltex (1)
LSI Systems (1972)	Newport Beach	Signetics (1)
Nitron (1972)	Sunnyvale	CMI (3), AMI (4), Fairchild (1)
Frontier (1972)	Santa Clara	
Interdesign (1972)		
Synertek (1974)		
Zilog (1974)	Cupertino	Intel (2)
Maruman (1975)	Sunnyvale	National Semiconductor (2)
Supertex (1976)	Sunnyvale	Fairchild (1)

Source: U.S. Senate, Committee on Commerce, Science, and Transportation, *Industrial Technology* (Washington, D.C.: U.S. Government Printing Office, 1978), p. 91.

hand-held calculators, digital watches, and computer main memory, sales of MOS IC products rapidly expanded between 1970 and 1975. In 1970 sales of digital MOS integrated circuits were only some $45 million; by 1975, however, MOS sales had reached $428 million and had surpassed the total value of digital bipolar IC sales.[38]

The surge in market demand for MOS circuits came largely from three market segments: consumer products, computer main memory devices, and microprocessors. Between 1969 and 1974 the consumer products market for digital ICs grew rapidly. From approximately $30 million in 1969, sales of ICs in the consumer product market grew to over $300 million by 1975, the bulk in special chips for calculators and watches. The consumer market's share of total IC production rose from a mere 4 percent in 1969 to over 15 percent in 1974.[39]

The first tentative steps toward structural consolidation of the fragmented industry structure occurred when more than a dozen of the U.S. merchant firms founded between 1966 and 1972 tried to integrate forward into the marketing and sale of their own calculators and watches for the consumer market. The move into final consumer product markets had three primary motives: (1) sales of consumer products would presumably allow the merchant IC producers partially to insulate themselves from the cyclical swings in the component market, (2) the consumer market offered the potential of a new mass market for integrated circuits, and (3) by integrating forward, the merchant firm would capture the higher margins available to systems producers. Of these rationales, only the second was substantiated in the marketplace. The consumer market did prove to be a mass market for special calculator and watch ICs, but intense price competition and the vagaries of consumer product marketing forced most of the merchant firms to abandon their consumer product lines by 1977.

The chief victors in the calculator wars were, of course, Japanese producers. Their success demonstrated that merchant U.S. chip producers were vulnerable to the problem of insufficient resources in competition with vertically integrated systems producers. The Japanese success simultaneously discouraged the merchants' attempts to become less vulnerable through forward integration. U.S. firms were thus dissuaded from pursuing reconsolidation, although the microprocessor was to give some of them a second chance.

The use of the new MOS circuits in computer main memories spawned the growth of a new mass market for IC devices. Between 1971 and 1979 the U.S. market for digital semiconductor memories grew at an extraordinary pace: From a base of $60 million in 1971, sales of semiconductor memories reached $500 million in 1976 and $1.290 billion in 1979.[41] The first major breakthrough was the introduction of the 1,000-bit random access memory (1K dynamic RAM) by Intel in 1970. The rapid sales growth in RAM devices since then has been a function of increasing memory device densities and decreasing chip costs. First, storage capacity per IC advanced from 1K in 1979 to 4K in 1973 to 16K in 1976 to 64K in 1979. Second, the price of storage fell from about 1 cent per bit in 1970 to 0.05 cents per bit in 1979.[42] Progressive increases in storage density per chip led the industry into the "virtuous circle" of increased production volume leading to lower cost per bit leading to jumps in demand and further increases in production volume. This circle came to be known as the "learning curve": For each doubling of cumulative output, the cost per electronic function declined on the average by 28 percent. Competition among the merchant producers on both circuit price and performance was the driving force behind the rapid diffusion of MOS-based circuits in the computer memory market. Of course the extraordinary growth of this market also invited foreign entry, becoming the target of Japanese strategy.

Finally, the introduction of the microprocessor (mpu) by Intel in 1971 offered "as big a step forward in digital systems as did the original integrated circuit."[43] The microprocessor launched "a virtual revolution" in the application of microelectronics to a variety of products and processes.[44] In essence, a microprocessor is a single-chip version of a computer's central processing unit. But its flexibility, a consequence of its capacity to be programmed for a variety of applications, introduced a new set of marketing challenges and strategic choices into the dynamic of market competition. While the relatively low-cost "intelligence" embodied in microprocessor hardware encouraged diffusion into new applications markets, the cost of developing application programs or instruction sets for specific applications emerged as the new barrier to penetration and development of those markets.[45]

In order to expand and penetrate the new applications markets that the relatively low cost of microprocessor hardware made possible, a number of the merchant firms established "teaming centers" and offered "development systems" that allow the microprocessor user to program, in high-level computer language, an instruction set for a specific application. A number of merchant firms integrated forward into computer markets in order to capture the higher value-added associated with the microprocessor.

By 1977, sales of peripheral and input-output devices exceeded sales of the microprocessor itself, and the market for memory chips associated with the use of the microprocessor—RAM, ROM (read-only memory), PROM (programmable ROM), and EPROM (erasable PROM)—was twice the value of microprocessor sales.[46] The total value of the market for the microprocessor and its family of peripheral and memory devices grew rapidly from $25 million in sales in 1974 to over $550 million in sales in 1979.[47]

In effect, the introduction and development of the microprocessor altered both strategies and structure of the merchant market. The microprocessor and its associated peripheral and memory chips were the third generation of computer technology, following mainframes and minicomputers. Each generation was born of advances in semiconductor technology, and each has had the effect of further diffusing computational power throughout society. The uniqueness of the microprocessor for the merchant firm lay in its more systemslike nature than any previous component the merchant sector had produced. Though both mainframe and minicomputer manufacturers have made ample use of the device in their own systems (to enhance both performance and cost), the microprocessor provided the foundation upon which merchant firms began gradually to evolve into sophisticated marketing vehicles for the third wave of diffusion of computer technology.

As manufacturers of a complex, systemlike component, the merchant firms faced the task of penetrating those markets in which electronic "intelligence" had yet to be applied because its cost had been prohibitive. The application of the microprocessor to new products and processes was not limited by size, complexity, or power consumption. As competition in the microprocessor field accelerated, prices fell rapidly. By 1980, standard eight-bit, single-chip microcomputers (a microprocessor chip that incorporates a main control program in ROM, a clock oscillator, some input-output capability, and some RAM capacity) were selling in the $8 to $5 range. Thus, hardware cost rapidly became marginal in a variety of application fields. The major barrier to diffusion and major marketing challenge for the merchant firms was applications software.

Early microprocessors forced programmers to program in the lowest (least English-like) of computer languages—machine language. For very short, simple programs this presented no problem, but as applications expanded, so did the length of the programs, causing software development costs to soar. A partial solution was the introduction of microprocessor development systems. These systems provided programmers with software tools (like editors) that eased some programming problems but did not allow the programmer to program in a high-level language, the easiest method of all.

Programming the 16-bit microcomputer was even more expensive. By 1980, a software application for a 16-bit microcomputer cost more than $5 million and accounted for 50–90 percent of total design cost, depending on the application. IC manufacturers reacted to this problem in two ways: by providing most 16-bit microcomputers with facilities for high-level languages, like PASCAL, and by implementing in hardware operations that had previously been done in software. This mix of hardware and software, or "firmware," helped the microprocessor firms solve some of the more basic marketing challenges of their new product. The emphasis on software development pushed the leading IC firms toward closer relations with systems companies and toward a second try at forward integration. As chips took on the character of complete electronic systems during the evolution of large-scale integration, the strategic importance of IC design became more acute for final electronic systems producers, both in the United States and abroad. As a consequence, between 1972 and 1979, systems producers began to integrate backward into IC design and production, either by creating their own IC capacity or by acquiring existing merchant producers. As Table 4-10 shows, from 1975 to 1980 at least 14 independent merchant houses, including Fairchild and Signetics, were acquired by foreign companies. With the notable exception of Fairchild, many of these merchant companies welcomed acquisition as a means of financing further growth or of establishing financial solidity in a period of financial crisis. The financial constraints imposed on smaller firms by the highly competitive and rapidly growing IC market in the 1970s made acquisition by a financially more secure parent an attractive option. Given the vicissitudes of the equity market and periodic downturns in the semiconductor business cycle, acquisition proved to be unavoidable.

While foreign companies played a dominant part in the wave of merchant acquisitions in the late 1970s, major U.S. users set up captive IC production and design facilities. The increasing number of U.S. firms involved in captive production included defense equipment companies such as Hughes, minicomputer companies like DEC, and electronic instrumentation manufacturers like Hewlett-Packard. Overall, systems producers set up captive facilities to give their final systems products a competitive edge through custom tailoring to deliver unique system features

Table 4–10. Corporate Investments in U.S. Semiconductor Companies Through 1979.

Company	Corporate Investor	Percentage Ownership	National Base
Advanced Micro Devices	Siemens	20%	West Germany
American Microsystems	Robert Bosch	12.5	West Germany
	Borg Warner	12.5	United States
Analog Devices	Standard Oil of Indiana		United States
Electronic Arrays	Nippon Electric		Japan
Exar	Toyo	53	Japan
Fairchild Camera	Schlumberger		Netherlands Antilles
Frontier	Commodore International		Bahamas
Inmos	National Enterprise Board		United Kingdom
Interdesign	Ferranti		United Kingdom
Intersil	Northern Telecom	24	Canada
Litronix	Siemens		West Germany
Maruman IC	Toshiba		Japan
Micropower Systems	Seiko		Japan
Monolithic Memories	Northern Telecom	12.4	Canada
MOS Technology	Commodore International		Bahamas
Mostek	United Technologies		United States
Precision Monolithics	Bourns		United States
SEMI, Inc.	GTE		United States
Semtech	Signal Companies		United States
Signetics	Phillips	Merger	Netherlands
Siliconix	Electronic Engineering of		United States
	California; Lucas Industries	24	United Kingdom

25

Solid State Scientific	VDO Adolf Schindling	West Germany
Spectronics	Honeywell	United States
Supertex	Investment Group	Hong Kong
Synertek	Honeywell	United States
Unitrode	Signal Companies	United States
Western Digital	Emerson Electric	United States
Zilog	Exxon	United States

[a]No entry indicates 100 percent (wholly owned), or presumed to be wholly owned in the absence of data.

Source: Morgan Stanley Electronics Letter, December 31, 1979; Dataquest, Inc., January 1979, for percentage of ownership; The Consulting Group, BA Asia Ltd., 1980, for Maruman IC data.

or to produce higher performance or reliability than was typical for merchant products.

THE INTERNATIONAL CHARACTER OF THE U.S. INDUSTRY, 1970–1980

The competitive dynamism spurred through the successive industry stages of development examined in the last sections also resulted in the increasing multinationality of U.S. firm operations during the periods under consideration. Direct foreign investment by U.S. merchant firms has been an integral aspect of their penetration of foreign markets and of their competitive position in the U.S. market.

Foreign investment has been of two types: investment in offshore assembly facilities and in point-of-sale affiliates.[48] Point-of-sale affiliates have been established primarily in Europe both to mitigate the impact of the relatively high EEC tariff and to coordinate circuit designs with European buyer demands. Offshore affiliates, on the other hand, have been established largely in Southeast Asia and Latin America to take advantage of low-cost foreign labor to assemble U.S. manufactured subassemblies for export back to the United States and to third markets.

The shift offshore was an aggressive move to reduce labor costs in the most labor-intensive stages of IC manufacture. It began in the mid-1960s with Fairchild's opening of assembly facilities in Hong Kong. The apparently natural division in IC production between wafer fabrication, assembly, and testing allowed the assembly stage of production to be located at a different facility from the fabrication and testing stages without any serious impact on learning economies. In turn, the substantial difference between wage costs in Southeast Asian developing countries and the United States offered a substantial economic incentive to shift assembly offshore. Finan estimates that the lower wage rates available in Southeast Asia and Latin America could yield up to a 50 percent reduction in total IC manufacturing costs: "For example, the total manufacturing cost for a MOS integrated circuit in 1973 was approximately $1.45 per device with assembly done in Singapore. If the same device was assembled in the U.S., the total manufacturing cost would be about $3.00."[49]

The timing and location of offshore assembly investment, however, was also conditioned by U.S. policies that provided an additional set of economic incentives. On the one hand, the Tariff Schedules of the United States were amended in 1963; under Items 807 and 806.30, imported articles assembled in whole or in part of U.S. fabricated components became dutiable only to the extent of the value added abroad. "Reductions in the duties achieved through use of Items 806.30 and 807 act to offset the transportation expenses incurred in using offshore facilities," thereby enhancing the final cost competitiveness of U.S. firm imports into the United States against foreign imports that do not receive similar tariff treatment.[50] On the other hand, beginning in 1967, the governments of Mexico, Taiwan, Singapore, Malaysia, and Korea established "export platforms" to encourage direct foreign investment in manufacturing for export. While the packages of economic incentives differed among developing countries, most involved duty-free export and import, property tax reductions, and some form of income tax holiday. While far from determinative, these various inducements were found in at least one survey to have ranked second behind the availability of low-cost labor among the reasons cited by industry executives for the shift to offshore production.[51]

The first great wave of offshore assembly affiliates was established during the 1964–1972 period, with Mexico, Hong Kong, Malaysia, Singapore, and Korea the leading offshore locations.[52] By 1974, the number of offshore assembly facilities in low-wage developing countries had risen to 69.[53] By 1978, the top nine U.S. IC manufacturers together had 35 offshore assembly facilities in 10 developing countries in Southeast Asia and Latin America.[54]

The second type of direct foreign investment, one with much more strategically beneficial consequences, has been the establishment of point-of-sale affiliates, primarily in Europe, to enhance the ability of U.S. firms to penetrate foreign markets. Finan lists five general factors that influenced the decision by U.S. firms to initiate assembly in the European market:[55]

1. The size of the European market
2. The relatively high EEC tariff (17 percent of value)
3. The competitive advantage over other U.S. firms which early investors, such as TI had derived from their European operations
4. British and French government pressure on U.S. firms, particularly those serving the European military market, to take on more of the character of domestic producers

5.   The fact that, as IC devices began to implement entire systems on a single chip, greater coordination in chip design between buyer and seller became a crucial factor influencing sales.

The major period of direct foreign investment by U.S. IC firms in Europe was 1969–1974. By 1974, U.S. firms had established over 46 point-of-sale affiliates within the EEC, of which at least 18 were engaged in complete manufacturing activities.[56] The early U.S. leaders in technology—TI, Fairchild, and Motorola—also led the move to European direct investment. As we shall see in Chapter 8, the U.S. entrenchment in Europe became a critical component underwriting the overall U.S. position in world chip markets.

The same factors that led U.S. firms to invest in point-of-sale affiliates in Europe also encouraged U.S. firms to invest in Japan, though with much less success. Only TI, with its strong patent position, was able to extract from the Japanese government permission to establish a wholly owned manufacturing subsidiary in Japan prior to 1978. To circumvent the Japanese 12 percent ad valorem tariff on imports of ICs from the United States, Finan suggests, other U.S. firms in the period prior to 1974 used offshore assembly affiliates in the developing countries of Southeast Asia as export platforms to the Japanese market. Imports into Japan from an affiliate located in a less developed country were duty-free.[57] However, prior to 1975, ICs that contained more than 200 circuit elements could not enter Japan from any point of origin without the permission of the Japanese government.[58] As a consequence, U.S. firms had relatively little success in translating their superior technological capabilities and production experience into a strong position in the Japanese market. Moreover, the Japanese "liberalization" that began in 1976, while eliminating the import quota system on advanced ICs, began, for tariff purposes, to treat imports from U.S. affiliates in less developed countries as coming directly from the United States.[59] Obviously, this nullified the tariff advantages to U.S. firms of exporting to Japan from Southeast Asian assembly affiliates.

This political structure governing market access and trade in ICs therefore influenced the patterns of exchange in which U.S. firms engaged. In order to exploit their lead in IC technology and production experience, U.S. firms were compelled by tariffs to invest in point-of-sale affiliates in Europe, while a variety of trade restrictions in Japan (investment controls, quotas, and tariffs) led them to license their technology to Japanese firms as a means of generating residual earnings in a market to which access was at best difficult.

The patterns of trade suggest the following conclusions. First, most U.S. exports of finished ICs serve four markets: Britain, France, West Germany, and Japan. Second, U.S. exports of unfinished ICs (chips, dice, and wafers) go primarily to five countries—Malaysia, Singapore, Hong Kong, Korea, and the Philippines—for final assembly and packaging by U.S. affiliates located there. Third, the reexport of finished integrated circuits out of Malaysia, Singapore, Hong Kong, Korea, and the Philippines primarily serves five markets: the United States, Great Britain, France, West Germany, and Japan. Thus, U.S. based IC manufacturers maximized scale economies and learning-curve efficiencies on wafer fabrication operations in the United States, where about 80 percent of all U.S. industry wafer fabrication occurred. They minimized labor costs by assembling finished ICs primarily in Latin America and Southeast Asia for export and final sale to the five major industrial nations. In the absence of Japanese competition, this was a prudent and efficient production structure.

Paradoxically, this efficient production structure also left U.S. firms vulnerable to Japanese competition and to the changing technical and market requirements of chip production in the early 1980s. The temptation to justify the investment in offshore facilities sapped resources that might have been used for experimenting with reorganizing and automating a fully integrated (design-fabrication-assembly-test) chip production process. This was, of course, precisely the area in which Japanese firms generated their manufacturing advantage. Moreover, with the capital costs of assembly and test radically increasing in the 1980s, U.S. firms could not take advantage of the plant-level economies that became the determinants of production costs (since total investment could be amortized over a greater share and more stages of production if assembly and test were combined with fabrication in the same place).

Moreover, the U.S. attempt to reintegrate onshore production through automation in the face of intensified competition, led to a series of costly false starts as U.S. firms attempted to acquire and match the know-how that Japanese companies had developed over several decades of heavy investment. Bifurcated production intensified international competition through technology transfer by inviting new entry in Taiwan and Singapore. Finally, bifurcated production also limited the ability of existing merchant producers—by adding lengthy turnaround time—to take advantage, as a strategic response to Japanese competition, of the design and market lead they possessed in the development and sale of semicustom chips.

Very little of this was foreseeable in the mid-1970s, as the U.S. industry piled up market successes in seemingly unstoppable fashion, Between 1974 and 1978, U.S. based shipments of ICs grew at an annual rate of 17.7 percent, from $1.056 billion in 1974 to $3.950 billion in 1978. If we exclude the recession of 1975, the annual growth rate over the period 1976–1979 was even more dramatic: shipments in 1976 were some $2.5 billion and by 1979 exceeded $5 billion—an annual average growth rate of 26 percent.[60] Investment in production equipment worldwide was over $355 million in 1974 and exceeded $662 million by 1978, with more than 75 percent of that investment being made in the United States.[61] Investment in new plants and in plant improvements was over $188 million in 1974 and exceeded $234 million in 1978, with more than 71 percent of that investment being made in the United States.[62] Expenditures on IC research and development by U.S. firms were $329 million in 1974 and exceeded $529 million in 1978. By contrast, in 1978, Japanese IC shipments still had not exceeded 30 percent of the value of total U.S. shipments of ICs. The situation was to change dramatically in the decade that followed. To see how and why, we turn now to the Japanese industry and its development.

NOTES

1. This chapter draws heavily from and in part reproduces the work of James Millstein in Michael Borrus, James Millstein, and John Zysman, *U.S.-Japanese Competition in the Semiconductor Industry: A Study in International Trade and Technological Development,* Policy Papers in International Affairs, 17, (Berkeley: Institute of International Studies, 1982), and in Borrus and Millstein, *Technological Innovation and Industrial Growth: A Comparative Assessment of Biotechnology and Semiconductors,* Report prepared for the U.S. Congress (Office of Technology Assessment, March 1983).

2. Bell Telephone Laboratories, *Impact,* (ATT, 1982), Introduction.

3. U.S. Congress, Senate Committee on the Judiciary, Subcommittee on Patents, Trademarks and Copyrights, *Patent Practices of the Department of Defense* (1961), pp. 127–128.

4. John Tilton, *International Diffusion of Technology: The Case of Semiconductors* (Washington, D.C.: The Brookings Institution, 1971), p. 76.

5. *United States v. Western Electric Co.,* 1956 Trade Cas. (CCH ¶ 68, 246 (D.N.J., 1956) (consent decree).

6. Tilton, *International Diffusion of Technology* p. 57, table 4–2.

7.   Ibid., p. 57. See ibid., pp. 16–17, tables 2–1 and 2–2 for a breakdown.
8.   *Electronic News,* June 16, 1958, p. 4.
9.   The 35 licensees were Arnold Engineering, Globe Union, Hanovia Chemical and Manufacturing Company, T. R. Mallory Company, Microwaves Associates, Minneapolis Honeywell, Raytheon Manufacturing, Radio Receptor Company, Sprague Electric Company, Texas Instruments, Tung-Sol Electric Company, Automatic Electric, Automatic Telephone and Electric Company, The Baldwin Company, Bowser, British Thomson-Houston Company, Bulova Watch Company, Crane Company, L. M. Ericsson, Felton and Guilleaume Carlfswerk, General Electric Company, Hughes Tool Company, IBM Corporation, IT&T Corporation, Lenkurt Electric Company, National Cash Register Company, National Fabricated Fabrics, N. V. Philips, Pye, Radio Development and Research Corporation, Siemens and Halske, Telefunken Gesellschaft, Transistor Products, English Electric Company.
10.   *Bell Laboratories Record* 29 (August 1951): 379.
11.   U.S. Department of Commerce, Report on the U.S. Semiconductor Industry (1979) p. 8.
12.   U.S. Department of Commerce, Business and Defense Services Administration, *Electronic Components: Production and Related Data, 1952–1959,* p. 3, table 2.
13.   Tilton, *International Diffusion of Technology,* p. 52, table 4–1.
14.   Ibid., p. 52, table 4–1.
15.   Ibid., p. 57, table 4–2; p. 60, table 4–3; p. 66, table 4–5.
16.   For a more detailed discussion of the impact of the Department of Defense on the development of the civilian electronics industry in the United States, see Norman Asher and Leland Strom, "The Role of the Department of Defense in the Development of Integrated Circuits," Institute for Defense Analyses, Arlington, Va., 1977; James Utterback and Albert Murray, "The Influence of Defense Procurement and Sponsorship of Research and Development on the Development of Civilian Electronics Industry," Center for Policy Alternatives, Massachusetts Institute of Technology, Cambridge, Mass., 1977.
17.   Ian Mackintosh, *Microelectronics in the 1980's* (London: Mackintosh Publications, 1979), p. 66, table II.
18.   John G. Linville and C. Lester Hogan, "Intellectual and Economic Fuel for the Electronic Industry," *Science,* v. 195, March 18, 1977, p. 1107.
19.   Ibid.
20.   U.S. National Commission on Technology, Automation and Economic Progress, *Technology and The American Economy* (Washington, D.C., 1966), p. II–24.
21.   Asher and Strom, "Role of the Department of Defense," pp. 4, 17.
22.   Ibid., p. 17.

23. Ibid., p. 45.
24. U.S. Federal Trade Commission (FTC), *Staff Report on the Semiconductor Industry* (Washington, D.C.: U.S. Government Printing Office, 1977), p. 11, table II-3.
25. U.S. Department of Commerce, *Report on the U.S. Semiconductor Industry,* p. 46, table 3.5.
26. Mackintosh, *Microelectronics in the 1980's,* p. 65.
27. Ibid.
28. For an excellent study of the evolution of the computer industry, see John T. Sima, *The Computer Industry* (Lexington, Mass.: Lexington Books, 1975).
29. Charles River Associates, "Innovation, Competition, and Government Policy in the Semiconductor Industry," Boston, 1980, p. 2-3. A more detailed analysis of the product "races" discussed below can be found in chapter 4 of that study.
30. FTC, *Staff Report on the Semiconductor Industry,* p. 26, table II-9.
31. Ibid., p. 11, table II-3.
32. Charles River Associates, "Innovation, Competition, and Government Policy," pp. 4-16, 4-17.
33. Ibid., p. 4-18.
34. SIA, *International Microelectronic Challenge,* p. 35.
35. U.S. Department of Commerce, *Report on the U.S. Semiconductor Industry,* p. 56.
36. FTC, *Staff Report on the Semiconductor Industry,* p. 26, table II-9.
37. Charles River Associates, "Innovation, Competition, and Government Policy," p. 2-9.
38. U.S. House of Representatives, Ways and Means Committee, Subcommittee on Trade, *Competitive Factors Influencing World Trade in Semiconductors* (Washington, D.C.: Government Printing Office, 1980), p. 64, table 1.
39. U.S. Department of Commerce, *Report on the U.S. Semiconductor Industry,* pp. 46, 50.
40. "The Mess in Consumer Electronics," *Dun's Review,* June 1977, p. 72, and "The Great Digital Watch Shakeout," *Business Week,* May 2, 1977, p. 78.
41. Charles River Associates, "Innovation, Competition, and Government Policy," p. 4-23.
42. Ibid., pp. 4-22–4-28.
43. Mackintosh, *Microelectronics in the 1980's,* p. 65.
44. Bob Lund, Marvin Sirbu, and Jim Utterback, "Microprocessor Applications: Cases and Observations," Center for Policy Alternatives, Massachusetts Institute of Technology, 1979, Cambridge, Mass., p. 1.
45. Two excellent studies should be consulted for greater detail on the development of microprocessor applications: Lund, Sirbu, and Utterback,

"Microprocessor Applications," and Economic Intelligence Unit, Ltd., "Chips in the 1980's: The Application of Microelectronic Technology in Products for Consumer and Business Markets," London, June 1979.

46. Based on statistics from industry sources.

47. Based on statistics from industry sources.

48. This terminology is borrowed from William Finan, *The International Transfer of Semiconductor Technology Through U.S.-Based Firms,* (Washington, D.C.: National Science Foundation, 1975). Finan adds a third category, "complete manufacturing facilities," which we shall treat under the discussion of "point-of-sale affiliates."

49. Ibid., p. 60.

50. Ibid., p. 69.

51. For a more detailed discussion of the factors influencing "offshore assembly" activity, see Richard W. Moxan, "Offshore Production in Less-Developed Countries: A Case Study of Multinationality in the Electronics Industry," *The Bulletin,* nos. 98–99, July 1974, and "Effects of Offshore and Onshore Foreign Direct Investment in Electronics: A Survey," Report for the Office of Technology Assessment, Washington, D.C., 1980.

52. Finan, *International Transfer of Semiconductor Technology,* p. 56.

53. U.S. Department of Commerce, *Report on the U.S. Semiconductor Industry,* p. 86.

54. Moxan, "The Effects of Offshore and Onshore Foreign Direct Investment in Electronics," p. 24.

55. Finan, *International Transfer of Semiconductor Technology,* p. 74.

56. U.S. Department of Commerce, *Report on the U.S. Semiconductor Industry,* pp. 84, 85.

57. Finan, *International Transfer of Semiconductor Technology,* p. 75.

58. Ibid., p. 95

59. U.S. Department of Commerce, *Report on the U.S. Semiconductor Industry,* p. 96, n.2.

60. U.S. Department of Commerce, *1980 U.S. Industrial Outlook* (Washington, D.C.: Government Printing Office, 1980), p. 268.

61. U.S. International Trade Commission (USITC), *Competitive Factors Influencing World Trade in Integrated Circuits,* p. 105.

62. Ibid., p. 104.

5 THE RISING SUN

On July 15, 1975 the Japanese Ministry of International Trade and Industry (MITI) and Japan's public telecommunications monopoly, Nippon Telegraph and Telephone (NTT), agreed to unite parts of their separate LSI R&D projects into a joint program aimed at developing the next generation of semiconductor technology, very large scale integration (VLSI). The four-year project began in 1976 and was funded at $250–350 million (72 billion yen). The funding was by government subsidies of some $150 million (30 billion yen) and by contributions from the program's private company participants, five of the six largest Japanese IC producers.[1]

Perhaps one-quarter to one-third of the project's funding was spent in the United States to purchase the most advanced semiconductor manufacturing and test equipment from U.S. equipment manufacturers.[2] As these purchases suggest, the VLSI program was aimed at catching up to U.S. industry production capability in advanced integrated circuits. The program freed Japanese firms to apply resources to the development of advanced, high value-added ICs aimed at the competitive penetration of the U.S. merchant semiconductor market.

The strategy coalesced with the domestic reorganization in 1971 of the Japanese semiconductor-electronics industry.[3] The major Japanese firms expanded their semiconductor production capacity to meet growing demand in the variety of their domestic end-markets. The firms moved from semiconductors for consumer electronic products to an advanced IC capability that could serve domestic computer and telecommunications demand.

From the mid-1970s, the major Japanese semiconductor firms also developed a solid marketing and distribution base in the United States— essential for penetration of a U.S. market completely dominated by U.S. firms. After 1977, demand in the United States for 16K RAM greatly exceeded supply. Excess demand meshed perfectly with the Japanese strategy for penetration. By the end of 1979, Japanese firms—led by NEC, Hitachi, and Fujitsu—had captured over 40 percent of the U.S. market for 16K RAM. Simultaneously, the Japanese VLSI project wound down with an output of 600–700 patents, and left the participating Japanese firms well aimed toward VLSI capability. At the start of the new decade, then, the once unchallengeable U.S. domination of the world IC market was very much in doubt.

The VLSI program and Japanese penetration of the U.S. integrated circuit market were (and are) part of a conscious national strategy of creating comparative advantage in the technology-intensive and knowledge-intensive industries. MITI has been explicit about its goal:

> [The] spirit of basing national development on technology should be our aim in the 1980s. . . . The basic course of knowledge intensification during the 1980s should be to increase the value added of products through technology intensification. . . . International specialization between Japan and advanced countries will also become possible as a result of the growth of industries where Japan has unique, creative technologies. . . . Possession of her own technology will help Japan to maintain and develop her industries' international superiority and to form a foundation for the long-term development of the economy and society.[4]

The rise of Japanese competitiveness in world IC markets, like the more general goal of creating comparative advantage, rested on a conscious state and industry strategy. Access to the domestic Japanese market was controlled, the terms of domestic competition were structured, the development of leading-edge user industries like computers and telecommunications was promoted, and cheap capital was made available for competitive investment. The controlled and structured domestic market was used as a secure base from which to create manufacturing advantage, develop competitive strengths, and establish competitiveness in international markets.

THE SYSTEMIC ADVANTAGES OF DOMESTIC STRUCTURE AND MARKET POWER

Since the end of the Second World War, the Japanese have been committed to rapid economic development. Economic growth has been the central political goal to which all other Japanese policies have been subordinated.[5] The conscious theme of policy has been to create comparative advantage in high value-added industries as an alternative to remaining dependent on the labor-intensive industries that might seem appropriate to an economy short on resources and capital. As a resource-poor nation dependent on the export of manufactures to pay even today for the importation of almost 90 percent of its energy needs, over half of its food, and the greater part of its chief resources, the Japanese chose industries for domestic development that could serve to expand overseas sales.[6]

The state aggressively promoted the shift out of agriculture into industry and out of low-wage into high-wage industrial sectors. Government policy served to channel resources into those industries for which there was growing domestic demand and potential economies of scale to facilitate export. The targets were machinery, metals, chemicals, and ships in the 1950s, then automobiles and heavy machinery, and by the 1970s, nuclear power and the information industries. The state played a crucial role in manipulating the access of foreign competitors to the domestic Japanese market, in restructuring the key domestic industries to promote their export competitiveness, and in helping to secure financial and technical critical mass. All of these tactics were an integral part of the development of the Japanese semiconductor electronics industry.

The theory underlying both control over access and the restructuring of domestic industry was

> to place undeveloped domestic industries with little competitive power under the government's active interference . . . to build up a large scale production system, while limiting entry into the domestic market of foreign enterprises with already established mass production systems and restricting the competition of foreign manufacturers in the domestic market.[7]

In the role of controlling access, the Japanese government was an "official doorman (between domestic Japanese society and the international arena), determining what, and under what conditions, capital, technology and manufactured products enter and leave Japan."[8] Selective control over internal foreign investment discouraged foreign efforts to control Japanese firms and to manufacture in Japan. Imports were limited through tariff and nontariff barriers to ensure that domestic firms would capture most of the explosive growth in domestic demand. Technology imports were controlled by MITI in order to force foreign firms, whenever possible, to sell technology and to be content with royalty payments rather than product sales in Japan. Thus, a "closed" market provided Japanese firms a stable base of demand on which to build competitive production and distribution networks.[9]

In its companion role as promoter of domestic industry, the state followed policies "which emphasized efficiency and rationalization."[10] It encouraged competition through extensive support for expanding firms. The state organized a stable availability of cheap capital; it provided tax breaks to assure cash flow liquidity, gave R&D support, and helped to promote the growth of domestic demand and of exports. Winners were encouraged, losers weeded out. In most sectors, a few large vertically integrated firms emerged and carved up the domestic market as a matter of company strategy and state policy. Markets were rationalized, and, in MITI's words, "intraindustrial specialization" was encouraged as a means of building efficient scale economies in market segments.[11] Capacity expansion was often planned with state help, and official or informal "recession cartels" were organized to manage periods of overcapacity. In these many ways, "disruptive" competition was avoided. Thus, vertical integration, "rationalization, oligopolization and cartelization were an integral part of the sectoral development policy."[12]

Deeply contrasting images characterize the dominant analytic descriptions of the resulting Japanese economic system. At one extreme lies the image of "Japan, Inc.," in which at every level of relations, businessmen and governmental promoters collaborate to further the development and international competitiveness of Japanese business. At the other extreme is "Japan, the Land of Fierce Competition," in which cutthroat competition is assumed to characterize domestic Japanese markets. The available evidence in a range of economic sectors—the semiconductor-electronics sector in particular—suggests that the extreme images are partial truths.

Especially in the face of foreign economic and political power, there is a collaborative unity within the conservative coalition of business and state actors that rules Japan. Such collaboration can be expressed through formal, state-sanctioned market sharing arrangements (like the recession cartels) or through less formal arrangements among economic actors (such as the strong preference to "Buy Japanese"). Simultaneously, among members of the ruling coalition—that is, among corporations and bureaucratic actors (such as MITI and NTT), as well as between business and the state—strong competition flourishes. Japanese firms do compete with one another in domestic and international markets. Japanese firms disagree about strategy, they can act independently of state strategies, and they often ignore the government pressures for market rationalization to compete fiercely and directly in segments of growing markets.

The Japanese economic system is thus one of controlled competition, in which the intensity of competition between firms in key industrial sectors is directed and limited both by state actions and by the formal and informal collaborative efforts of industrial and financial enterprises. The limits of competitive behavior change over time and from sector to sector. As a general rule, Japanese firms within market segments tend to tolerate existing market shares, in part because these shares are partly captive of long-established business relations among firms in the same family of companies. Meanwhile, the firms compete over expanding shares of growing markets. This has been the case during Japan's period of rapid growth, when increasing investment at a pace at least equal to the pace of domestic market growth was necessary merely to maintain market position; that is, if the market grew from year to year by 50 percent, so investment in production capacity had to also.[13]

Such competition probably shades into collaboration in the face of foreign penetration of domestic Japanese markets. Thus firms compete but they also collaborate. In turn, the state has resources and authority that permit it to alter the pattern of constraints and opportunities facing firms in the market. By providing funds to mitigate the riskiness of R&D spending here, or organizing a cartel to deal with overcapacity there, the government adopts the guise of an actor in the market. In essence the state becomes an industrial institution in its own right with the capacity to affect market outcomes by altering the logic of market dynamics facing firms.

When most successful in its dual role of doorman and promoter, the state has helped in a detailed way to develop conditions of investment, risk, and collaboration that have helped to establish the long-term development and international competitiveness of favored industries. But state policy in this image can also be misguided and can even fail. Government intervention to alter constraints and opportunities facing firms in the market does not in and of itself dictate firm strategies or the outcomes of competition. It simply creates a differently structured business environment in which the choices facing firms change. Some firms will succeed by operating in conjunction with the logic of changed circumstances—as, for example, Japan's major telecommunications firms have succeeded by operating in conjunction with NTT.[14] Other firms can and do succeed by developing a strategy that plays against the apparent logic of the new structured environment—as, for example, small, innovative machine shops did during the 1960s and 1970s in developing new customers and lobbying for new financing mechanisms to reduce their dependence on Japan's large corporations and to resist MITI-guided consolidation.[15]

State policy would not have succeeded without the efforts, investments, and strategies of Japanese industry, but industry would almost certainly have failed without the state. It is the character of the interaction that matters, not the credit for success which each side might claim.

The character of the interaction in semiconductors finds parallels in other major industries. In automobiles, for example, the domestic market was closed to foreign producers, a competitive components industry was established under government leadership, and the infrastructure was laid down by public investment to permit a rapid increase in automobile usage.[16] In 1960 Japan produced 160,000 automobiles; by 1970, the figure was 3.1 million; by 1980, Japan was producing over 8 million automobiles a year. The consequent Japanese success in the U.S. automobile market needs no recounting here. The story is similar in steel. State intervention closed the domestic market to preserve it for Japanese firms, provided cheap investment capital, staged investment through a series of rationalization plans to avoid overcapacity, and helped to manage excess capacity when it occurred.[17] Firms did not always follow state policy, however, and by risking competitive expansion in the face of state (and sometimes industry) opposition, some firms prospered. In 1950 Japan produced about 5 million net tons of steel, by 1960 some 24 million net tons, and by 1970 over 100 million net tons per year. It was also the lowest cost volume steel production in the world, with a full 40 perent of production exported every year.

Control over access, on the one hand, and promotion of market rationalization, oligopolization, and financial stability on the other hand, have thus created certain commonalities in Japanese business strategies across a range of sectors. Initial production volume is built on a tacitly closed domestic market with different firms achieving large-scale economies in part through intraindustrial specialization in subsegments of each market. Intense competition between firms appears to be centered on the expanding share of the market. Volume production is steadily expanded through selective exploitation of market niches abroad. Those niches provide an initial penetration of foreign markets and are followed by full-scale export drives. The growing domestic market requires increases in production capacity. Each increase provides a new opportunity for production reorganization in order to generate a production cost advantage or an increase in product variety permitting successful differentiation in the market. Steadily increasing production volumes at home thus generate the production economies that have often made Japanese producers the low-cost international competitors.

The characteristic features of Japan's developmental system and the company strategies it encourages and sustains have contributed to Japan's international competitiveness in semiconductors. In pursuit of MITI's goal of creating comparative advantage in the knowledge-intensive and technology-intensive industries, the Japanese had to turn a relatively backward semiconductor industry into a world-class competitor. During the 1970s, the Japanese industry moved from a consumer product orientation and a position of relative technological inferiority in components toward a state-of-the-art capability in components, telecommunications, and computers.

Domestic Structure And Market Power

The six major Japanese producers of semiconductors are large multidivisional, vertically integrated firms that manufacture electronics systems products serving end-markets primarily in consumer electronics, computers, and communications. The six firms, roughly in order of their share of the domestic Japanese IC market, are NEC, Hitachi, Toshiba, Fujitsu, Mitsubishi, and Matsushita. These six firms dominate the Japanese domestic semiconductor market and accounted for approximately 89 percent of domestic sales in 1979. The percentages of their total sales in 1986 accounted for by semiconductor sales (in comparison with a sample of representative U.S. merchant firms) are as follows:[18]

Japanese Firms		U.S. Firms	
NEC	20%	AMD	89%
Fujitsu	14	Fairchild	69
Toshiba	9	Intel	75
Hitachi	8	Mostek	93
Mitsubishi	9	Motorola	31
Matsushita	4	National	60
		Texas Instruments	36

These figures indicate why it is misleading to label the Japanese companies simply as semiconductor producers. Gresser's characterization of the industry as a unitary semiconductor-computer-telecommunications industry captures its systems character and the slant of its growth but understates the industry's continued heavy involvement in consumer electronics (which still consumes roughly 35–40 percent of ICs).[19] In order to emphasize the systems orientation of the industry, the major firms must be briefly profiled (see Table 5–1).

NEC is Japan's leading communications systems and equipment producer, its second leading computer manufacturer, and the largest producer of integrated circuits in the world. It is a domestic leader in metal oxide on silicon very large-scale integration, and especially in memory and microprocessor technology. Fujitsu is Japan's leading mainframe computer manufacturer and a leader in advanced MOS memory and digital bipolar semiconductor producton. Hitachi is Japan's largest diversified electronic systems producer serving computer, communications, and consumer markets, and is a major producer of heavy industrial equipment and electrical machinery. It is strong in MOS memories and is Japan's largest producer of logic circuits. Toshiba is also a large conglomerate which produces heavy electrical equipment, instrumentation, appliances, and electronic systems. It is a leader in standard and custom CMOS and linear semiconductor devices. Mitsubishi is a large diversified producer of electronic systems, Japan's largest manufacturer of small business computers, and a manufacturer of industrial and heavy electrical machinery and applicances. It has adequate capability in MOS and digital bipolar and good capability in industrial and consumer linear devices. Matsushita is Japan's, and one of the world's, largest consumer electronics and home appliance producers. It derives most of its IC income from consumer linear ICs and while not a major force in the domestic MOS LSI and bipolar markets,[20] it has demonstrated impressive MOS memory and processor capabilities. All of these six large firms are multibillion dollar companies, with sales in 1986 ranging from Fujitsu's $8–9 billion to Hitachi's $28 billion. Japan's other major producers include the consumer electronics giants Sharp, Sanyo, and Sony, and telecom producer Oki Electric. There are several other secondary producers who produce largely in-house, like Canon and Ricoh, and several new entrants like NMB, division of ball-bearing maker Minebea, who do not as yet account for much production volume.

It is important to emphasize the degree to which, though vertically integrated, these companies are composed of smaller, partially autonomous

Table 5–1. Dominant Firms in the Japanese Semiconductor (SC) Industry, 1986.

Firm	Total Sales ($billion)	Semiconductor Sales ($billion)	% SC Sales	Semiconductor Strength	Systems Market Segments
NEC	13	2.5	20	MOS memory and micropro-cessors, ECL bipolar, linear and discretes	Leading IC powerhouse Leader in telecommunica-tions, computers
Hitachi	28	2.3	7	MOS memory and micropro-cessors, digital bipolar, linear and discretes	Leading diversified systems in computers, communications, con-sumer, heavy industrial, and electrical machinery
Fujitsu	9	1.3	14	MOS memory, gate arrays, bipolar logic	Leader in computers, audio products, communications
Toshiba	22	2.2	10	CMOS logic, MOS memory, gate arrays, microprocessors, linear	Diversified systems, esp. consumer, industrial, instrumentation, and elec-trical equipment
Mitsubishi	12	1.1	9	MOS memory, discrete and linear	Diversified systems for small business, com-puters, industrial and heavy machinery
Matsushita	27	1.2	4	Consumer linear, microprocessors	Leader in consumer and ap-pliances, home computers

divisions quite different from the American vertical integration model.[21] While some divisions are closely consolidated on the U.S. model, other divisions are more or less autonomous, often vying for financing with the parent company, and pursuing independent purchasing and investment policies. While core businesses, like semiconductors and computers, may be closely and strategically interconnected, other divisions, like semiconductor materials or applications software, may not be. In this way Japanese firms can take advantage of the pressure of market competition to ensure that internal divisions are competitive for the parent in price and quality. In that sense the large Japanese firms are a microcosm of the horizontal and vertical relations that obtain in the broader industrial groups of which they are each a part.

Each of the top six Japanese semiconductor companies is tied to a *keiretsu,* a conglomerate industrial grouping of companies arranged around either a single large bank or large industrial firm (or several firms).[22]

Keiretsu Affiliations

Fujitsu Ltd.	Dai-Ichi Kangyo Bank (DKB) Group
Hitachi Ltd.	Hitachi Group and others
Matsushita Electronics Industrial	Matsushita Group
Mitsubishi Electric Corporation	Mitsubishi Group
NEC	Sumitomo Group
Toshiba Corporation	Mitsui Group

The *keiretsu*'s form ranges from groups with close intercompany ties, like the Sumitomo and Mitsubishi groups, to looser, basically financial arrangements, like the Dai Ichi Kangyo Bank group. *Keiretsu* members are bound by equity cross-ownership and interlocking management, financing, and buying-selling arrangements. Of course there is also equity cross-ownership outside of the *keiretsu* structure, for a majority of company stock in Japan is held by other companies or banks.[23] However, recent research indicates that that *keiretsu* affiliation predominates among the top 20 or 25 shareholders, those who could be expected to exert some influence in company decision-making.[24]

The *keiretsu* structure itself provides decisive advantages. First, and most critically, the *keiretsu* members provide important internal markets and supply for the firm's products and operations (as, for example, when the Dai Ichi Bank replaced its IBM banking system with a Fujitsu product).

These kinds of loose, quasi-ownership, quasi-market ties obtain up-stream, downstream, and horizontally. Thus, for example, NEC's ties to affiliated supplies of semiconductor material, like Sumitomo metals, and semiconductor production equipment like Anelva, ensure early, primary access to new innovations and prevent disruption of critical supplies when market conditions tighten. Similarly, NEC's downstream links to semiconductor users like Nitsuko (telecom) and Sumitomo Machinery ensure a guaranteed level of stable demand that, combined with NEC's internal consumption, mitigate the risk of aggressive investment in new chip production capacity. Other Sumitomo companies, like the insurance and heavy equipment affiliates, can be counted on to purchase NEC communication and computer systems, again providing a large internal market that mitigates investment risk and permits the attainment of initial production economies and associated debugging of new products. The Sumitomo bank and other financial sources can also be counted on to supply capital for expansion, virtually on an as-needed basis. In addition, each *keiretsu* usually includes a large trading company that has been frequently used by Japanese firms to perform overseas sales, distribution, and financing. The trading company thus provides increased access to international semiconductor markets. This was particularly true when Japan's major producers were smaller and far less experienced in dealing in foreign markets.

Intraindustrial specialization has enabled each firm to exercise a degree of control over different product segments of the overlapping systems markets it serves. Such specialization enables these Japanese firms to maximize economies of scale and scope, thereby optimizing the production cost efficiencies of their systems products. Again, this is not to suggest a lack of serious competition among Japanese firms in major final systems products; for example, NEC and Hitachi are currently engaged in a battle for the number two spot in large-scale computers behind Fujitsu. Rather, it appears that final systems markets have been rationalized, that individual firms specialize within market segments (Table 5–2), but that markets are growing fast enough to permit serious competition over increasing shares in segments where the systems product strengths of the major firms overlap.

The major Japanese firms slant their semiconductor production mix to meet the needs of the different markets which their systems products serve (see Table 5–2). Indeed, early on, the Japanese firms rationalized their semiconductor device production as a logical outgrowth of specialization in final systems markets. Such component-product rationalization

Table 5-2.   Domestic Market Share, by Semiconductor Type (%).

Firm	Digital MOS	MOS Memory	MPU	Logic	Digital Total	Bipolar ECL	Linear Bipolar
NEC	25	20	33	18	10	40	20
Hitachi	16	23	20	14	24	30	13
Toshiba	15	13	12	25	2	2	13
Fujitsu	7	17	5	4	20	20	2
Mitsubishi	6	10	7	7	9	2	7
Matsushita	5	4	7	—	4	—	17

Source: Japanese industry data, Japanese consulting sources.

among Japanese firms apes the market segmentation that can be found among merchant U.S. firms serving different systems markets in the United States. Thus, the two leading Japanese exporters of semiconductors to the world merchant market—NEC and Hitachi—are the firms whose systems capability in computers and communications use most technologically advanced devices.

However, while production mix correlates strongly with system product markets, internal (captive) consumption by the largest firms of their own production is relatively low.[25] Approximately 21 percent of the value of production is consumed internally by the 10 largest producers. The figure varies among firms. Toshiba, for example, internally consumes only 15 percent of total sales, while Fujitsu's internal consumption rate rises to perhaps 50 percent, which suggests a primary orientation toward computer sales. See the list below. Moreover, internal consumption is particularly low in MOS devices (10 percent on average among the top four firms in 1979).[26]

Such low internal consumption figures might seem peculiar because these same producers are also the largest consumers of domestic semiconductor devices. Indeed, the top 10 firms consume at least 60 percent of total Japanese domestic production, and the percentage of their consumption of the most advanced IC devices is undoubtedly even higher.[27] This juxtaposition of low internal with high overall consumption is complemented by another set of aggregate figures:

Captive Consumption (%)

NEC	22	Fujitsu	50	Oki	14
Hitachi	20	Matsushita	50	Sanyo	25
Toshiba	15	Mitsubishi	10	Sharp	30

These suggest that 80–90 percent of semiconductor output is consumed within the *keiretsu* of the major semiconductor producers. Two possible arguments can account for these aggregate figures. The figures illustrate trade among the major Japanese firms and their *keiretsu* based on a pattern of component and systems specialization; or they show extremely high intra-*keiretsu* consumption (and thus a captive market at the level of the *keiretsu*). Of course, both patterns of behavior could be operating simultaneously, with interfirm and inter-*keiretsu* trade probably dominating early on as Japanese firms specialized to try and reach sustainable production scale in the 1960s and early 1970s.

The implications of intercompany trade are important and mesh neatly with the observation that component specialization occurs among Japanese firms. The systems strengths of each firm rest in segmented but overlapping final markets. A more sophisticated specialization in certain devices and technologies may occur among Japanese firms in which they supply each other with semiconductor devices to meet the component needs of their overlapping systems products. Specialization would enable sophisticated rationalization of device production among the different firms. Indeed, one Fujitsu executive commented about specialization in certain components: "In a small market like Japan's, it is the only way to attain scales of production."[28] Interfirm trade in components necessary for specific final systems products may occur only minimally among the few direct competitors in each specific final market subsegment, however. Thus, NEC may be more likely to buy bipolar logic circuits from TI than from Fujitsu or Hitachi. The result of rationalization, wherever it occurs, is cheaper devices and cheaper systems that use these devices.

The argument about component specialization and consequent collaborative Japanese interfirm trade has been criticized because it allegedly "fails to answer why one Japanese firm would sacrifice profits by purchasing from another rather than from cheaper foreign supply."[29] When the Japanese industry was technologically backward and facing technologically advanced foreign competitors, collaborative interfirm trade would be a perfectly rational response: profits would be sacrificed simply to prevent the low-cost foreign competitors from overrunning the Japanese domestic market.

There is a crucial point to be made from the fact that the largest firms control over 60 percent of Japanese semiconductor consumption (and a higher percentage of advanced IC consumption). Hence they control the pace and direction of growth in that market. By altering the composition of their production and demand, these firms can control the share and composition of imports entering their domestic market. During the 1970s U.S. firms succeeded in penetrating the domestic Japanese market primarily with advanced product innovations that Japanese firms were not yet producing. As Japanese firms became competent in the production of such devices, U.S. firms found that their shares of the Japanese market in such devices leveled off or declined—even as domestic Japanese demand grew explosively—as the major Japanese firms replaced U.S. imports with devices produced internally and by other Japanese firms. Even if this pattern is no more than a straightforward import substitution, the ability to control even fully competitive imports still exists. Table 5–3 gives a rough indication of this ability.

The collaborative arrangements that control access to the Japanese market would thus appear to derive logically from past government-industry efforts to rationalize production in the domestic Japanese market when that market was small and Japanese firms were vulnerable to foreign competition. On the one hand, the arrangements would endure to the extent that each firm continued to enjoy benefits consonant with its own strategic conception of which products it wants to produce itself (given its long-term aims in systems markets). On the other hand, since domestic Japanese policies and practices have controlled new entry and regulated the pace of interfirm diffusion of new

Table 5–3. Consumption of Integrated Circuits in Japan, 1975–1980.

Year	Domestic Consumption (billions of yen)	Imports	Imports as a Percentage of Domestic Consumption	Percentage Change in Imports from Previous Year	Percentage Change in Consumption Previous Year
1975	Y 160	Y 59	31%		
1976	252	74	29	+48.0%	+57.5%
1977	272	64	24	−13.5	+ 7.9
1978	306	68	22	+ 6.2	+12.5
1979	403	111	27	+63.2	+31.7
1980	527	118	22	+ 6.3	+30.8

Source: Figures through 1978 based on data from The Consulting Group, BA Asia Ltd., 1980; MITI, Ministry of Finance from 1978–1980 from BA Asia Ltd., 1981 (unpublished).

technology through cooperative R&D like the VLSI project, the ability to sustain such collaborative behavior against outsiders would also endure.

Internal *keiretsu* demand appears to provide a stable, long-term and high-volume base of essentially captive demand on which each firm can rely for a substantial portion of sales—in most cases at least 35 percent and in some cases approaching 80 percent. Again, "essentially captive" means that each major producer either consumes internally a large percentage of its own production in its consumer electronic, computer, telecommunication, or other major end-use products, or that it can count on a high percentage consumption of its production by companies to which it is affiliated by virtue of *keiretsu* or other family ties.

Table 5–4 estimates the percentage of production accounted for by essentially captive sources of consumption for each major Japanese producer. It is quite interesting to note that these figures are confirmed if we start at the applications end and work backward from figures for the total available market for semiconductor consumption, as Table 5–5 shows.

Cheap and Abundant Capital

The infrastructural features permit the most significant advantage offered by the Japanese industrial and financial structure compared to its U.S. counterpart, a stable availability of (probably cheap) capital for continued growth—the basic need for semiconductor companies whose markets are expanding and whose products are changing rapidly. This point requires elaboration because stable access to capital would

Table 5–4. Essentially Captive Consumption (%).

Firm	Internal	Affiliated	Total
Fujitsu	48–55%	21–25%	70–80%
Hitachi	18–22	20–25	38–47
Matsushita	47–53	5– 7	52–60
Mitsusbishi	10–15	60–63	70–78
NEC	20–25	35–45	55–70
Oki	12–15	35–40	55–70
Toshiba	15–20	28–31	43–51

Source: Japanese industry sources.

Table 5–5. Selected Japan Applications and Semiconductor Consumption (Y-100M, Unit-100s).

Product	Monthly Production Value	Unit	Semiconductor Consumption Total	TAM	Captive%
Consumer	5,628.6	19,728	540.1	374.6	30.6
VCR	1,779.3	2,249.6	261.6	176	32.7
TV	655	1,284	101.5	61	39.9
Audio	1,465.3	3,076.5	105.5	71.2	32.5
Industrial	6,948.4	7,429	796.8	418.9	47.4
Office	1,704	250.6	163.6	155.4	5.0
Calculator	131	6,870	25.7	25.7	0
Facsimile	396.5	87	51.1	39.9	21.9
PC/WP	481.8	198.7	183.7	73.8	60.3
Office computers	189.8	7.3	73.8	26.2	64.5
Computer/terminal	1,904	3.4	112.3	36	67.9
Robot	22,138.3	27,156.7	1,336.9	793.5	40.6

Source: Japanese industry sources.

seem to be an odd attribute, given the financing structure of the Japanese industry, particularly during the 1970s. As every observer has noted, the Japanese semiconductor companies, with the exception of Matsushita, have (until recently) debt-to-equity ratios of 150–400 percent, compared with U.S. firm ratios of 5–25 percent. In an industry as volatile as semiconductors, where innovation can easily upset the plans of corporate investment, such high debt/equity ratios, with their attendant fixed costs, would normally imply instability rather than stability in the availability of capital. The more volatile an industry, the riskier it is for the lender and the less willing normally to lend. What, then, are the infrastructural advantages that mitigate the risk of carrying debt in Japan and that provide Japanese firms stable access to debt capital?

It should first be noted that Japan's remarkably rapid postwar development was of necessity debt-financed. Rapid expansion could not be sustained from internal profits alone, and the state could control the allocation of debt in a way that it could not control equity. The state indirectly influenced capital allocation toward favored industries, and as Ueno has shown, private lending followed shifts in public lending:

Broadly speaking, the total supply of funds in Japan was controlled by the Bank of Japan, the level and structure of interest rates were artificially regulated by the Ministry of Finance, and private funds were allocated, under the guidance of public financial institutions, by city banks which competed for market shares.[30]

Corporate debt was shared by the banks, which diffused the risk to each. But collapse of a highly leveraged firm could threaten the banks as well as the company and its suppliers. Since a bank collapse could spread throughout the economy, company troubles became a matter of public policy. Indeed, as Wellons argues, the Japanese government has permitted no bank to fail since World War II.[31] At bottom, then, despite the risks of high leverage, the resulting system is stable because government concern with the well-being of firms in favored sectors, like semiconductors, is taken as an implicit guarantee of loans made to them.[32]

The long-term risk born by lenders is thus reduced by the structural participation of the Japanese government, working through the Bank of Japan, in assisting financially troubled firms. Famous cases involving Mazda and Oki Electric attest to the system's patience.[33] Lending risk is further reduced by a number of additional structural features. As the Chase study noted:

> To the extent that a *keiretsu* bank directly or indirectly owns a significant interest in the shares of a borrower, it has a continuing voice in establishing corporate policy and direction. This control, coupled with the assurance of financial assistance or loan guarantees from the borrower's *keiretsu*, reduces the risk taken by lenders.[34]

The huge size and product line diversification of the Japanese electronics firms also make them a more secure investment risk. Indeed, the structure of market rationalization and group ties also mitigates risk because firms are less exposed to competitive failure in the market segments they dominate. These Japanese firms normally hold relatively large portfolios of cash, time deposits, and securities. Large time deposits held in lender banks compensatorially balance the loan exposure of these banks, and large security holdings of relatively liquid assets mitigate investment risk. Most of the older Japanese firms also have enormous real estate holding acquired in the nineteenth and early twentieth centuries, which are carried on their books at purchase value, but are orders of magnitude more valuable at current market prices.[35] Since debts can be translated into lender claims on this valuable asset, lending risk is reduced even further. In sum, low risk for investors means greater willingness to lend, and that translates into relatively stable access to debt capital for Japanese semiconductors firms.

The same infrastructural features also appeal to U.S. investors. U.S. banks that lend to Japan understand that Japanese banks and ultimately the Japanese government and the Bank of Japan are the sources of security for U.S. bank loans. Thus, for example, when the Ataka trading company went bankrupt in the early 1970s, Sumitomo and Kyowa Banks intervened, salvaging the investments of unsecured foreign creditors until a buyer could be found.[36] Here, the Japanese domestic structure provides important advantages for Japanese firms that compete with U.S. firms for international debt capital from "American" multinational banks.

Finally, the large diversified operations of the Japanese electronics companies add to the stability of capital. Funding of electronics projects is generated by other operations of the corporation—this has been critical during semiconductor recessions. Profits earned in older, declining sectors are used to finance expansion of the growing operations. The money may be used directly or to make interest payments on debt incurred in financing expansion.

The availability of capital provides crucial advantages for growth and competitive development. The stability of capital allows Japanese firms' managers to plan for the long term. The extensive use of bank-financed debt provides additional freedom to Japanese managers. The banks can give them commitments for a series of loans over many years. The funds that the corporation will have available are not dependent on the immediate earnings of its operations or the price of its stock, as in the United States. Short-term fluctuations in the companies' operations can be more easily explained and communicated to a small group of cooperative banker-owners than to participants in an impersonal capital market.

Capital is much less consistently available to U.S. firms, who raise most of their capital through retained earnings and equity investment (as their debt/equity ratios suggest). Since U.S. merchant firms lack those infrastructural advantages that mitigate the risk of carrying debt in Japan, they simply cannot operate at comparable debt levels: lenders would see the risk as so extreme that they would refuse to provide capital. Furthermore, U.S. firms operate with certain other disadvantages compared to the Japanese industry. The financing of projects from current earnings could well force a firm to forgo promising projects, which would ultimately yield market share and profits, because of a current slump in sales. Long-term planning is much more difficult. Moreover, a return to the equity markets might not provide a meaningful choice much of the time. New equity issues must be timed to coincide with variable evaluation of the stock in the market. High stock prices may be poorly correlated with a firm's internal requirements for capital. And whether or not they actually need do so, U.S. managers are highly sensitive to expectations for quarterly improvements in earnings to raise the price of shares and generate higher dividends.[37] The firm may be unwilling or unable to inform the public of its long-term projects and thus unable to prevent a fall in the price of shares when current earnings falter. A reduction in the value of the stock decreases the ability of the firms to raise not only equity but also additional debt. With or without a sustained decline in the price of the stock, a takeover of the company by unfriendly outsiders is always a threat.

Aside from the advantages provided by access to debt capital, Japanese firms may also enjoy access to cheaper capital. This is the central claim of the Chase Econometrics study and of several successor studies over the years.[38]

The lower prime lending rate is often mistakenly identified as prima facie evidence of a Japanese cost of capital advantage, especially given the greater dependence of Japanese firms on debt. Yet, the compensatory account balances required by Japanese lenders, collateralization of loans, and the equity positions of lenders would all tend to raise the effective lending rate in Japan closer to market rates elsewhere.[39] Nonetheless, Phillip Wellons offers a convincing analytic argument to support the lower cost of capital thesis.[40] He shows that in various ways Japan induces its savers and financial intermediaries to accept lower real rates of return, thereby lowering the cost of capital. In addition, Japanese banks manage the flow of credit in ways that, compared to equity markets, reduce firms' vulnerability to recessions, thus providing cheaper capital over the full business cycle. Finally, Wellons suggests that the overall structure of the Japanese financial system, in which policy substantially influenced the flow of funds, created a highly segmented capital market in which intense competition among lenders within segments lowered capital costs to borrowers.

Since large size, diversification, and a tacit government guarantee against failure reduce the likelihood that Japanese firms will be unable to repay a loan, lower interest costs should result. The risk to lenders is generally perceived to be smaller when financing a $200 million expansion for a corporation with $2 billion in assets than when financing the same expansion for a corporation with only $100 million in assets.

Since the late 1970s, there has been a marked move toward less reliance on debt and greater reliance on retained earnings and bonds and equity by Japan's large firms.[41] Evidence suggests, however, that diversification of credit sources has not eliminated cost of capital advantages probably enjoyed by Japanese firms. First, stable equity sources in Japan, where 70–80 percent of stockholding is essentially not traded, are compensated by the long-term receipt of free shares rather than by the payment of a premium on dividends. This would tend to reduce the short-term costs of capital below U.S. market-equivalent rates.[42] Finally, the move to external (foreign) funding sources permits Japanese firms to shop for the best deal; in conjunction with their size, group ties, and other implicit guarantees of stability, they must be seen as low-risk investments. The result is undoubtedly lower cost of capital than for their U.S. counterparts.

Cheap and available capital is a special advantage in an industry like semiconductors, resulting ultimately in cheaper final product. As the industry has matured, the contribution to total device cost that comes from capital equipment has increased. In turn, the cost of capital has become a much more significant component of final product cost. For example, in the early 1970s the ratio of capital investment to annual revenues for wafer fabrication was on the order of approximately 1:15. By the early 1980s, that ratio had already declined to on the order of 1:2. The figure may be closer to 1:1.5 today.[43]

The stable capital supply allows Japanese firms to finance R&D and capacity expansion, engage in price competition to expand market share and finance penetration of foreign markets with relative unconcern for current earnings, even in a recessionary environment. By contrast, growth, development, and the ability to compete over market share are all less stable for U.S. firms because they are subject to the vicissitudes of the business cycle. U.S. firms must be very profitable to attract or generate sufficient capital to grow and compete.

Effects of the Domestic Structure

As in numerous other Japanese industrial sectors, vertical integration, oligopolization, and *keiretsu*-rationalization stabilize the domestic market environment and permit the Japanese firms in this industry to build massive production volumes in devices and systems destined for export. Control over access further stabilizes the domestic market and prevents U.S. firms from consolidating their innovations and victories in the international marketplace into long-term advantage in the Japanese market. The domestic market thus serves as a stable, mass production base from which to launch penetration of foreign markets, particularly the U.S. market. Stability of capital secures the domestic base and underwrites the Japanese ability to bear short-run adjustment costs in order to gain increasing shares of foreign markets over the long run.

These domestic features provide potentially formidable advantages for Japanese firms in international competition, but of course they do not guarantee success. They could not, for example, overcome Japan's absolute feedstock cost disadvantage in petrochemicals, especially when the larger, entrenched European and U.S. firms that dominate that industry chose aggressively to defend their market position. Nor, for example, could a closed domestic market compensate for too small demand to support independent Japanese entry into the aircraft industry. But in the semiconductor industry, as in consumer electronics, steel, autos, and so many others, the advantages of domestic Japanese market structures proved decisive.

STATE ACTION AND THE PROMOTION OF INTERNATIONAL COMPETITIVENESS

By 1968, the Japanese semiconductor-electronics industry was almost completely dominated by production for consumer electronic products. The industry was weak in IC capability, and IC production accounted for only about $24 million out of a semiconductor production of some $252 million, and a total component production of some $1.4 billion.[44] By 1978, a majority of Japanese semiconductor production was still in the consumer area, but production for computers and telecommunications had brought Japanese firms near international state-of-the-art capability in IC production. IC production accounted for some $1.2 billion out of a semiconductor production of some $2.4 billion and a total components production of some $18.75 billion.[45]

The weakness of Japanese markets in computers and telecommunications (compared to the U.S. markets), and the complete lack of military demand, meant that the domestic semiconductor industry's development was not pulled toward innovation except in consumer products at first. This situation posed a central dilemma for Japanese policymakers. Under conditions of free trade and open market access, they faced a risk that U.S. firms might dominate Japanese markets in semiconductors, computers, and telecommunications. If they protected their markets and denied U.S. firms open access, they risked severe technological backwardness in those sectors. The solution the policymakers chose was characteristic of postwar Japanese development strategy. They used trade policy to limit foreign penetration of the domestic market while deploying a range of financial and promotional policies to assist the industry's growth. Simultaneously, Japanese firms purchased huge amounts of foreign technology, mostly from the United States, and used their strength in consumer products to subsidize a limited price competition with U.S. firms in international semiconductor markets. Only after 1975, when Japanese firms had grown in their technological competence and domestic market dominance, did the government begin to move toward a partial dismantling of the restrictions on foreign penetration.

In 1968 the estimated share of Japanese firms in their domestic semiconductor market was as follows:[46]

Hitachi	23%	Mitsubishi	3%
Toshiba	21	Sony	2
Matsushita	15	Fujitsu	1
Sanyo	13	Other,	
NEC	7	including imports	12
Kobe Kogyo	3		

Japanese production was dominated by a consumer-electronics orientation. Note in particular that NEC, the industry's largest producer of semiconductors and integrated circuits at the end of the 1970s, had only a 7 percent market share in 1968. At that time also, NEC was the Japanese industry's largest producer of integrated circuits, which suggests the degree to which IC production was a relatively insignificant segment of total semiconductor production. Note also that Japan's largest computer manufacturer at present, Fujitsu, accounted for only 1 percent of semiconductor production in 1968. Fujitsu did not produce semiconductors for consumer product markets until its merger in 1968 with Kobe Kogyo, which again suggests that firms that did not produce semiconductors for consumer products could not grow effectively in the 1960s.[47]

In 1968 consumer products accounted for at least 60 percent of electronic systems production. The significance of this domination for

Japanese semiconductor production cannot be overemphasized. NEC began limited commercial production of the IC and the MOS transistor only one year after their commercial introduction by Texas Instruments and Fairchild in the United States. However, with no significant military or computer demand to stimulate the production and innovation of those devices, they remained a relatively insignificant part of Japanese semiconductor production. By the end of the 1960s Japanese firms had achieved only rough technological parity with U.S. firms in producing ICs with under 100 gates. Japanese firms lagged in basic LSI research and capabilities and were simply not an important factor in international competition.[48]

There was, however, one area where the Japanese industry's consumer product orientation was to pay vast dividends. Chip production for calculators and other consumer products required very high volumes. As Japanese labor costs rose in the 1970s and IC demand took off, Japanese producers discovered that dramatically increased production capacity and automation of assembly could sufficiently lower unit costs to compensate for U.S. technological advantages, at least in the domestic Japanese market. In the bargain, increased capital investment in assembly led to lower defect rates. The Japanese industry's consumer production orientation thus established both the logic of capital-intensive, high-volume commodity manufacture, and the strategy of higher quality at low cost, that were to dominate Japan's chip production and sustain its international competitiveness by the late 1970s.

The Japanese developmental strategy of creating comparative advantage in advanced technology sectors centered in the late 1960s and early 1970s on promoting the domestic computer industry.[49] If the Japanese developmental strategy was to succeed, Japan needed a competitive semiconductor sector. Thus the Japanese government, principally through MITI, sought to build a competitive semiconductor industry by limiting foreign competition in the domestic market and acquiring foreign technology and know-how. Foreign investment laws created after World War II required the Japanese government to review for approval all applications for direct foreign investment in Japan.[50] The government consistently rejected all applications for wholly owned subsidiaries and for joint ventures in which foreign firms would hold majority ownership. It also restricted foreign purchases of equity in Japanese semiconductor firms. Simultaneously, the government limited foreign import penetration of the home market through high tariffs and restrictive quotas and registration requirements on advanced IC devices in particular. For example, until 1974, ICs that contained more than 200 circuit elements simply could not be imported without special permission. Penetration was also managed by exclusionary customs procedures and "Buy Japanese" procurement and jawboning policies.[51]

The price to U.S. firms for limited access to the Japanese market was their licensing of advanced technology and know-how. Since MITI controlled access to the Japanese market and its approval was required for the implementation of licensing deals, it was in the powerful monopsonist's position of being able to dictate the terms of exchange. Its general policy was simple and effective. It required foreign firms to license all Japanese firms requesting access to a particular technology. It limited royalty payments by Japanese firms to a single rate on each deal, thereby preempting the competitive bidding-up of royalty rates among Japanese firms. MITI often linked the import of certain technologies to the acquiring firm's ability to develop export products using that technology.[52] MITI also conditioned approval of certain deals on the willingness of the involved Japanese firms to diffuse their own technical developments, through sublicense agreements, to other Japanese firms. The result of these policies was a controlled diffusion of advanced technology throughout the Japanese semiconductor industry. John Tilton gives a convincing measure of the extent of Japanese firm dependence on the acquisition of U.S. technology: By the end of the 1960s, Japanese IC producers were paying at least 10 percent of their semiconductor sales revenues as royalties to U.S. firms—2 percent to Western Electric, 4.5 percent to Fairchild, and 3.5 percent to TI.[53]

Royalty income may have been substantial for a number of U.S. firms, but market access (with one notable exception) was ephemeral indeed. Diffusion of advanced technology meant catching up, during the 1960s and 1970s, to successive generations of technological innovation by U.S. firms. As this occurred, domestic Japaness production displaced U.S. imports, and U.S. firms maintained Japanese market share only by shifting the composition of their imports toward products that Japanese firms were not yet producing themselves. But for the Japanese firms, the experience drove home a lesson that was to dominate their international strategy: U.S. firms could be driven from market segments if prices fell rapidly enough to eliminate profits on the product in question. U.S. firms would move to the next innovation rather than slugging it out through capacity investment to become the low-cost producers.

The one successful entry into the Japanese market by a U.S. firm came when Texas Instruments reached agreement with Sony on a joint venture in 1968. In fact, TI's entry strategy was really a replication of IBM's earlier success at establishing a wholly owned subsidiary in Japan in 1960 in exchange for IBM's industry-leading technology. Indeed, the very existence of the system of control over access and diffusion of technology described above is an acknowledgment of IBM's success at penetrating and then dominating the Japanese computer market. The Japanese did not want to allow IBM's success to be repeated by other foreign firms in other sectors—especially a sector as crucial as semiconductors. In that light, the TI story is significant for what it reveals about Japanese government policies, attitudes, and strategy in this period.[54]

Texas Instruments petitioned the Japanese government for a wholly owned subsidiary in the early 1960s and was offered a minority-share joint venture that it rejected. Its chief bargaining chip during these negotiations was its continuing refusal to license its critical IC patents to Japanese firms without gaining a substantial production subsidiary in Japan. In turn, the Japanese government stalled approval of TI's patent application in Japan, enabling NEC and the other domestic firms to play technology catch-up and forcing TI to negotiate for quicker access. The Japanese government then held up Japanese exports of IC-based systems to the United States because TI threatened infringement action. A compromise was finally reached in which TI got a 50 percent share of a joint venture with Sony. In return, it agreed to license its IC patents to NEC, Hitachi, Mitsubishi, Toshiba, and Sony, and agreed further to limit its future share of the Japanese semiconductor market to no more than 10 percent.

TI bought Sony's share of the joint venture in 1972 and through 1980 remained the only U.S. merchant firm with a wholly owned manufacturing subsidiary in Japan. Yet, TI's very market presence in Japan was sufficient to dissuade Japanese producers from challenging the U.S. industry in its area of greatest technological expertise, bipolar circuits. When the Japanese challenge came, it was premised on the opening provided by the shift to MOS. To this day, Japan is not a dominant producer of most older bipolar circuits—almost certainly a consequence of TI's Japanese market presence.

The strategy of technological diffusion and limited market access implied in the TI story enabled Japanese firms to mimic technological developments in the United States. However, the pace of semiconductor innovation in the United States was accelerating, driven by the computer market, and Japanese semiconductor-computer firms were lagging behind despite a decade of Japanese government promotion. These

policies included the creation of a specialized infrastructure of advisory
bureaus, promotional institutions and laboratories, preferential government procurement, credit allocation, and tax incentives, and direct and
indirect R&D subsidization.[55] As Gresser summarizes it:

> By 1969 it was obvious that the six major computer and semiconductor
> manufacturers were operating inefficiently. MITI well understood that if
> the Japanese firms continued to produce similar systems for a domestic
> market a fraction of the size of the U.S. market, the Japanese industry would
> not be able to compete internationally despite the most generous govern-
> ment assistance. MITI therefore decided to expedite the development of
> core technologies and to realign the industry.[56]

Through 1970, direct Japanese government subsidization of advanced
IC and production technology R&D by Japanese firms was not significant, although significant basic research was carried out in government
and especially NTT laboratories. Moreover, private company funding
of R&D was not at all competitive with U.S. firm spending. Indeed, in
the early 1970s, combined spending by Fujitsu, Hitachi, and NEC on
semiconductor and computer R&D was less than TI's R&D budget.[57]

In 1971 the Japanese government introduced a national policy for
the promotion of certain industries that targeted the development of
advanced technologies.[58] The Law for Provisional Measures to Promote Specific Electronic and Machinery Industries designated three
strategic categories: (1) advanced technologies needing direct R&D support, especially technologies like LSI, where Japanese firms lagged con-
siderably behind U.S. firms, (2) production technologies, like those
demanded in LSI production, which were intimately linked to device
or system cost, quality, and performance, and (3) high-volume production technologies. MITI was given responsibility for financing R&D
and rationalizing production, NTT for developing product innovations
and process technology. By 1977, over 60 different projects had received
total financial support in the multihundred million dollar range in such
areas as electron-beam exposure and LSI production equipment, high-
performance discrete devices, basic materials research, low-power, high-
performance ICs, and VLSI. Along with advances in fabrication and
materials, NTT was directly responsible for pioneering the introduction of successive generations of MOS dynamic RAM into large-scale
electronics systems in this period.[59]

The target of MITI's reorganization of Japanese industry was IBM's
370, which dominated world mainframe computer sales and utilized

IC but not LSI technology. Entry into world computer markets could be gained by leapfrogging the IBM technology and introducing an LSI-based computer system. Semiconductor R&D funding was aimed, therefore, at final usage in next-generation computers.

In 1971 the six semiconductor-computer firms formed three paired groups: Fujitsu-Hitachi, NEC-Toshiba, and Mitsubishi-Oki. Through these pairings MITI hoped to force a specialization of development efforts and long-term competitive segmentation of the computer market. Also in 1971, MITI and Japan's Electronics Industry Association formed an LSI cartel among the 10 major semiconductor producers. Its purposes were to standardize LSI basic structures and packages, to streamline and standardize manufacturing processes, and to develop LSI test equipment.[60] This cartel may indeed have been the seedbed for device specialization among the major Japanese firms.

The government's strongest and most coherent support may well have been in the form of R&D subsidies and the creation of demand for leading-edge components. Under the 1972 financial assistance programs for promotion of the development of new computer types and of peripheral devices,[61] grants covering up to 50 percent of the cost of developing new model computers were made to the three consolidated industry manufacturing groups. These programs led directly to NEC's ACOS series, Hitachi and Fujitsu's M series, and Mitsubishi's Cosmo series computers.

Demand creation was just as critical. Following a cabinet resolution of 1968, Japanese government offices were used as domestic procurement mechanisms for office computer systems.[62] In 1961 the Japan Electronic Computer Corporation (JECC) was set up to be a leasing intermediary. It bought domestic computer systems and leased them to users, thereby easing the costs of technology diffusion to users. Between 1972 and 1976 about 160 billion yen in loans to JECC were made by Japan's public financial arm, the Japan Development Bank.[63] Along with various tax measures, including depreciation provisions that permitted the writing off of over 50 percent of the acquisition costs of new computer systems in the first year, these provided critical stimuli to use of new computer systems. The resulting demand pull helped Japanese producers push their semiconductor production mix toward leading-edge devices.

These efforts to shift semiconductor production and development to meet the needs of Japan's fledgling computer industry must be located within the context of the continuing demand pull from consumer electronic markets. Through 1979, consumer discrete semiconductor devices and consumer linear ICs still accounted for well over 50 percent of the value of Japanese domestic semiconductor production. Moreover, all of the major producers, with the exception of Fujitsu, were heavily involved in calculators and consumer linear ICs.[64] During the late 1960s, the move abroad of major U.S. semiconductor and consumer electronic companies undercut part of the Japanese comparative advantage in consumer electronic products. As LSI technology penetrated consumer product markets in the early 1970s, the U.S. shift abroad and the relative technological weakness of Japanese producers presented a serious challenge to their strength in international consumer markets.

The case of calculators is illustrative.[65] In 1971 Japanese firms held approximately 85 percent of the domestic U.S. market for calculators. By 1974, under severe price competition from U.S. producers, that share fell to 25 percent. At the beginning of the period, Japanese firms like Sharp, Sanyo, Canon, and Casio entered into long-term contracts with Rockwell, General Electric, TI, and Fairchild for calculator chips and technical assistance to close the technology gap. The largest Japanese semiconductor producers capitalized on their emerging MITI-coordinated LSI capability to produce competitive calculator chips.

After 1974, when semiconductor-calculator technology stabilized and production costs equalized, the Japanese share of the U.S. market began to rise again. It was then that Japanese firms learned that U.S. producers could be pushed out of chip market segments through concerted investment in manufacturing capacity and the resulting erosion of margins on the product in question. As Japanese firms began to wrest control of the world calculator market from U.S. producers again, their investment in production capacity for calculator ICs grew accordingly.[66] Although the strategy was costly,[67] it succeeded in regaining market share and set the tone for future competitive confrontations.

By the end of 1975, the cooperative computer efforts, MITI's subsidization and coordination of R&D for LSI, and shifting consumer product market demand had succeeded in raising the value of the industry's IC portion of domestic semiconductor production from 27 percent in 1971 to about 42 percent.[68] While MITI's promotion of LSI capability had worked well, its attempt to consolidate the computer operations of the six semiconductor-computer companies had largely failed. The attempt at consolidation did produce joint marketing ventures, notably (in 1974) NEC-Toshiba Information Systems (NTIS) and Fujitsu-Hitachi's ACOM-HITAC, and coordinated R&D had benefited each of the participating firms. However, there was continuing strong competition in computer system products among the three groups and among each group's members, and the six firms remained largely independent. More important, by mid-1975 it was clear that the MITI-industry effort to leapfrog into an internationally competitive position in computers had fallen victim to changes in the international computer market.

The most significant market development was the introduction by U.S. computer companies of low-cost, LSI-based plug-compatible mainframes (PCM). PCMs were made economically possible by advances in LSI technology and the continuing decline in cost per function generated by them. They offered superior performance per dollar and generally utilized IBM's software. U.S. innovation in the market thereby rendered Japanese goals obsolete. If Japanese computer companies wanted to break into the international market for computers in a big way, they were going to have to do so on the basis of the next generation of semiconductor-computer technology—VLSI. (A complementary response was acquisition of a growing PCM firm, as Fujitsu did with Amdahl in 1976.)

It is within the context of these events that MITI's liberalization of some of the restrictions on foreign access to the Japanese market in semiconductors and computers, announced on December 24, 1975, must be understood. During the previous four years of market protection and industry promotion, Japanese semiconductor-computer firms had developed a significant LSI capability, and by 1976 they dominated their domestic market in all but the most advanced IC devices. Thanks partly to the government efforts aimed at demand creation, they had also succeeded in raising their share of the domestic installed base of general purpose digital computers to over 60 percent. They were thus in a dominant position in their domestic market at a time when the issue of a protected domestic base from which to enter international competition in LSI-based mainframes had been mooted by international market developments. Liberalization of trade in components and computers, with continued structural control over the character and composition of penetration, thus made sense, especially when combined with a program of promotion aimed at VLSI. Moreover, liberalization also made great political sense because the industrialized West was in the middle of a cycle of recession and recovery, and Japan was exporting excess domestic capacity in a range of economic sectors (such as steel, consumer electronics, and autos). The beginning clamor in the United States and Europe for domestic protection against Japanese imports could best be countered by liberalizing access to the Japanese market.

In preparation for liberalization and the push toward advanced LSI, the Japanese semiconductor-computer industry regrouped in late 1975.[69] Fujitsu, Hitachi, and Mitsubishi formed a joint venture—Computer Development Industries—to develop VLSI and the next generation of computer prototypes. Mitsubishi also joined with Hitachi and Fujitsu in their MITI-sponsored research. Oki Electric, no longer among the elect, split off to specialize in terminals, though its tight ties as a supplier to NTT would keep it in the chip game. Also in 1975 NTT formed an LSI group with Hitachi, Fujitsu, and NEC to develop advanced communications systems. Just after liberalization, the corporate articles of NEC-Toshiba Information Systems were amended to emphasize VLSI development, and a VLSI laboratory was established within NTIS. Finally, MITI, NTT, and the five major semiconductor-computer firms organized the VLSI project, and in March 1976 they formed the VLSI Technology Research Association.

Trade liberalization in 1976, contemporaneous with the Japanese industry's regrouping, was more than a little ambiguous. Gresser summarizes:

> Foreign capital investment was greatly expedited and the burdensome import quota system was eliminated. Trade and investment in computers was completely liberalized on schedule by April 1976. . . . The Cabinet released the following statement . . . "The Government . . . will keep an eye on movements in the computer market so that liberalization will not adversely affect domestic producers nor produce confusion.
>
> To mitigate liberalization, the government expanded its support for research and development of "core" technologies; foreign penetration of the Japanese market was checked, principally by limiting foreign procurement opportunities and by other administrative means.[70]

Indeed, the newspapers of this time are full of references to "liberalization countermeasures," meaning government policies adopted to mitigate the impact of an increase of foreign competition in the domestic market.[71] The *Nihon Keizai Shinbum* of June 15, 1973 is illustrative:

> MITI Minister Nakasone [yes, the retired Prime Minister] reported MITI's plan . . . to strengthen the computer industry . . . to meet liberalization by . . . (1) to step up efforts for development of new kinds of electronic computers and improvement of the efficiency of IC's; (2) to strengthen the power of the software industry; (3) to enforce measures for dissemination of computers among small enterprises; and (4) to strengthen and expand . . . JECC.[72]

Indeed, it has been estimated that as a condition of their support for liberalization, Japan's major firms demanded, and received, almost 150 billion yen in "liberalization countermeasures" funds, including subsidies to the Japan Electronic Computer Corporation (JECC) from the Japan Development Bank (JDB).[73]

Such policies for mitigating the impact of liberalization generally continued in force into the 1980s. Moreover, the ability of the largest Japanese semiconductor firms to collaborate in playing the role of doorman acted structurally to mitigate the impact of liberalization on the domestic market. In the late 1970s, then, both trade policy and industry structure combined to regulate access to the domestic market for semiconductors.

The VLSI program was the major promotional vehicle to assist the competitiveness of the Japanese semiconductor computer firms during the late 1970s. Developing semiconductor technology for the next generation of computers meant developing state-of-the-art capability in the production of both memory devices and logic circuits. Figure 5–1 gives a rough organizational picture of the project. The stated aims of the program were:

1. Development of microfabrication methods to handle submicron lithography, especially electron beam lithography
2. Development of low-defect, large-diameter silicon wafer substrates
3. Development of improved computer-aided design technology
4. Development of improved LSI microfabrication processing techniques and equipment
5. Development of VLSI evaluation and testing techniques and equipment
6. Definition of logic and memory devices that could utilize 1–5.[74]

As this list suggests, much of the VLSI program was aimed at catching up to the U.S. industry's capabilities in advanced IC process technology. Toward that end, as described in the introduction to this chapter, a significant portion of the program's funding was spent in the United States to purchase production and test equipment. Such purchases were not surprising, for in the first years of the VLSI program, imports of foreign (mostly U.S.) production equipment accounted for at least an estimated 80 percent share of the domestic Japanese market.[75] In 1976 Japan's indigenous capital equipment industry for semiconductor manufacture was small. Since the import share of production equipment

Figure 5–1. Structure of VLSI Project in Japan.

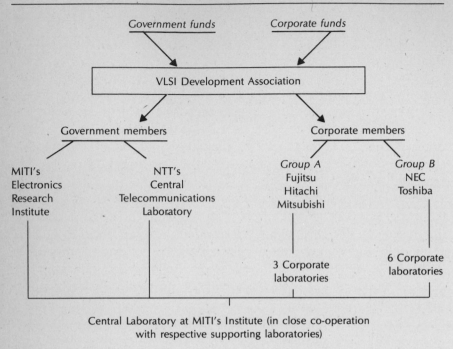

Source: Ira Magaziner and Thomas Hout, "Japanese Industrial Policy," Institute of International Studies, University of California, Berkeley, 1981, p. 104.

fell to about 50 percent in 1980, one result of the VLSI program was a strengthening of the domestic Japanese infrastructure in production, and especially photolithography and test capabilities. Indeed, the general manager of NEC's VLSI development division admitted, for example, that his firm would have had to spend five times as much on the development of electron-beam technology without the VLSI program.[76]

An equally important impact of public subsidies and nonduplicative research coordination in the VLSI program was the release of company funds for capacity expansion (and eventual penetration of the U.S. market). In 1977 the top six Japanese semiconductor producers spent a total of some $116 million on new plant and equipment.[77] That figure rose to an estimated $212 million in 1978, with NEC accounting for $66 million and Fujitsu for $42 million. Most of the investment made by NEC and Fujitsu went to build IC and especially MOS RAM production capacity. In 1979 spending by the top 10 semiconductor producers in Japan climbed to an estimated $420 million. This pattern of heavy spending was a response to increasing demand in the domestic Japanese market and to rapidly growing export opportunities, which were carefully nourished by Japanese companies.

The exploitation of export opportunities was particularly apparent in the domestic U.S. market. During the first two years of the VLSI program, the major Japanese firms (led by NEC and Fujitsu) rapidly built up a distribution system in the United States.[78] Prior to 1976 major U.S. distributors had been hesitant to serve Japanese producers who could not meet commitments for large volumes and continuous supplies of high-margin memory and microprocessor devices. This situation changed as the Japanese rapidly expanded production capacity and advanced their technology. By the middle of 1977, NEC, Fujitsu, Hitachi, and Toshiba were all moving toward broad-based distribution channels, which were frequently managed by marketing experts recruited from U.S. companies. NEC, Fujitsu, and Hitachi each set up wholly owned domestic U.S. subsidiaries for marketing LSI products. Toshiba sold its LSI devices through an OEM sales group attached to Toshiba America Corporation. NEC and Fujitsu each developed extensive ties to a large number of U.S. distributors, which gave them access to most regions of the country. By the beginning of 1978, when MOS memory demand jumped in the United States, Japanese firms were well placed to take advantage of the situation. From supplying only 1 percent of U.S. consumption of integrated circuits in 1976, Japanese firms were supplying 8 percent in 1980.

Japanese firms could take advantage of export opportunities in the U.S. market because the growth of production for their own domestic market had brought them toward international state-of-the-art capability by the late 1970s. Table 5–6 shows the composition of domestic Japanese IC production, by units and value, in 1974 and 1978; Table 5–7 shows the composition of Japanese IC consumption, by units and value, in 1979; and Table 5–8 shows the percentage of Japanese IC consumption in 1979 by major market segments.

These tables reveal important shifts in the growth and composition of Japanese production. The quantity and value of Japanese IC production almost tripled from 1974 to 1978. Linear ICs as a percentage of unit production rose to 53 percent. Note that linear ICs are relatively low value-added devices. Since most linear ICs are consumer linear devices, the growth in their production suggests the continued demand pull of the consumer electronics market on the composition of Japanese IC

Table 5-6. Composition of Domestic Japanese IC Production, 1974 and 1978 (units in millions; values in $millions).

	1974				1978			
Category	Units	Percent of Units	Value	Percent of Value	Units	Percent of Units	Value	Percent of Value
Total IC	340	100%	$429	100%	1,063	100%	$1,260	100%
Linear	154	45	110	25.2	561	53	363	29
Digital	152	45	273	62.3	450	42	769	61
Bipolar	106	31.5	109	25	222	21	183	14.6
MOS	46	13.5	163	37	228	21	585	46.4
Hybrid	34	10	54	12.4	52	5	126	10

Note: Yen/dollar conversion at 286/1 in 1974 and 212/1 in 1978. Figures may not add due to rounding.

Source: The Consulting Group, BA Asia Ltd., 1979, pp. 89-94.

production. Indeed, Table 5-8 indicates that consumer electronics, calculators, and watches still consumed approximately 50 percent of the ICs that entered the domestic market. Recall, however, how important consumer production was during the 1970s in establishing the characteristic volume production strategy, in providing an extra bin for

Table 5-7. Composition of Domestic Japanese IC Consumption, 1979 (units in millions; values in $millions).

Category	Units	Percent of Units	Value	Percent of Value
Total IC	2,056	100%	$1,604	100%
Consumer linear	700	34	300	19
Other linear	150	7	80	5
Digital bipolar	550	27	304	19
Digital MOS	576	28	760	47
Hybrid	80	4	160	10

Note: Yen/dollar conversion at 250/1. Figures may not add due to rounding.

Source: BA Asia Ltd., 1980, p. 113.

Table 5–8. Domestic Japanese IC Consumption, by Major Market Segment, 1979 (%).

Consumer	29%
Computer	35
Communications	6
Test and measurement	2
Calculators	11
Other (including watches, automotive)	17
Total	100

Source: The Consulting Group, BA Asia Ltd., 1979, pp. 89–94.

increased yields, and in providing operating funds from sales of consumer systems to subsidize expansion in chip production.

The continuing importance of consumer production must be viewed in the context of the rapid growth of digital IC capability between 1974 and 1978. Those years witnessed a rapid changeover from digital bipolar production to MOS (as had occurred by 1975 in the United States). The deemphasis on bipolar production again suggests a strategic evaluation of where the best prospects lay for rapid growth and international competitiveness of Japanese production, particularly given TI's entrenched bipolar position in Japan. The most important market factor in the growth of MOS production was Japan's burgeoning computer industry, which by 1979 accounted for 35 percent of domestic Japanese IC consumption.

This shift had finally positioned Japanese firms internationally, since technical sophistication in MOS memory is directly transferable to the design and production of other complex products. Indeed, the rapid growth of MOS LSI capability to serve domestic computer demand increasingly displaced complex MOS imports to the Japanese market, and forced U.S. firms to shift the composition mix of their exports to supply devices not yet produced in quantity in Japan. Equally important, by 1978 that growth had enabled Japanese firms to enter the U.S. markets for MOS memory and later microprocessor devices.

The domestic computer market in 1978 and 1979, by sales value of the major producers, is given in Table 5–9. The increasing market share taken by domestic firms continued through the 1980s, with a resulting favorable impact on the technological competitiveness of these Japanese semiconductor firms.

Table 5–9. Japanese Domestic Computer Sales, 1978–1979
(billions yen; $millions).

	1978		1979	
Fujitsu	Y303	($1,420)	Y340	($1,360)
Hitachi	190	(896)	220	(880)
NEC	167	(787)	200	(800)
Matsubishi	45	(212)	53	(212)
Oki	48	(226)	50	(200)
Toshiba	60	(283)	55	(220)
IBM Japan	315	(1,480)	324	(1,290)

Note: Yen/dollars conversions are 274/1 for 1977, 212/1 for 1978, and 250/1 for 1979. The fall of the yen versus the dollar in 1979 accounts for the rise in yen value and the decline in dollar value between 1978 and 1979.

Source: BA Asia Ltd., 1980, p. 47.

Demand from the growing telecommunications sector also stimulated Japanese LSI capability in the late 1970s, and this growth was tied to the policies of NTT. During this period, NTT bought almost all of its equipment from NEC, Hitachi, Fujitsu, and Oki, the Big Four, and also played the characteristic role of doorman for telecommunications. NTT's procurement was completely closed to foreign firms; moreover, it did not allow the Big Four to use imported semiconductors in the equipment they supplied to NTT. Magaziner and Hout described the promotional character of NTT's impact on technological development and market rationalization.

> NTT makes all decisions on technical specifications, and engineers of the Big Four manufacturers are invited to develop new equipment partly after basic research is completed by NTT's own engineers. Therefore, all research and development expenses incurred by manufacturers are mostly application and production related. . . . NTT assigns actual production and supply to each manufacturer, depending upon availability of technical capacity and actual performance of the company on past assignments.[79]

Under such guidance, the production value of communication equipment rose steadily from under $2 billion in 1973 to over $2.6 billion in 1977.[80] The Bank of America study estimates that communication equipment consumed approximately $235 million worth of semiconductors in 1978, with NEC and Fujitsu combined accounting for about 35 percent of that total.[81]

Apart from financing and directing research and development, NTT also helps indirectly to finance exports. Since NTT negotiates its equipment purchases on a cost-plus basis, it acts to provide "monopoly-like" prices in a manner similar to U.S. military purchases. The exclusion of foreign procurement stabilizes prices and production volumes. NTT also advances part of the purchase price, thereby providing interest-free loans to the manufacturer. The result is great flexibility in export pricing. As Magaziner and Hout describe the resulting export growth during the 1970s:

> Japanese companies got off to a late start in telecommunications exports, in large part because of their undistinguished technology. However, the boom in the OPEC and developing Asian markets in the middle and late 1970s, combined with lower growth at home, brought them into export markets. Exports, only 8 percent of sales in the early 1970s, are now 18–20 percent.[82]

The international markets expanded during the 1980s, with a resulting favorable impact on the technological sophistication of the largest semiconductor producers.

The separate but rapid growth during the 1970s of the three markets discussed above—the consumer, computer, and telecommunications markets—produced conflicting demands on the major Japanese semiconductor electronic firms. In conjunction with the MITI and NTT promotional policy actions, the various demands of rapid growth were responsible for the specialization of product and semiconductor technology among Japanese firms described at the beginning of this chapter.

Through most of the 1970s, Japanese government policies limited foreign access to the domestic market and ensured that the advantages of rapid domestic growth would accrue mostly to domestic Japanese firms. Growth was underwritten partly through public subsidies, but mostly through the stable access to capital delivered by the structure of domestic Japanese business and finance. By 1978, a decade of Japanese government assistance and protectionist policies had finally coalesced with the growth of domestic IC markets to create a strong domestic semiconductor sector. Moreover, the industry was rapidly expanding its export penetration of important and growing international electronics markets, which further strengthened its semiconductor capability. Through its industry structure and domestic market power, the Japanese semiconductor industry dominated its domestic market and achieved near state-of-the-art capability in the fastest growing segments of the international IC market. For the first time in history, major Japanese IC firms were positioned to enter world MOS LSI memory markets on a roughly equal technological footing with their U.S. merchant competitors.

NOTES

1. The five are Nippon Electric Company (NEC), Hitachi, Toshiba, Fujitsu, and Mitsubishi. The nondirect participant was Matsushita, Japan's largest consumer electronics company, whose autonomous research capacities and relative independence from the government's "administrative guidance" have been much heralded. The VLSI participants were roughly aligned during the project into two groups that mirrored formal working arrangements developed during the early 1970s. These were NEC and Toshiba, with their joint NEC-Toshiba Information Systems Company (NTIS), and Fujitsu-Hitachi-Mitsubishi, with their Computer Development Laboratory (CDL). The subsidies for the VLSI program were in the form of a combination of *hojokin,* success-conditional loans, repayable without interest only if the R&D becomes profitable, and *itakuhi* grants, provided on a contract basis and not repayable. The public subsidy represented perhaps 10 percent of the value of these companies' combined production of digital MOS ICs during the years of the VLSI project. This is a rough estimate based on MITI's figures for digital MOS IC production in Japan and an estimate of the percentage of that production which is accounted for by these five firms. Since most of the VLSI project's thrust involved development of digital MOS ICs, the percentage figure given here should show a reasonable representation of the impact of public spending in the VLSI program.

2. Figures vary, but purchases in the first two years were at least some $42 million worth. Purchases in the last two years were roughly comparable.

3. The linked characterization of the industry is suggested by Julian Gresser, "High Technology and Japanese Industrial Policy: A Strategy for U.S. Policy Makers," (Washington, D.C.: U.S. Department of State, June 26, 1980).

4. *Vision of MITI Policies in the 1980s* (Tokyo: MITI, 1980), pp. 136, 199, 200.

5. T.J. Pempel, "Japanese Foreign Economic Policy: The Domestic Bases for International Behavior," in Peter J. Katzenstein, ed., *Between Power and Plenty* (Madison: University of Wisconsin Press, 1978), p. 157.

6. Import percentages are from *Vision of MITI Policies in the 1980s,* p. 30.

7. Edward F. Denison and William K. Chung, "Economic Growth and Its Sources," in Hugh Patrick and Henry Rosovsky, eds., *Asia's New Giant* (Washington, D.C.: Brookings Institution, 1976), p. 67.

8. Pempel, "Japanese Foreign Economic Policy," p. 139.
9. John Zysman, *Governments, Market, and Growth* (Ithaca, N.Y.: Cornell University Press, 1983), p. 241.
10. *Vision of MITI Policies in the 1980s,* p. 31.
11. The term is from ibid., p. 196.
12. Pempel, "Japanese Foreign Economic Policy," p. 159.
13. James C. Abegglan and George Stalk Jr., *Kaisha: The Japanese Corporation* (New York: Basic Books, 1985).
14. Michael Borrus, et al. "Telecommunications Development in Comparative Perspective: The New Telecommunications in Europe, Japan and the U.S.," BRIE Working Paper 14, 1985.
15. David Bennett Friedman, "The Misunderstood Miracle: Politics and the Development of a Hybrid Economy," Unpublished Ph.D. dissertation, Massachusetts Institute of Technology, Cambridge, Mass., May 1986.
16. See discussion in Robert E. Cole and Taizo Yakashuji, "The American and Japanese Auto Industries in Transition: Report of the Joint U.S.-Japan Automotive Study," Center for Japanese Studies, University of Michigan, Ann Arbor, 1984; and Alan Altshuler et al., *The Future of the Automobile: The Report of MIT's International Automobile Program* (Cambridge, Mass.: MIT Press, 1984).
17. Michael Borrus, "The Politics of Competitive Erosion in the U.S. Steel Industry," in Laura Tyson and John Zysman, eds., *American Industry in International Competition: Government Policies and Corporate Strategies* (Ithaca, N.Y.: Cornell University Press, 1983).
18. Chase Financial Policy, "U.S. and Japanese Semiconductor Industries: A Financial Comparison," 1980 (hereafter cited as Chase), pp. 1.5, 1.6.
19. The Consulting Group, BA Asia Ltd., The Japanese Semiconductor Industry, 1980 (hereafter cited as BA 1980), p. 113.
20. Descriptions are culled from The Consulting Group, BA Asia Ltd., "The Japanese Semiconductor Industry: An Overview," April 1979 (hereafter cited as BA 1979), pp. 160–78; BA 1980, pp. 134–35, 184–204; and Gresser, "High Technology and Japanese Industrial Policy," pp. 1–3.
21. Iwao Nakatani, "Technological Innovation and the Role of Corporate Groups in Japan," presented at the international symposium, Technological Competitiveness in the 21st Century, Duisburg, West Germany, August 3–8, 1987.
22. Dodwell Marketing Consultants, *Industrial Groupings in Japan* (Tokyo: Dodwell, 1975).
23. S. Miyaski, "Japanese-Type Structure of Big Business," and Yusaku Futatsugi, "The Measurement of Interfirm Relationships," in Kazuo Sato, ed., *Industry and Business in Japan* (White Plains, N.Y.: M.E. Sharpe, 1980).
24. Michael Gerlach, *Alliances and the Social Organization of Japanese Business,* Ph.D. dissertation, Yale University, 1987.

25. Figures that follow are from BA 1979, pp. 80, 115.
26. BA 1980, p. 148.
27. BA 1980, p. 129.
28. Quoted in Leslie Donald Helm, "The Japanese Computer Industry: A Case Study in Industrial Policy," Unpublished M.A. thesis, University of California, 1981, p. 34.
29. Based on conversations with industry sources.
30. H. Ueno, "The Conception and Evolution of Industrial Policy," in Sato, ed., *Industry and Business in Japan,* pp. 400–407.
31. See the discussion in Phillip Wellons, *Passing the Buck: Banks, Governments, and Third World Debt* (Boston: Harvard Business School Press, 1987).
32. Richard Caves, "Industrial Organization," in Patrick and Rosovsky, eds., *Asia's New Giant,* p. 488.
33. For Mazda story, see Altshuler, *The Future of the Automobile*; For Oki Story, see Hitachi Hiromatsu, *Denwa no Muko wa Konna Kao: Denden Kosha KDD no Uchimaku* (1980), as cited in *An Assessment of International Competition in Microelectronics: The Role of Government Policy in Enhancing Competitiveness* (Semiconductor Industry Association, 1987).
34. Chase, p. 23.
35. Stalk and Abegglan, *Kaisha.*
36. See the account in Andreas R. Prindle, *Japanese Finance* (New York: John Wiley, 1981).
37. See, for example, Robert S. Kaplan, "What You See [in Accounting Earning] is Not What You Get," Workshop on Competitiveness, Harvard Business School, July 12–18, 1987; and Carliss Baldwin, "The Capital Factor: Competing for Capital in a Global Competition," in Michael E. Porter, ed., *Competition in Global Industries* (Boston: Harvard Business School Press, 1986).
38. See Chase; M. Therese Flaherty and Hiroyki Itami, "Financial Systems and Capital Acquisitions," Stanford University, Stanford, Calif., 1982; George N. Hatsopoulos, "High Cost of Capital: Handicap to American Business," American Business Conference, April 1983; and U.S. Department of Commerce, "A Historical Comparison of the Cost of Financial Capital," April 1983.
39. Yoshio Suzuki, *Money and Banking in Contemporary Japan* (New Haven, Conn.: Yale University Press, 1980), pp. 50–51.
40. Wellons, *Passing the Buck,* ch. 2.
41. Koichi Hamada and Akiyoshi Horuchi, "The Political Economy of the Financial Market," in Kozo Yamamura, ed., *The Political Economy of Japan* (Stanford, Calif.: Stanford University Press, 1987); see also, Michael A. Rappa, "Capital Financing Strategies of Japanese Semiconductor Industry," *California Management Review* (Winter 1985): 85–99.

42. Ibid.
43. These ratios are based on information supplied by industry sources.
44. Figures are from Japan Electronics Industry Development Association (the predecessor to the present Japan Electronics Industry Association).
45. BA 1979, pp. 83 and 48; yen conversion at 212/1 for 1978.
46. Source is John E. Tilton, reprinted in U.S. Federal Trade Commission (FTC), *Staff Report on the Semiconductor Industry* (Washington, D.C.: U.S. Government Printing Office, 1977), p. 33. Kobe Kogyo and Fujitsu merged in 1968.
47. On NEC and Fujitsu's orientation, see John E. Tilton, *International Diffusion of Technology* (Washington, D.C.: The Brookings Institution, 1971), pp. 143, 145.
48. Estimate from industry sources.
49. See generally, Helm, "Japanese Computer Industry."
50. Chalmers Johnson, *MITI and the Japanese Miracle: The Growth of Industrial Policy* (Stanford, Calif.: Stanford University Press, 1982), ch. 1.
51. On these points, see Tilton, in FTC, *Staff Report on the Semiconductor Industry,* p. 146; Gresser, "High Technology and Japanese Industrial Policy," pp. 15, 45, 93 (fn. 42), 95 (fn. 46); and William Finan, *International Transfer of Semiconductor Technology Through U.S.-Based Firms* (Washington, D.C.: National Science Foundation, 1975), p. 95.
52. Helm, "Japanese Computer Industry," p. 76.
53. FTC, *Staff Report on the Semiconductor Industry,* p. 148.
54. Ibid., pp. 146–47.
55. For an elaboration of these policies, see Gresser, "High Technology and Japanese Industrial Policy," pp. 22–23, 88–91 (fns. 27–41).
56. Ibid., p. 16.
57. Ira Magaziner and Thomas Hout, "Japanese Industrial Policy," Institute of International Studies, University of California, Berkeley, 1981, p. 103.
58. See Gresser, "High Technology and Japanese Industrial Policy," pp. 16–17, and Ian Mackintosh, *Microelectronics in the 1980's* (London: Mackintosh Publications, 1979), p. 18.
59. See discussion in Makoto Watanabe, "Electrical Communication Laboratories," *Japan Telecommunications Review* (January 1979): 4–5.
60. Sources on these points are Gresser, "High Technology and Japanese Industrial Policy," p. 19; Magaziner and Hout, *Japanese Industrial Policy,* p. 103; and Helm, "Japanese Computer Industry," p. 34; for a detailed look at government support to the Japanese Computer Industry, see, Marie Anchordoguy, *The State and the Market: Industrial Policy Toward Japan's Computer Industry* (UC Berkeley, unpublished Ph.D. dissertation, 1986).

61. See the discussion in JIPDEC Reports and Computer White Paper, various editions 1976–1980, Japan Information Processing Development Center (hereafter, JIPDEC reports).
62. Ibid., 1977, p. 6.
63. Ibid., pp. 36–38.
64. BA 1979, pp. 96, 110, 128.
65. This account is largely from Charles River Associates, "Innovation, Competition, and Government Policy," Boston, 1980, pp. 4-36–4-39.
66. *Japan Economic Journal,* various issues 1970–1974; e.g., February 23, 1971.
67. Eiji Kawamura, "Quality and Commitment Are the Keys to Selling Imported IC's in Japan," *JEE,* (March 1976): 21.
68. Percentages are estimated from figures in U.S. Department of Commerce, *Report on the U.S. Semiconductor Industry,* 1979, p. 82.
69. This material is from Gresser, "High Technology and Japanese Industrial Policy," pp. 7, 17–18, 20, but Gresser does not analyze the regrouping of the industry or liberalization within the domestic and international market context we have elaborated here.
70. Ibid., p. 20.
71. The general policies associated with liberalization countermeasures are well examined in Stephen D. Krasner and Daniel Okomoto, "Japan's Trade Posture: From Myopic Self-Interest to Liberal Accommodation?" Department of Political Science, Stanford University, February 1985, mimeo.
72. See also, e.g., *Sankei Shinbum,* March 7, 1973; *Asahi Shinbum,* March 8, 1973; *Nihon Keizai Shinbum,* March 15, 1973; and *Nihon Kogyo Shinbum,* June 25, 1973; SIA translations in "Japanese Protection and Promotion of the Semiconductor Industry," October 1985.
73. *Mainichi Shinbum,* March 8, 1973.
74. BA 1979, p. 122.
75. These import percentage estimates are from BA 1980, p. 137.
76. *The Economist,* April 5, 1980, p. 75.
77. These investment figures are from BA 1979, p. 133 and BA 1980, pp. 136–138, 153. Yen/dollar conversions are 274/1 for 1977, 212/1 for 1978, and 250/1 for 1979.
78. On the following, see in particular *Electronic News,* December 6, 1976, p. II–33; April 18, 1977, pp. 1, 4; October 17, 1977, p. 56; January 30, 1978, p. 58.
79. Magaziner and Hout, *Japanese Industrial Policy,* p. 108.
80. BA 1979, p. 57.
81. Ibid., p. 35.
82. Magaziner and Hout, *Japanese Industrial Policy,* p. 108.

6 THE JAPANESE CHALLENGE, 1978–1984

By the late 1970s, the Japanese had established a thriving domestic IC sector to serve growing domestic computer and telecommunications needs. The growing convergence in demand for advanced ICs between international and Japanese markets provided the basis upon which international competition among U.S. and Japanese IC producers accelerated.

JAPANESE ENTRY AND SYSTEMIC STRENGTHS IN INTERNATIONAL COMPETITION: THE FIRST ROUND

From their secure domestic base, the leading Japanese firms entered those international markets in the leading-edge IC memory devices whose standard, commodity-product character had been developed and dominated by U.S. merchant firms. The value of Japanese IC exports to the United States rose from about $50 million in 1977 to just under $300 million in 1980.[1] The value of Japanese IC exports to Europe rose from $12 million in 1976 to about $165 million in 1980.[2] While Japanese IC firms had clearly matured enough to expand competitively in international markets, they chose not to accept the full brunt of competiton in their domestic market. As Japanese demand for the most advanced IC devices began to increase, the domestic Japanese market share held by U.S. firms narrowed rapidly.[3] Figure 6–1 sketches the pattern of domestic Japanese IC consumption accounted for by imports from U.S. controlled sources (domestic and offshore facilities combined).[4]

If U.S. firms were consolidating their product innovation advantages into enduring market positions, we would expect the percentage of consumption accounted for by a progressively higher value-added mix of U.S. exports into Japan to increase. As Figure 6–1 indicates, this was not the case; rather, a pattern of organized import substitution seems to have occurred. The rise in 1979 in the U.S. controlled import share of Japanese IC consumption is accounted for by an increase in 16K RAM sales,[5] while the decline in 1980 again reflected the general pattern.

Competitive interaction of the U.S. and Japanese semiconductor industries in the late 1970s centered on Japanese entry to the domestic

Figure 6–1. Estimated Percentage of Domestic Japanese IC Consumption Accounted for by U.S.-Controlled Imports, by Value: 1975–1980.

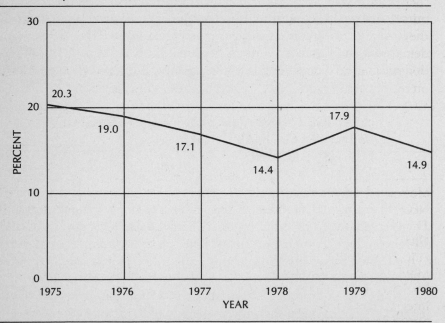

Source: Michael Borrus, James Millstein, and John Zysman, "U.S.–Japanese Competition in the Semiconductor Industry," Institute of International Studies, University of California, Berkeley, no. 171, p. 85.

U.S. market for ICs. The first battle took place in the MOS memory market. With price-per-bit equivalency between 4K and 16K dynamic RAM in 1978, came accelerating demand for 16K RAM. On top of the demand generated by this crossover, IBM entered the merchant market with a huge demand for 16K RAM to meet the memory needs created by the rapid market acceptance of its new Series 4300 computer.

The increasing demand for 16K RAM met a production capacity shortfall in the United States. This stemmed largely from the failure or inability of merchant U.S. firms to expand capacity during the 1975 recession and from their cautious investment policies following the recession. Reliance on internal funds and equity markets constrained the business strategy choices of U.S. firms. Japanese firms were able to build up capacity rapidly. By the end of 1979, the major Japanese firms had taken 43 percent of the domestic U.S. 16K RAM market. Table 6–1 summarizes 16K RAM production in 1979 by major producers.

The 16K RAM story offers important insights into the ways in which the Japanese industry's domestic market structure and power give Japanese firms an initial advantage in international competition. First, they were better able than U.S. firms to add production capacity and pursue a high-volume production strategy because capital was available, they could be relatively unconcerned with current earnings, and captive demand existed. Second, their characteristic rationalization of production enabled the major Japanese firms to concentrate capacity expansion on the high-volume production of a single memory product, 16K RAM,

Table 6–1.   16k RAM Production, by Major Producers, 1979 (thousands of units).

Firm	Units	Firm	Units
Mostek	16,800	Fairchild	1,900
NEC[a]	11,300	ITT	1,700
TI	9,000	Mitsubishi[a]	1,250
Hitachi[a]	7,100	Siemens	875
Fujitsu[a]	6,500	Zilog	190
Motorola	4,700	Signetics	175
Toshiba[a]	3,475	AMD	65
Intel	3,250	Intersil	10
National	3,200	SGS-ATES	3

[a] Japanese firm.
Source: Dataquest

destined for the U.S. market while meeting their other product needs through specialization and trade between domestic firms. Third, since they exercised dominant market power over consumption in their domestic market, the major Japanese firms could play the role of doorman and control the growth and composition of imports entering their market.

This meant two things. First, until late 1978, Japanese producers apparently used a two-tier pricing strategy. They kept RAM prices high in their controlled domestic market, thereby subsidizing their ability to offer lower prices in the U.S. market. (Prices only came down in response to the U.S. International Trade Commission's investigation of "dumping" initiated by the Semiconductor Industry Association in the United States.[6])

More important, as domestic Japanese demand for 16K RAMs rose in 1978 and 1979, Japanese IC firms chose to let imports meet domestic Japanese demand—and, by implication, to meet a part of their own consumption needs. This enabled Japanese producers to divert their own production to the United States in order to increase their share of the U.S. market. Thus, as we have seen, exports by U.S. firms of 16K RAMs to Japan actually rose in 1979. Since the major Japanese producers of 16K RAMs also dominated 16K RAM consumption in Japan, they were able to limit and displace future U.S. imports, as occurred in 1980 after additional domestic Japanese production capacity came on line. The cost to U.S. firms of temporarily increased access to the Japanese market was a significant and enduring Japanese presence in the domestic U.S. market.

The successful Japanese strategy was premised on investment in manufacturing in more ways than simply having needed capacity in place in a timely fashion. Since the VLSI project had concentrated on refining generic process techniques and diffusing them widely to Japan's chip producers, Japanese firms achieved a roughly common level of improved process expertise as they invested to build RAM production facilities. Improvements in fabrication precision and automated assembly delivered the now characteristic advantage in production yields, and also delivered, as a by-product, higher quality devices (with fewer device failures per user incoming lot). While higher yields and greater financial muscle permitted entry to the U.S. market through low-pricing strategies, it was higher quality that carried the day for Japan's first successful push into the U.S. market.

A number of U.S. consumers of Japanese 16K RAMs, notably Hewlett-Packard and NCR, suggested that the failure rates of the Japanese products were significantly lower than those of U.S. devices.[7] While U.S. devices met the existing quality standards of U.S. purchasers, there was unexploited market demand for higher quality devices. U.S. manufacturers had used postmanufacturing testing to eliminate device failures, in much the same way that U.S. automobile producers used buffer stocks and postproduction inspection to achieve quality control. By contrast, the Japanese approach was to eliminate product-quality variations in the manufacturing process itself—in essence, using tight process control, manufacturing refinement and precision to ensure uniform high quality of components coming out of the production process.[8] The result was higher yields *and* higher quality at lower costs.

THE SECOND ROUND: JAPAN WINS THE MEMORY WARS

Japanese producers leveraged their entry to the U.S. market by engineering a system of commodity component manufacturing that allowed rapid entry with relatively simple components of high quality and low cost. Japanese firms thus changed the terms of market competition by imposing new basic manufacturing parameters that favored Japanese strengths. By putting a premium on manufacturing in the context of rapidly escalating capital costs, Japanese firms speeded the maturation of the industry and enhanced their own competitive position. The formidable ability of Japanese firms to build on their success in 16K RAMs was amply demonstrated in the early 1980s. In 1981 and 1982, Japanese electronics companies captured 67–69 percent of the world market for the then latest generation of dynamic RAM, the 64K dRAM, and captured about 95 percent of the market for 16K static RAM.

The 64K dRAM represents the first commodity IC device for which Japanese firms *led* U.S. merchants in new product and market development. Because the 64K dRAM required relatively high capital investment, generated very high-volume demand among a few large purchasers, was relatively less complex than other dense circuits, did not require much servicing or support, and involved iterative production know-how and capacity that was fairly easily transferred from the manufacture of earlier generation RAMs, it meshed perfectly with Japanese strengths and manufacturing strategies. Nevertheless, Japanese success at developing the product market and *sustaining* a leadership position in the device represented the first clear departure from the established strategy of following the market.

The early Japanese lead in the 64K dRAM was not based on product innovation. Rather, the strategy used illustrates the characteristic production-refinement approach and manufacturing systems strength of the Japanese. Japanese firms chose, essentially, a straightforward scale-up to 64K of their 16K dRAM, based on U.S. merchant Mostek's industry-standard 16K design. They accomplished this through incremental improvement of older photolithographic techniques—proximity aligners, which few U.S. firms believed capable of reaching the 2–3 micron design rules of the 64K device.[9] U.S. firms, in turn, moved to projection aligners and wafer steppers, equipment they believed necessary to produce subsequent generations of dRAMs, from the 256K on up. If they could successfully use steppers in production of the 64K dRAM, U.S. firms would gain an edge in producing future devices. Unfortunately, the newer process techniques required much longer for debugging and know-how acquisition. Moreover, U.S. producers adopted a range of novel approaches to the 64K device (such as redundancy and self-refresh) which made their development times longer and their production problems greater than those experienced in the straightforward Japanese effort. Thus, although Motorola and TI managed through major investment efforts to approximate the pace of Japanese introduction and scale-up, other U.S. merchants ran into difficulties. Intel withdrew its initial 64K entry in August 1981; Mostek was forced to redesign its first device; and National encountered manufacturing problems with its three-layer polysilicon approach and eventually licensed the part and manufacturing techniques from Japan's Oki Electric.

As demand for the device grew, the market gap created by the delays in production by U.S. firms was filled by the aggressive and rapid Japanese production strategy. Japanese firms spent heavily to increase yields and quality while bringing down production costs. Automation permitted Japanese firms to hold their production processes to closer tolerances. The result, as before, was higher yields and quality. They continued to invest in highly automated capacity expansion for 64K dRAM during the 1981–1982 U.S. recession, unlike U.S. firms.

The ability to spend heavily during rough economic times, and the move to automation, illustrate again the characteristic domestic-based strengths of the Japanese industry. The ability to spend was based on consistent access to cheap capital (which was undoubtedly much cheaper for Japanese firms, given the grossly high interest rates that obtained in the United States from 1980 to 1982). The point to be made about automation is more complex. First, automation implies high initial fixed manufacturing costs, which entail two kinds of vulnerability. One is vulnerability to product innovation, where automated production that is optimized for a product or design is made obsolete by a new product or design that becomes an industry standard. Japanese 64K dRAM producers were helped in this area because no single 64K design became an industry standard as Mostek's 16K design had been in the previous generation. Moreover, the Japanese financial structure and government policies generally decrease this kind of vulnerability by permitting cheap reinvestment combined with rapid tax write-offs and less concern about the impact of obsolescence and reinvestment on current earnings.

The related vulnerability is to fluctuations in demand, because the higher fixed costs of automated production place a premium on the use of full capacity. If demand drops but capacity is fully used, over-supply could eliminate profits on the device in question. Production can then be automated successfully when some major portion of demand is guaranteed to be stable, when overall demand is growing rapidly, and when a firm is more interested in gaining market-share than short-term profits (by selling as much output as it can produce at whatever price is necessary). Japanese demand is stable and high because a substantial portion of each firm's output is either used captively or sold within the essentially captive market of the firm's own *keiretsu*.[10] With the assist from stable internal demand in their home market, Japanese firms again used their domestic base to launch high-volume export penetration of world markets.

The rapid production expansion and the move to automotion pushed Japanese firms further down the learning curve, lowering costs and consequently prices, faster than most U.S. firms.[11] Very aggressive price competition was led by the second-tier Japanese producers, Mitsubishi and Oki, who needed to establish a quick market presence. The strategy was simple and effective, as epitomized in a comment by Mitsubishi's Hideo Ohta: "The introductory price of 64K [dynamic] RAMs was dictated by market conditions—they had to be priced at slightly less than four times the price of 16K RAMs."[12] Despite the offhand reference to "market conditions," the pricing strategy operates independently of actual production costs and market conditions: Japanese firms forced a demand crossover from 16K to 64K by pricing the latter "at slightly less than four times the price of" the former.

They rapidly shifted capacity from 16K to 64K, and forced the crossover more quickly than U.S. firms anticipated. When one or two

Japanese firms moved in this fashion, the other firms were forced to move in parallel, and they did.[13]

With learning economies and high yields driving device costs down, Japanese firms easily sustained their initial leadership position as merchant firms like Mostek, Intel, and Fairchild entered the market in earnest in 1983. The manufacturing-based Japanese strategy of rapid entry and production of a relatively simple first-generation 64K device, was combined with their pricing strategy to buy the time needed to develop and introduce more advanced, second-generation devices using smaller die sizes and generating even higher yields. Although additional U.S. production after 1982 narrowed the Japanese market share, the Japanese industry had captured the lead and would use its new advantage to ensure dominance of future production of memory devices.

THE TRANSITION TO VLSI

During the early 1980s, international competition in semiconductors entered a period of rapid change, in which features typical of a maturing industry paradoxically coincided with continuing rapid innovation. Signs of maturity included extremely high capital costs for production, strategic emphases on marketing, and the Japanese-led focus on reducing production costs. Simultaneously, however, the pace of innovation associated with the development of the technological capabilities of very large scale integration (VLSI) accelerated. New markets for new commodity semiconductors opened up, and dramatically new commercial possibilities for the design and implementation of custom and semicustom circuits were concurrently developed. Hence, along with signs of maturity, semiconductor technology was changing and new competitive strategies emerging, so that instability continued to mark competition in semiconductors.

The industry had entered a fourth stage of development, loosely associated with the move to even greater levels of complexity in integrated circuits that is characteristic of VLSI. This phase intensified some of the trends of the LSI phase. The production of more systemslike components, forward integration into systems markets by merchant firms, the increasing penetration of markets such as factory and office automation, and the rising presence of captive production had their roots in the era of LSI. To these should be added a number of new structural trends that began to take shape, the most important of which can be characterized according to the innovation cum maturity theme. Pushing toward innovation are four factors:

1.   The emergence of potentially large markets for nonstandard application-specific (custom and semicustom) integrated circuits made possible by the design capabilities of VLSI
2.   Entrance of the latest wave of new merchant firms
3.   The identification of new standard systemlike commodity components, along with the emergence as commodity products of certain formerly low-volume market niches
4.   Closer strategic cooperation in some areas between merchant producers and final-systems manufacturers

Pushing toward maturity are two other factors:

5.   The enduring presence of Japanese competition, with the manufacturing-based strategy described earlier
6.   High and rising capital costs of R&D and production

Viewed from the perspective of competition in the industry, the new developmental phase can be called the era of strategic diversification. A diversified range of old and new strategic approaches to market success in the industry highlighted semiconductor competition during the 1980s. These approaches should be viewed as responses both to the potentials of VLSI and to the Japanese presence.

Very Large Scale Integration

As an industry matures, product design parameters become standardized and the focus of competition shifts toward incremental manufacturing refinement and marketing.[14] Technological innovation, which upsets established design parameters, refocuses the search for competitive advantage on new products and processes. VLSI upset established semiconductor design parameters.

VLSI rests on technological advances in semiconductor fabrication that permit the dense packaging of extremely complex circuits on a single silicon chip. Viewed as a process innovation, VLSI permits the production of increasingly dense standard circuits, such as semiconductor memory with a transistor count starting at roughly 100,000 per chip.[15] The 64K dRAM, which approaches this complexity, should thus be viewed as a transitional device, bridging the industry's move from LSI to VLSI. Yet the ability to implement such increasingly higher densities on single chips of silicon suggests that VLSI should not be viewed merely as process innovation. A defining characteristic of LSI for semiconductor producers was the ability to implement relatively less complex, existing electronics systems architectures in silicon (like the microprocessor); VLSI implies the ability to implement more complex and radically new systems achitectures directly in silicon. VLSI is thus an innovation in product technology at the systems level, where silicon becomes the design medium for application-specific electronic systems and subsystem components.[16] The limit to implementing the complex large circuits that VLSI makes possible is the great difficulty of design.[17] The high cost of VLSI design has precluded the widespread use of application-specific circuits. One solution to this dilemma is design automation, the use of computer-aided-design (CAD) systems to simplify and reduce the cost of designing VLSI circuits.

The dilemma surrounding custom circuits is not a new one for the industry's producers. Throughout their short history, the position of merchant firms as innovators and diffusers of semiconductor technology has rested on their ability to achieve commodity positions in standard components of ever greater complexity, thereby delivering increasing performance at decreasing costs. The ability to define and implement logic, then memory, and then microprocessor components in each phase of the industry's development allowed it to break out of the vicious circle whereby greater component complexity would lead to higher costs, which would lead to smaller markets. Indeed, the historical unwillingness of most merchant producers to undertake the custom design of integrated circuits rested on their inability to amortize the high costs of design, development, and production over the typically small volume (say 10,000 units) of custom logic circuits required by any individual purchaser who sought to give its final systems an edge in performance (by incorporating customized components).

The rise of captive production has been a response to this situation, because the high per-unit costs of custom component design, development, and production could be recouped by the systems manufacturer in the sale of the final end system. Prior to VLSI, however, the ability to implement complex logic systems in custom circuits did not exist. Indeed, all systems manufacturers with captive semiconductor operations combine standard memory, microprocessor, and logic components with their custom logic chips to form the microelectronic architecture of their systems products. Their captively produced custom circuits provide certain performance advantages over what might be achieved by interconnecting standard logic components to perform the same function, but they do not design the entire logic system in silicon.

For merchant semiconductor companies, then, the vicious circle of greater component complexity confronted them anew as the application-specific capabilities of VLSI became clearer. VLSI thus reopens the old custom-versus-standard debate that characterized semiconductor competition in earlier development phases, but with a new twist. The old solution of creating more complex and less costly standard circuits that can be interconnected in place of more costly custom logic chips appears to be less feasible at the density levels VLSI makes possible:

> Logic circuits tend to be less general purpose as they become more complex. As a result, the semiconductor manufacturer's available market for a standard logic product decreases as the implemented complexity increases. That is not to say that systems-level manufacturers do not require VLSI logic components. In fact, they do, but in order to be truly cost-effective, they must be custom.[18]

The microprocessor solved this problem for some uses, because the cheap commodity computer architecture, combined with the versatility of programming software, could substitute readily for many systems based on logic design. But software solutions to the customizing of logic systems can be both expensive and less efficient compared to custom hardware if the hardware components can be produced cost-effectively. Hence, semiconductor firms now find themselves in a position where their VLSI device technology, which permits the design of logic systems in silicon, is so powerful that it forces a reconceptualizing of the design and production of final systems products. The potential impact of VLSI, in short, is to upset established design parameters in final systems, as well as in components, thereby forcing innovation in final-systems products as well. The capabilities of the new component technology are now defining a whole new range of applications for which the difficulty of design (its high cost), combined with low production volumes, is the major barrier to commercial market penetration.

The picture is complicated, however, because over the last decade intermediate solutions to the custom-versus-standard question have arisen. In the late 1960s a number of attempts were made to reduce design costs by harnessing computers to aid in custom design. But computer-run costs were high, the design software was generally inadequate, and the approach was more expensive than interconnecting standard components.[19] The advent of the microprocessor offered a cheap, standard alternative to custom logic for many uses, and the existence of growing markets for standard commodity logic devices and microprocessors kept merchant semiconductor firms from major efforts at automating custom circuit design. Major systems houses, however—particularly IBM, Bell Labs, and RCA (through the Defense Department)—continued to develop approaches to custom design in order to enhance the performance of their system products.

In the early 1970s, two major approaches emerged. IBM introduced "masterslice gate arrays" in which logic "gates" are laid out on a chip in a standard production process and physically customized in the last stage of manufacturing by selectively interconnecting the gates to form unique logic structures. The IBM 4300 Series computer used gate arrays and set new price and performance standards for the computer industry. DEC, Amdahl, Fujitsu, and other computer companies thereafter committed themselves to gate-array technology. Its increasing popularity for data processing and military system applications has led almost all merchant producers, at least some 80 firms, to offer gate arrays on the merchant market. Since gate arrays are essentially commodity products until the final customization stage, they complement the merchant's basic commodity strategy.

Bell Laboratories concurrently developed an alternative approach to custom design, dubbed "standard cell," together with computer-automated tools, to achieve the layout of such circuits. In the standard-cell approach, a computer library of standard logic functions, each designed and tested in advance, is built up.[20] The automated layout tools then combine logic sets from the library into custom configurations on chip. The Defense Department also promoted standard cells through RCA. Hence, some defense contractors and some telecommunications companies (following Bell's lead) adopted this approach to custom circuit design for their system products. Neither gate arrays nor standard cells are pure custom devices, because they rely on the configuring of standard blocks (the array of logic gates or the libraries of functions). They constitute intermediate approaches to custom design, and have therefore been labeled semicustom devices. Open-market consumption of semicustom ICs reached somewhere between $100–$200 million by 1982, predominantly in gate arrays.[21] The standard cell design approach, unlike with arrays, involves customization of all mask layers. While this permits much greater flexibility in designing a functional chip, and in the efficiency of using the chip's available real estate, the trade-off is much higher design and manufacturing costs.

In the late 1980s standard-cell approaches have begun to be subsumed within a more general approach to IC design, called macro-cells. In this style, a circuit library is built up of large, functional circuit-building blocks, customized to specific functions (for example, blocks of RAM or ROM, of logic in array form or of core processor components). These blocks are of irregular shape and size and can be customized through physical interconnection (as in array technology) or at each mask layer with a unique topology (such as a unique configuration of the irregular functional building blocks). The larger the macro-cell library, the more inherently flexible and powerful this approach becomes, but the more computer memory is consumed in storing the ever growing library. Partly to solve this problem, computer programs called module generators have been developed, which automatically generate the layout of complex functional circuit blocks from a characterization of basic circuit parameters.

Newer approaches to the full and semicustom design of VLSI circuits are based on advances in CAD for IC design automation and on new methods of conceiving the design problem. The new techniques abandon logic-level design in favor of so-called structured design.[22] Structured IC design is modeled after structured approaches to software design, in which complex programming tasks are broken down into a hierarchy of subtask "modules" and then related back to form the complete program. The aim of these new design approaches is to start with high-level descriptions of the circuit and what it should accomplish (algorithmic, behavioral, or functional descriptions), and then to automate the translation of the high-level description through successive domains of representation to the specification and layout of circuit geometry at the mask-making level. Such a complete synthesis system would, in essence, be based on the macro-cell design approach, and would automatically generate layout masks from inputs composed of the functional description of a VLSI system, a description of the process technology to be used, and a description of constraint and cost functions. Much work needs to be done, however, to accomplish the full-blown synthesis system of wholly automated structured design, layout, and testing.

U.S. ADJUSTMENT IN AN ERA OF INTERNATIONAL COMPETITION

The U.S. industry responded to the interrelated market and financial challenges represented by the transition to VLSI and Japanese competition politically and through new market arrangements. The major political response was the formation of the Semiconductor Industry Association, which coordinated intensive lobbying of the U.S. government. Through political action the industry sought both to sensitize the U.S. government to the nature of the Japanese "threat" and to generate policies that would facilitate the industry's future growth (see Chapter 7).

Responses in the market centered on moving new product innovation in semicustom and commodity chips into the market and on developing looser ties to customers. For these purposes, it was necessary to generate capital for continued competitive growth and to spread the costs of new product development and market penetration. This was accomplished through venture-capital-backed new entry, a series of cross-licensing and technology-exchange agreements, acquisitions and equity investments, product-development contracts with electronic systems manufacturers, integration forward into systems markets by merchant producers, and integration backward into captive production by a variety of systems producers.

The Commercial Development of Custom Circuits

The continuing development of automated design for custom and semicustom circuits began drastically to reduce the design costs associated with VLSI. In turn, broad new merchant markets began to emerge for application-specific circuits, especially among the vast majority of U.S. systems manufacturers with no captive semiconductor production. In past phases of the industry's evolution, new merchant firms were the development vehicles by which major technological advances were diffused into commercial use. In this regard, application-specific VLSI is no exception. The entrenched positions of the captive and established merchant producers—the strategic focus of the former on keeping custom circuits proprietary, and of the latter on standard commodity components—militated against their developing and bringing the new technology to market as fast as its potential applications warranted. As a consequence, many new merchant firms entered the semiconductor business over the past decade, with the avowed aim of developing markets for application-specific circuits. Table 6–2 lists over 40 of the new firms, most of which entered in 1982–1983.

The strategies of these new entrants represent a distinct departure from the commodity focus that has until now dominated merchant production. Traditionally, the entire process from design conception through volume production of semiconductors has rested with the merchant (or fully captive) producers. By retaining control over the entire process, merchant firms could potentially generate competitive advantage at any point in the process; but, of course, controlling all stages is costly, because the final product must generate sufficient revenues to cover the costs of design, development, and manufacturing—as well as generating a margin for work on new products. Recall, then, that the traditional merchant strategy has rested on achieving a strong enough commodity position in standard circuits to amortize the costs of the entire process; their interest in custom circuits has been limited by their inability to amortize the high costs of custom design over the typically low volume of individual custom circuits required.

In response to this dilemma, the new entrants have attempted to lower the costs of custom circuits by unbundling the overall process of making semiconductors from design through production. The new entrants have chosen to carve up that process in a variety of ways. They tend, first, to be specialists in design and specific process implementation (such as CMOS, cell-based telecom chips). They often transfer (or diffuse) semiconductor design technology to systems producers. Some retain production technology and offer it as a foundry service on the open market, while others have no production, and buy it as a foundry service on the open market. Some of the new firms like VLSI Technology (VTI), LSI Logic, and Weitek offer a variety of proprietary and licensed automated IC design tools, from software packages to turnkey CAD systems for the design of custom or semicustom circuits. In this way, the costs of design and development are both reduced through automation and transferred to systems producers, who undertake the actual design using the automated tools. Completed masks can then be farmed back to the new merchants for prototyping and final production in foundries. The new start-ups are highly responsive to customers' needs in the market, and rapid turnaround time, a result of advanced design tools and focused efforts, is a major competitive advantage.

Equally important, however, this strategy of unbundling semiconductor services alters the traditional economics of semiconductor production. The key for a new firm engaged in ASIC production is the sharing of production costs across a large number of designs. By aggregating a large number of different designs, each of which requires low volumes of finished circuits, the new entrants hope to achieve sufficient volume to amortize the high capital costs of production. Their success depends on advances in semiconductor production equipment

Table 6–2. ASIC Market Positioning of the Start-up Companies.

	Process			Products			
	CMOS	Other MOS	Bipolar	STD Logic	ASICs Gate Arrays	Cell Based	PLD
ACTEL	X						
Acumos	X				X		
Altera	X						X
AMCC	X		X		X	X	
Atmel	X						X
BRI	X		X		X	X	
CDI	X				X	X	
CMA	X				X	X	
CSI	X		X		X	X	
Custom arrays			X		X		
Cypress	X						X
ESS	X						
ETC	X		X		X	X	
Exel	X						X
ICI array	X				X	X	
ICS	X				X		
ICT	X						X
IDT	X			X			
ILSI	X				X		
IMP	X				X	X	
Insouth	X				X	X	
Intercept	X				X		
Laserpath	X				X		
Lattice	X			X			X
LSI logic	X				X	X	
Matra-Harris	X				X		
MCE	X		X		X	X	
Micro linear	X		X		X	X	
Mietec	X	X	BiMOS		X	X	
Panatech	X						X
Performance	X			X			
Samsung	X			X			
Sierra	X					X	
S-MOS	X				X	X	
Telmos	X				X	X	

Table 6–2.   (continued)

	Process			Products			
	CMOS	Other MOS	Bipolar	STD Logic	ASICs Gate Arrays	Cell Based	PLD
UMC	X				X		
Universal	X				X	X	
VLSI	X				X	X	X
VTC	X		X	X	X	X	
WSI	X					X	
Xilinx	X						X
ZyMos	X					X	

Note: Spectrum Semiconductor Inc. will be offering its ASIC products in 1987.

Source: Dataquest, Inc. *Start-ups 1987* (San José: Dataquest, Inc., 1987).

and in the management of manufacturing systems which will allow different custom circuits to be produced in the same facilities with a minimum of disruption for new set-up.

As Table 6–3 shows, the typical new U.S. start-up with fabrication capability produces between 100 and 200 different types of chips in the same facility, compared to 10–20 for a traditional merchant, and

Table 6–3.   Production Indicators: U.S. Versus Japanese IC Companies, 1985.

Category	Unit Manufacturing Costs ($/sq. inch silicon)	Plant Size (wafer starts per week)	Average Number of Products per Line
Large Japanese firms	17.52	5,000	1–2
Large U.S. firms	24.76	2,500	10–20
Small U.S. start-ups	49.32	1,000	100–200

Source: Figures quoted in *VLSI Research Newsletter*, VLSI Research Inc., San José, Calif., February 1986, p. 6.

1–2 in the typical, highly automated giant Japanese memory plant. The higher per-chip costs associated with flexibility and limited volumes is more than compensated for by the premium chargeable for semi-customized performance and rapid turnaround time.

This new strategy has been further fragmented by some of the new entrants. Rather than combining design services with foundry production, some firms concentrate exclusively on design and perform only limited prototype production. They farm out finished designs to foundries or foundry lines of captive or merchant producers, for production. Because they are not burdened by the capital costs of production, these nonmanufacturing service merchants generate revenue through development contracts and royalties from systems producers. Here again, the capture of a high number of designs is crucial to competitive success. But there is a question as to whether such firms can maintain their market position as technology changes if they do not manufacture.

In sum, as the new entrants pursue their alternative approaches, a growing segment of the U.S. industry is becoming, in effect, an engineering service business tied to silicon-foundry production strategies. The new entrants have fragmented the traditional commodity strategy of the merchant producers in order to pursue new potential markets in custom design. Indeed, the transfer of design technology is a new strategy for creating market demand by educating the user to the potential of VLSI custom design. In that sense, the new merchants have taken a strategic page from the book of earlier merchant producers like Intel, who introduced microprocessor development and support systems to expand their markets by educating users to the virtues of the microprocessor.

As users become educated to custom design, the markets for application-specific ciruits have expanded rapidly because the potential competitive advantages of the new approaches are numerous. For the systems manufacturer, the cost of building a system can be reduced by some 60–80 percent, depending on the system in question and the approach to custom circuits chosen (gate arrays versus cells versus full custom).[23] Moreover, the development time from design through production of custom circuits is radically reduced by using the new techniques. Hence, in addition to cost-savings, application-specific designs offer greater potential flexibility for systems producers in responding to changing demands in their own markets.

The growth of application-specific markets, and the market presence of the new merchant entrants seeking to push along the use of custom circuits, has created new dynamic instability in existing component markets. Virtually every major established merchant firm has committed resources to respond to the new opportunities and competitive challenges associated with semicustom circuits. TI, Motorola, Intel, National, Fairchild, Signetics, Mostek, Harris, and RCA, among many others, are all offering parts of the range of semicustom or custom services, from IC design centers to silicon foundry divisions. The sudden profusion of merchant players in the custom game has altered the strategies of many of the systems manufacturers who have or were planning captive semiconductor facilities. Systems companies like NCR and GE have opened semicustom design centers; others like Wang, Prime, Unisys, and Data General have limited their captive operations and are turning to the merchant market for design or prototyping and production of various custom devices.

It is difficult to estimate the relative competitive position of U.S. and Japanese firms in custom and semicustom markets. It appears, however, that the intense competitiveness surrounding emerging custom markets in the United States and the emphasis on moving custom techniques into commercial production have given U.S. producers a lead. Except for the gate-array area, in which Japanese firms have become leading participants, there is comparatively little Japanese presence in semicustom markets outside of Japan. Japanese producers do appear, however, to produce a substantial number of custom and semicustom circuits for the Japanese market, although probably two-thirds of production is consumed captively.

The relative lack of Japanese participation in the U.S. custom arena is due in part to the market's small size relative to standard component markets. However, the nature of the custom business also cuts against Japanese participation. Very close cooperation is required between the systems manufacturer and semiconductor supplier in the development of custom circuits. At the end of the development process, the semiconductor supplier will have intimate knowledge of the proprietary circuits that give the systems product its performance characteristics. Very few U.S. systems companies ought to be willing to divulge such proprietary information to potential Japanese competitors before they are ready to take their products to market. U.S. systems companies should be prepared to avoid designing custom circuits with the semiconductor divisions of the same Japanese electronics firms who compete with them in final systems markets. Here, the vertically integrated, multidivisional structure of Japanese electronics companies, which has been a great strength in commodity component markets, might actually impede their ability to compete for design wins in foreign semicustom markets. Of course, if Japanese producers have a sufficient technical lead over merchant U.S. producers, then U.S. systems houses may have little choice but to rely upon their Japanese competition for the technology they need to be competitive.

Commodity Opportunities and Diversified Strategies

While the advent of custom capabilities associated with VLSI is an important competitive development, standard commodity components continued to dominate semiconductor production during the mid-1980s. This was so because VLSI permits the commodity production of increasingly dense and versatile memories, microprocessors, and peripheral circuits that opened new markets in areas like factory and office automation, and also because complex systems products continued to use standard components in tandem with custom-designed circuits. By the mid-1980s, standard devices still accounted for approximately 85 percent of the total market for semiconductors, a percentage that is unlikely to undergo drastic deterioration before the end of the 1980s.[24] The semiconductor sales of five major U.S. merchant firms in the early 1980s, shown in Table 6–4, suggest both the wide range of commodity market segments and the strategic differences in emphasis.

Motorola, TI, and National are all broad-based suppliers in the entire gamut of semiconductor market segments, whereas Intel and AMD are more narrowly focused on MOS and on MOS and biopolar production. Among the three broad suppliers there are differences, such as Motorola's relative emphasis on discrete devices and CMOS, and TI's and National's emphasis on bipolar devices. Intel has the heaviest focus on nonvolatile MOS memory and MOS microprocessors, whereas AMD's MOS participation is balanced and roughly equal to its bipolar production.

The diversity of focus among these and other merchant firms is broader, however, than the aggregate figures of Table 6–4 suggest. Any segment can be broken down into subsegments (for example, the MOS RAM segment into dynamic and static) and each subsegment broken down further according to device density (16K and 64K, for example), access time, and other performance specifications. A firm locates itself on this spectrum of products according to its perspective of where the

Table 6-4. Semiconductor Sales, by Market Segment, 1982 ($million).

Company	Total Sales	Discrete	Linear IC	Logic/Memory Bipolar	MOS RAM	MOS ROM/ EPROM	MOS MPU	CMOS Logic/Memory
Motorola	1,300	475	180	200	100	110	110	175
TI	1,300	170	220	530	130	130	130	20
National	745	35	220	325	70	25	30	40
Intel	615	—	—	20	100	280	215	—
AMD	325	—	30	160	40	45	50	—

Source: John J. Lazlo, Jr., "The Japanese Semiconductor Industry," (Hambrecht and Quist, January 31, 1983), p. 14.

best possibilities for growth lie given its technological capabilities and investment resources. As the competitive environment changes, a firm can also make its limited resources of talent and capital go farther by entering into selective arrangements with its competitors to share the costs and risks of development through technical exchanges and cooperative R&D. Both of these strategic moves, shifting the product focus and entering into cooperative arrangements, were characteristic of U.S. merchant firms during the early 1980s as they struggled with increasing capital costs and Japanese competition.

Table 6–5 breaks down the 1982 world MOS memory market by major segment. It suggests that although dynamic RAMs constituted the largest part of the market, static RAMs, read only memories, and erasable programmable ROMs were becoming segments nearly as large. Moreover, the electrically erasable PROM portion of the market was projected to grow much faster than the others and to rival the other major segments in size by the early 1990s. In 1978, only five years earlier, the MOS dRAM segment was valued at $235 million, static RAM at only $162 million, and the others were smaller or nonexistent.[25] Hence the rapid growth of these and the other MOS memory subsegments permitted *each of the segments to take on a commodity character* and to offer the promise of sufficient returns to sustain merchant firm growth. This led to new strategic choices for existing merchant firms, and to the potential for new entry. For example, when U.S.-Japanese competition in dRAMs limited the profitability of the segment, many established merchants like Intel shifted resources to concentrate on other products, in particular microprocessors and EPROM.

Table 6–5. World MOS Memory Market, 1982 ($million).

Device	Sales	Percentage of Market
RAM	$ 800	27%
Static RAM	650	22
ROM	699	23
EPROM	650	22
EEPROM	70	2
PROM and others	120	4
Total	2,990	100

Source: Integrated Circuit Engineering Corporation, *Status 1983*, p. 101.

Moreover, as VLSI technology and markets developed in this fashion in the early 1980s, more and more opportunities emerged to fragment the different commodity market segments into profitable niches. Adopting a page from the application-specific IC (ASIC) start-up book, many of these new merchants became process and design specialists relying on foundries for production. Combined with the ability to shift resources rapidly, specialization appeared to represent at the aggregate industry level a dynamic response to changing opportunities in the market.

However, there were major questions in the early 1980s concerning the efficacy of shifting resources and specializing in this fashion. The constraints revolved around the issue, alluded to earlier, of where firms gained design and production experience for moving to ever more complex devices. Would it be possible to generate sufficient experience from the manufacture of complex commodity devices other than RAM, so that if existing merchant U.S. firms were forced to abandon the RAM market, a viable merchant commodity strategy could still be preserved? And what of the nonmanufacturing start-ups? Could they retain their distinct advantages as process specialists if they engaged in no manufacturing?

Participation in the dRAM market had thus far been critical for two reasons. First, as the highest volume product market, dRAM generated the sales revenues critical to sustaining long-term investment in next-generation R&D and capacity. Second, and equally important, the dRAM was an unparalleled state-of-the-art process development vehicle: dRAM density evolution was straightforward and predictable, hard-tooled fabrication lines could be ramped up very quickly in anticipation of stable market expansion as costs fell, and the regular, repetitive memory arrays that compose a dRAM chip could be debugged with relative ease. However, as major U.S. merchants were forced by Japanese competition to look elsewhere than dRAM for sustained revenues, they also discovered that they could use other products as process development vehicles. As Table 6–6 shows, while all major Japanese producers, IBM, AT&T, and TI still use the dRAM as their principal process development vehicle, major U.S. merchants are using a variety of chips ranging from static RAM to nonvolatile EPROM to microcontrollers to proprietary logic and even gate arrays.

As the major U.S. merchants attempted to stay at the state of the art and eliminate their exposure in dRAM, they discovered that avoiding participation in dRAM markets might pay for itself in a new-found flexibility to produce related families of products on the same non-RAM

Table 6–6. IC Process Development Drivers.

Company	Driver
Japanese	Dynamic RAM
ATT	Dynamic RAM
IBM	Dynamic RAM
TI	Dynamic RAM
AMD	EPROM, with limited in-house dRAM
Intel	EPROM, static RAMs, single-chip microcontroller
Motorola	Static RAM, EPROM, limited dRAM
National	Proprietary logic, gate arrays

fabrication lines. Indeed, the flexibility required approaches that needed in the ASIC end of the IC business.

For both established merchants and new start-ups, the moves into new VLSI products, whether semicustom or standard commodity, could not be accomplished without an acceleration in cooperation. Cooperative agreements were, however, more than solutions to the clearly defined problems of product development and market penetration. They represented solutions to the problems posed by innovation and maturity: how to position a firm to meet an uncertain future, how to meet Japanese competition and the push toward industry maturity that it partly represents, and how to cope with burgeoning development, manufacturing, and marketing costs.

Cross-licensing, technology exchanges, and less formal second-source arrangements were a major way in which U.S. firms spread these risks over the last decade. For example, by developing and cross-licensing different components within a family, U.S. firms were able to spread the risks and share the costs of development and production. U.S. firms also were able to enter markets with assured second sources tied together through cross-licensing arrangements. The assurance of supply and support which these actions represented enabled easier market access and more rapid customer acceptance. Moreover, cross-licensing and technology exchanges dispersed technical know-how among the partners and thereby enhanced the technology position of each. The different deals struck during the late 1970s captured different aspects of these opportunities, depending upon the strengths, needs, and strategies of the partner firms. Table 6–7 summarizes many of these proliferating deals during the early 1980s.

Table 6–7.　Representative Technology Exchanges, Cross-licenses, and Second-source Arrangements.

Firm	Partner	Products
AMD	Intel	Microprocessors, peripherals
	LSI Logic	Gate arrays
	Mostek	Communications
	Signetics	Bipolar
	Thomson-EFCIS	Modem
	Zilog	Microprocessors, peripherals
AMI	Wang	Custom
GI	Hitachi	EEPROM
GTE	Mitel	CMOS communications

The advantages and opportunities of exchange can best be seen in the proliferating deals centered on the rapidly expanding markets for microprocessors (MPU) and related devices. Market penetration required not only that MPUs be supported with a supply of memory and peripheral chips, which would in effect create an MPU-based systems product, but also that second sources be available. The costliness of developing and adding peripherals and the need for second sources resulted in mask exchanges and cross-licensing agreements. Through these actions, total system development costs were spread and the complete MPU and peripherals family second-sourced, which made market penetration easier. The challenges of high development cost and market entry, which might have overtaxed individual firms acting alone, were successfully met through cross-licensing.

Other patterns of cross-licensing involved the exchange of differing proprietary technologies. These deals broadened the potential markets for products and process technology, spread the cost of technology development, and broadened each participating firm's technology base. Through such deals, partners could take advantage of each other's competitive strengths to build market position and simultaneously reduce the risks and costs of product development. Cross-licensing and related arrangements thereby seemed to help meet the problems of rapid market growth and technology development which dominated the industry's agenda in the late 1970s and early 1980s.

Acquisitions and major equity purchases of merchant U.S. semiconductor firms were another broad competitive response to the challenges of rapid growth and international competition. For the smaller U.S. firm, faced with costly problems of growth, development, and competition, acquisition often delivered a number of advantages. First, it provided an infusion of capital to meet the demanding requirements of capacity expansion and continued technology development. It also held out the promise of future access to cheap debt capital for continued expansion. Second, acquisition often meant access to new geographic and product markets through the marketing resources and systems products of the parent. Third, acquisition offered access to the parent firm's technological and production resources, which meant the ability to acquire technology and to move forward into production of more complex systemslike devices. In many cases, of course, acquisition held out the notable long-run disadvantage of the loss of corporate autonomy or identity. For the parent firm, acquisition offered several obvious advantages. For foreign electronics firms, acquisition meant instant access to the U.S. market in both semiconductors and electronic systems. Equally important, it meant access to advanced semiconductor technology. For original equipment manufacturers (OEM) integrating backward into semiconductors, acquisition provided a cheap, rapid way of "installing" a captive semiconductor division. The acquisitions and equity investments listed in Table 6–7 express different aspects of these advantages.

Of course, many of the outright acquisitions showed a mixed record of success. For example, United Technology's investment in Mostek was eventually abandoned after years of losses in the mid-1980s, and, after major investments and continuing losses, Schlumberger finally disposed of Fairchild in 1987. Here as elsewhere, there was no guarantee that a well-heeled parent would be willing or able to sustain the kind of investment necessary, and permit the autonomy required, to restore competitive health to a troubled merchant firm. Indeed, succeeding best were those acquisitions or equity infusions that either focused the merchant firm on specific niches serving the parent company (for example, GTE-Semi), or provided a timely capital infusion and greater market stability without disrupting the merchant's aggressive autonomy (for example, Siemens-AMD, IBM-Intel).

The infusion of IC technology into rapidly growing new or changing markets which required significant development and applications expenditures was also sometimes picked up through technology development contracts by the equipment manufacturer whose specific needs had to be met. The competitive benefits to IC firms were obvious: they developed new technologies at minimal cost to themselves and often gained market access for their resulting products. While such contracts were given in most major market segments, the notable example for its size and impact was the series of development contracts given by the U.S. automotive industry (particularly, General Motors) to develop IC based automotive electronics systems.

Perhaps the most significant response by U.S. firms to the challenges of market growth in the late 1970s was a continued forward integration into systems by the largest merchant firms and the exceptionally rapid backward integration into semiconductor production by a wide range of OEMs. During the late 1970s and early 1980s, there was a literal explosion of backward integration by OEMs into semiconductor production (see Table 6–8). These companies spanned all of the major semiconductor markets: computers, data processing, telecommunications, industrial, consumer, and military.

There were four major competitive reasons for the growth in backward integration. First, with VLSI increasingly providing systems in silicon, backward integration became a strategic necessity where it could be afforded, at least to assure control over proprietary custom chip technology. Second, as microelectronic products increasingly infiltrated new systems markets, OEMs integrated backward to ensure themselves a competitive position in those markets. Third, the serious supply shortages in the merchant market during some periods forced OEMs into captive production to ensure supply for their needs and to supplement purchased inventories. Fourth, captive production provides an attractive secondary source of supply. Table 6–8 is a representative list of large-sized captive and mostly captive suppliers.

It is important to remember that the growth in captive facilities was made possible in part by the emergence in the 1970s of the sophisticated infrastructure of independent firms described earlier—manufacturers of materials and equipment for testing and production, and suppliers of analysis, consulting, and design services to both captive and merchant semiconductor producers. This infrastructure had developed during the 1970s to support merchant firms, but its capacities were ideally suited to the needs of backwardly integrating OEMs.

The forward integration of the largest merchant U.S. semiconductor firms during the LSI period (described in Chapter 4) also continued apace in the late 1970s and early 1980s. As development and design costs rose with the complexity of IC devices, these firms moved forward into systems production to recapture the higher value-added that systems represented. The move forward was also aimed at meeting the

Table 6–8. U.S. Captive Suppliers: Semiconductor Production.

Company
Aerojet Electro Systems
Amdahl Corporation
Ampex Corporation
Bell Telephone Labs
Boeing Company
Burroughs
Chrysler Corporation
Control Data Corporation
Cutler-Hammer/Eaton
Data General
Datel Systems
Delco Electronics Division
Digital Equipment Corporation
Eastman Kodak
E-Systems
Essex Group
Fluke Automatic Systems Division
Ford Aerospace Communications
Foxboro Company
Four-Phase System
General Dynamics
General Electric
SSAO
Corporate R&D
Aerospace Electronics Systems
Gould
GTE Laboratories
Hewlett-Packard
General Systems Divison
Santa Clara Division
Microwave
H.P. Labs
Optoelectroncis
Stanford Park Division
Instrument Division
Desktop Computer Division

Table 6–8. *continued*

Company

Instrument Division
Handheld Calculator Division
Honeywell
   Solid State Electronics Center
   SSEC Center
IBM
   Corporate
   General Systems Division
   Data Systems Division
   General Technology Division
   System Development Division
   Data Products Division
   General Systems Division
   Federal Systems Division
Lockheed Missiles and Space
Magnavox
Martin Marietta Aerospace
McDonnell-Douglas
   Astronautics
Micro-Rel
NCR
Northern Teleocm
Northrup
Rosemount
Sandia Labs
Sperry
Storage Technology Corporation
   Microtechnology
Stromberg-Carlson
Tektronix
Western Electric
   Teletype Corporation
Westinghouse
   Friendship Solid State Research
Xerox
   PARC

Source: Integrated Circuit Engineering, *Status*, 1980, pp. 59–61.

applications needs of users in systems markets, thereby serving to enhance and establish positions in expanding markets, and also to generate additional revenues to stabilize the semiconductor business cycle. Some of the move forward was achieved through the cross-licensing arrangements, acquisitions, and development contracts. In addition, the largest firms integrated forward by establishing systems subsidiaries and through forward mergers.

Once again, the movements forward by different firms spanned the major markets for semiconductor devices. Texas Instruments continued to expand into a broad range of consumer and computer systems markets, though not always successfully. Motorola continued to expand its telecommunications capability, and built an automotive electronics expertise. National moved further forward into plug-compatible mainframes (PCM) through merger with its formerly independent marketer, Itel, to form National Advanced Systems. All of the major MPU manufacturers moved forward into microcomputer board-level systems, into MPU based industrial control systems, and toward distributed processing systems. These moves included further refinement of microprocessor development systems and entry into software support, notably by TI, Motorola, and Intel, in the form of ROM-based "firmware."

Finally, the other significant developments in the cooperative arena centered on research. The formation of two new arrangements, the Semiconductor Research Corporation (SRC) and Microelectronics and Computer Technology Corporation (MCC), to pursue basic and applied research on the one hand and VLSI-related product development on the other, were particularly noteworthy. Table 6–9 lists the membership of each.

The SRC effort is aimed at increasing the level of focused semiconductor research for both the long term (5–10 years) and the near term (3–5 years). It is not expressly aimed at product development; rather, the participating companies use the results of cooperative research to develop their own new products and technologies.[26] SRC research focuses on three broad areas: microstructure sciences, systems and design automation, and production and engineering. The intent is to involve universities directly in the research in order to upgrade their participation and increase their ability to fill industry's employment needs. As Japan has done through its cooperative research programs, the SRC hopes to reduce the per-firm risks and costs of basic research by sharing, eliminating duplicative research, and achieving a broad-based program

Table 6–9.   Membership of SRC and MCC.

SRC	MCC
AMD	AMD
Applied Materials	Allied
ATT	Bell Communications Research
Control Data	(BELCOR)
DEC	Boeing
Dupont	Control Data
Eastman Kodak	DEC
Eaton	Eastman Kodak
E Systems	GE
GE	Harris
GM	Honeywell
GTE	Hewlett-Packard
Harris	Lockheed
Hewlett-Packard	3M
Honeywell	Martin Marietta
IBM	Motorola
Intel	National Semiconductor
Loral Systems	NCR
Monolithic Memories	RCA
Monsanto	Rockwell International
Motorola	Unisys
National Semiconductor	Westinghouse
Perkin-Elmer	
Rockwell International	
Silicon Systems	
Texas Instruments	
Union Carbide	
U.S. Government	
(NSF, DOD, NSA)	
Westinghouse	
Varian Associates	
Xerox	
SEMI (representing	
36 SEMI	
member companies)	

Source: Semiconductor Research Corporation; Microelectronics and Computer Technology Corporation.

for the development of new technologies. SRC members pay a fee proportional to their integrated circuit sales volume (or purchase volume for the systems companies).

A number of cooperative university-industry research centers were also funded, some through National Science Foundation sponsorship. Table 6–10 lists a sample of these centers. They represent an increased awareness of the crucial role in basic and some applied research that

Table 6–10   Representative University/Industry Microelectronics Research Centers.

Center	Focus
Center for Integrated Systems (CIS) Stanford University, Stanford, Calif.	VLSI systems and integrated circuit research, including task turnaround fabrication facility, laser annealing, artificial intelligence
Communications and Signal Processing North Carolina State University, Raleigh	Speech and image processing; transmitting data over power lines; VLSI algorithms and architecture; computing communications architecture
Electronics Research Laboratory University of California, Berkeley	Microelectronics; microfabrication; CAD and computer sciences
Engineering Excellence for the 80's Arizona State University, Tempe	Solid-state electronics; computer science; CAD; energy systems
Microelectronics and Information Sciences (MEIS) University of Minnesota, Bloomington	Information science and technology
Microelectronics Center of North Carolina N.C. State, Duke, Univ. of N.C./Chapel Hill, N.C. A&T Research Triangle Institute, Univ. of N.C./Charlotte, Raleigh	Microelectronics and chip research

Source: *High Technology*, May 1983, p. 16.

universities play, together with an acknowledgment that the U.S. research infrastructure in microelectronics needed to be strengthened.

In great part, all of the cooperative activities described above were responses to the quality of products and research coming out of Japan. Why and how these adjustment moves by U.S. industry in the late 1970s and early 1980s were insufficient to stem the Japanese challenge, and the corresponding adjustment activities of the mid-1980s, are the subjects of the next chapter.

NOTES

1. Estimated from figures in *Fortune,* March 1981, p. 116.
2. *Business Week,* March 30, 1981, pp. 86–87.
3. Based on conversations with industry sources.
4. Authors' estimates based on data in The Consulting Group, BA Asia Ltd., (BA 1980), *The Japanese Semiconductor Industry, 1980,* pp. 117, 123. Estimated percentages for 1975 and 1976 assume that the U.S.-controlled percentage of total Japanese imports remained roughly the same as in 1978 and 1979. The 1980 figure is an estimate based on industry sources.
5. BA 1980, pp. xix–xx.
6. Ibid.
7. *The Economist,* April 26, 1980, pp. 54–55; see also, *Rosen Electronics Letter,* July 7, 1980, p. 59.
8. T. Abe, "Robust Design, a Cost Effective Method for Improving Process Variations," *Japan Semiconductor Journal 2,* no. 1 (February 1983).
9. Ultratech Stepper's C. Woodrow Rea, "Impact of VLSI on Lithography," Dataquest, Semiconductor Industry Conference, October 18–20, 1982, p. 9; *Electronic News,* May 31, 1982, p. 20.
10. The major Japanese electronics firms are each members of a different *keiretsu,* a conglomerate industrial grouping of companies arranged around either a single large bank or large industrial firm (or several firms).
11. John J. Lazlo, "The South Korean Electronics Industry," Morgan Stanley, 1986.
12. *Electronic News,* March 8, 1982, p. H–4.
13. This does not mean that Japanese firms necessarily collaborated to force crossover. Crossover may have been the result of each firm competing individually on price. The distinction is drawn in U.S. antitrust law between parallel behavior resulting from each firm's individual strategy and resulting from an agreement to collude. Generally, only the latter is actionable under U.S. antitrust law.

14. See the discussion in William J. Abernathy, Kim B. Clark, and Allan M. Kantrow, *Industrial Renaissance* (New York: Basic Books, 1983), ch. 2.

15. A rough estimate of the point of transition from LSI to VLSI in the memory and microprocessor areas is "when the number of 'things' on a chip exceeds, say, a hundred thousand." Paul Penfield, Jr. "Small Is Big: The Microelectronic Challenge," VLSI memo 82-94, Massachusetts Institute of Technology, Cambridge, Mass., April 1982, p. 4.

16. The process-versus-product innovation perspective on VLSI is suggested by Weitek's Arthur J. Collmeyer, "Custom VLSI and CAD in the 80's," Dataquest, CAD/CAM Industry Conference, September 29–October 1, 1982, pp. 1–2.

17. Penfield, "Small Is Big," p. 4.

18. VLSI Technology's Alfred J. Stein, "Systems and Silicon—A Partnership," Dataquest, Semiconductor Industry Conference, October 18–20, 1982, p. 2.

19. United Technology's Gordon Hoffman, "CAD and Semiconductor Technique: Tools for System Integration," Dataquest, Semiconductor Industry Conference, October 18–20, 1982, p. 1.

20. I am indebted to discussions with my colleague Alberto San Giovanni-Vincentelli, for the following description of standard-cell, macro-cell, and procedural design methodologies. He, of course, bears no responsibility for my interpretations.

21. Compare *Electronics,* January 12, 1983, pp. 129 and 151, with *Electronic News,* April 20, 1981, p. 50.

22. *Electronics,* "VLSI Special Report," February 10, 1983, pp. 134–145.

23. Bogert, "Semiconductor Market Overview," Dataquest Semiconductor Conference, October 18–20, 1982, p. 5. Northern Telecom's Lloyd A. Taylor gives an identical estimation of potential cost-savings based on his company's actual experience, in "The Efficient vs. the Effective Use of Silicon," Dataquest, Semiconductor Industry Conference, October 18–20, 1982, p. 5.

24. The 88 percent estimate is based on Dataquest's $2.1 billion estimate of the 1982 nonstandard market and Integrated Circuit Engineering Corporation's figure of $17.675 billion for world semiconductor production in 1982, ICE, *Status 1982,* p. 3.

25. *Electronics,* "World Market Survey," January 1978.

26. Erich Bloch, "Industry and Universities Cooperative Action by the Semiconductor and Computer Industry," Dataquest Semiconductor Industry Conference, October 18–20, 1982.

7 JAPAN ASCENDANT: 1984–Present

By 1986, Japanese producers dominated world production of dynamic and static RAM. They held approximately 90 percent of the then leading-edge 256K dRAM market, 55 percent of the 64K market, 70 percent of the total dRAM market, 75 percent of the 64K dRAM market, 50 percent of the fast 16K sRAM market, and about 50 percent of the total sRAM market. Moreover, they were moving to introduce the 1Mb dRAM well ahead of all U.S. competitors except IBM, AT&T, and Texas Instruments, and of these, only TI would compete in the merchant market. So dominant had Japanese producers become that they had easily attained the major world market share in total MOS memory production by 1983 (see Figure 7–1).

Japanese success in memory derived from sustained investment creating leadership in manufacturing. Japanese producers took RAM production to a new level by investing in extremely large, highly automated facilities dedicated solely to RAM production and capable of operating at 10,000 wafer "starts" (wafers started into production) per month, compared to the typical merchant U.S. facility's capability of perhaps 2,500 wafer starts per month.[1] Only one or two types of chips were producible in these facilities, but the monster plants featured extremely low unit production costs once they were operated at peak volumes. Since the process rarely had to be changed to accommodate changes in product, once the process was fine-tuned for dRAM production, and process

Figure 7–1. MOS Memory World Market Share (percent of world shipments).

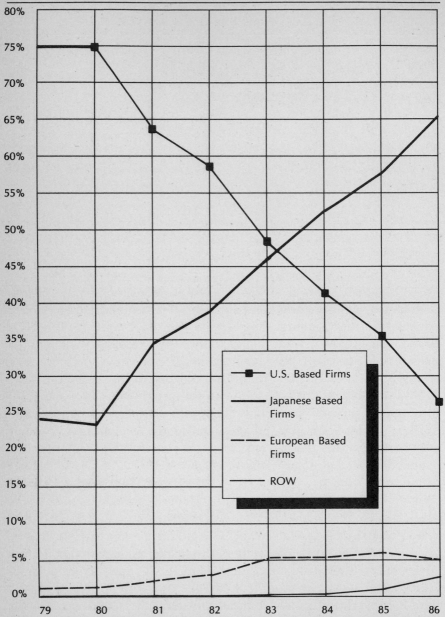

Source: Reprinted by permission of Westview Press from *The Microelectronics Race: The Impact of Government Policy on International Competition,* edited by Thomas R. Howell, William A. Noellert, Janet H. MacLaughlin, and Alan W. Wolff. Copyright © Westview Press, 1987, Boulder, Colo.

variability for this type of chip was eliminated the plants could be turned on and run essentially nonstop. The result was not only low unit costs but uniformly high quality as well.

Japanese producers were able to speed up the product life cycle of dynamic RAMs. As Figure 7–2 suggests, sustained Japanese investment from the 64K generation in early 1980 to 1987 compressed product life cycles and forced costs and average selling prices to decline at a rate faster than the industry's prior historical experience.

The dramatic result of aggressive Japanese investment practices in the face of stagnant demand was to force U.S. merchant firms, with the exception of TI and struggling Micron Technology, to abandon the dRAM market entirely by the advent of the 256K generation. Prices simply collapsed in the 256K market in 1985-in both Japan and the United States, falling to roughly $1.50, just one-tenth of their original volume price. These prices were well below the production costs of most Japanese firms; indeed all producers lost money on dRAM production in 1985 and probably did little better than break even in 1986.

The loss of U.S. position was not quite so rapid in nonvolatile MOS memory, particularly erasable programmable read only memory (EPROM) and electrically erasable PROM (EEPROM), market niches into which U.S. merchants retreated as they lost the RAM battle. By 1985, EPROM and EEPROM accounted for close to $1 billion in sales, largely in EPROM. Although the technology was pioneered by American firms and is dominated by Intel and AMD in the highest densities, Japanese firms emerged during the mid-1980s to capture majority shares of the high-growth markets, and to challenge for leadership at the leading edge. Table 7–1 estimates worldwide EPROM production ranking for each generation in 1986.

Intel and small U.S. start-ups like Xicor and Seeq dominated the small but fast-growing EEPROM market in the mid-1980s. Whether they could maintain leadership as the market grew and attracted Japanese investment was very uncertain.

Japanese success in EPROMs was intimately tied to characteristic near-cost or below-cost pricing strategies. Sustained price declines increased the Japanese 128K market share from 1 percent in 1983 to 60 percent in 1985, and the 256K share from 3 percent in the third quarter of 1983 to 20 percent by the third quarter of 1985. Since, as argued in the last chapter, EPROMs became critical process drivers for major U.S. producers as they were forced out of the RAM market, they chose to defend their market position in EPROMs through political and legal

Figure 7–2. Transition in Dynamic RAM Products, by Date of Product Introduction.

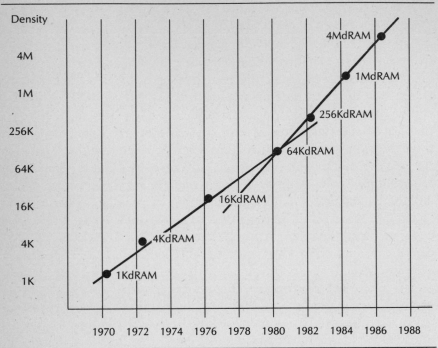

Source: Robertson, Coleman and Stephens and Toshiba data.

tactics. They filed dumping suits under U.S. trade laws, accusing their Japanese competition of selling EPROMs in the United States at less than fair value.

By 1986, U.S. producers saw their once unchallenged dominance of the microprocessor (MPU), microcomputer (MCU), and peripherals market also come under severe challenge. Japanese producers leveraged their accumulated IC production experience and strong demand in the domestic Japanese market to garner an increasing share of worldwide sales. Japanese producers prospered by embedding low-end MCUs (4- and 8-bit) in their consumer electronic and consumer durable equipment, and by becoming aggressive second sources of U.S. designed 8-, 16- and now 32-bit MPU families from Intel, Motorola, and Zilog in particular. In addition, NEC introduced its V-series, a competitive 8-, 16-, and 32-bit family that represents the first serious bid to have a proprietary Japanese MPU family accepted as a design standard in the market.

Table 7-1. World EPROM Production Leaders, 1986.

16K	32K	64K	128K	256K
National	TI	Hitachi	Intel	Intel
TI	AMD	Mitsubishi	Hitachi	AMD
NEC	Intel	Intel	Mitsubishi	Fujitsu
AMD	Hitachi	Fujitsu	AMD	Hitachi
SGS-Ates	Fujitsu	TI	Fujitsu	—
Japan: 15%	Japan: 35%	Japan: 60%	Japan: 60%	Japan: 20%

Source: Morgan Stanley, ICE, and author's estimates.

In addition, Hitachi and Toshiba, among other Japanese firms, are completing work on the government-organized TRON project, an ambitious attempt jointly to develop a design standard for high-performance MPUs for industrial and data-processing applications. Table 7–2 ranks the major MPU/MCU producers for each major product generation in the market by 1986.

The principal technical reason for U.S. dominance at the top end of the market is the U.S. lead in the design and implementation of high-level computer architectures on-chip, stemming from both the U.S. lead in design software and CAD, and in the nature of implementing high-level architectures, still largely a craft.

The following list breaks out the total $2.9 billion 1985 MPU and related chip market according to the percentage of sales value accounted for by each subsegment.

Microprocessor	25%
8-bit	14
16-bit	11
32-bit	1
Microcontroller	20
4-bit	6
8-bit	13
16-bit	1
Peripherals	55

In 1985 in the leading-edge U.S. market alone, about 85 percent of the MPU chips shipped were 8-bit, and the 8-bit sales value about equaled the combined value of shipments of the higher value-added 16- and 32-bit chips. In both value and volume terms, 8-bit MCUs thoroughly

Table 7-2.   World MPU/MCU Production Leaders, 1986.

4-bit MCU	8-bit MCU	8-bit MPU	16-bit MPU	32-bit MPU
NEC(P)	NEC(IN.P)	Intel(P)	Intel(P)	Intel(P)
Toshiba(P)	Intel(P)	NEC(IN/ZI/P)	Motorola(P)	Motorola(P)
Matsushita(P)	Motorola(P)	Zilog(P)	NEC(IN.P)	National(P)
Japan: 80%	Japan: 40%	Japan: 33%	Japan: 17%	Japan: negligible

Source: Morgan Stanley, ICE, and author's estimates.

dominated controller sales. The 8-bit MPU was then about 12 years old. Thus, unlike dRAM, the market life of MPU/MCU chips can be quite long, particularly if their applications do not require much computational power beyond that available from current generations.

Several factors account for the unusual longevity of each MPU generation. First, chip makers upgrade the functionality of each generation, either by incorporating peripheral functions on-chip or by changing internal architectures to accommodate longer bit-lengths. Second, well-established software support is built up for each generation. Third, as the chips drop in cost, the low price, combined with the versatility of programmability and with functional enhancements, generates increasingly large and wide-ranging applications. For example, 8-bit chips can be found in applications ranging from cellular mobile phones, to low-cost engineering work stations, to automobiles, to industrial control and factory automation systems.

U.S. producers have managed to maintain the leading edge in this market, in part because there are very few dominant product families in each product generation. Product dominance depends heavily on the number of systems manufacturers who design the MPU family into their systems products, and that in turn depends most heavily upon the base of software written and peripherals developed for the MPU family. Moreover, since the 8-bit generation, U.S. producers have designed their next-generation products to be upwardly compatible with the base of software written for the prior generation. This has tended to lock in succeeding generations of systems products, which have migrated upward with the MPU family chosen earlier in order to retain software compatibility. Once the MPU family is locked in to a systems product, the U.S. chip manufacturer prospers because, over time, the sale of support peripherals constitutes a more lucrative market than the MPU itself.

The need for peripherals support and customers' demand for multiple suppliers has typically engendered a wide variety of second-sourcing arrangements for MPU families. In the case of Intel's leading 16-bit family, primary second sources included AMD, Fujitsu, NEC, Harris, Oki, and Siemens; for Motorola's MPU family, the second sources were Hitachi, Thomson, Rockwell, Philips-Signetics, and Mostek. Paradoxically, it was these arrangements that permitted Japanese firms to gain MPU technology and production expertise, thereby enabling them to challenge U.S. leadership. As a result, the number of licensed second sources for the new 32-bit MPU families is likely to be much more limited than in the past.

By contrast to MOS markets, the digital bipolar market segment is one semiconductor market in which U.S. firms managed to maintain overall world market share through the mid-1980s, as shown in Figure 7–3. Unfortunately, U.S. leadership here is not necessarily an indication of future strengths. Bipolar logic devices, particularly the ubiquitous TTL family, are the oldest and were the most widely used of all IC families until surpassed in the late 1970s by the growth of MOS technology. TTL's variations, notably Schottky TTL, low-power Schottky TTL, and advanced low-power Schottky, have sufficiently improved on TTL's speed and power consumption to make the TTL family still the most widely used digital logic for electronic design. U.S. companies pioneered the technology and most of its enhancements over time. They have decades of accumulated production experience in the device family's manufacture, and very well-established customer/distributor relations. As an older product family dominated by entrenched U.S. suppliers, the overall bipolar logic market simply was not as attractive an investment in the 1970s for Japanese companies as the fledgling MOS market. Its growth was demonstrably slower than MOS, and Japanese firm entrants were chary of trying to dislodge the large U.S. producers.

In turn, of course, Japanese producers—like smaller, newer U.S. entrants—have concentrated on developing competitive alternatives to TTL in order to displace the established market with newer technologies. These alternatives, including ECL bipolar for very-high-speed applications, semicustom (ASIC) arrays and cells, programmable logic (PLA and PAL), and CMOS logic, are finding increasing acceptance among growing numbers of users.

Indeed, given the relative attractiveness of the market for ECL digital bipolar and the bipolar replacement technologies, Japanese producers have honed their internal bipolar manufacturing processes to emerge

Figure 7-3.   Bipolar Digital World Market Share
(percent of world shipments).

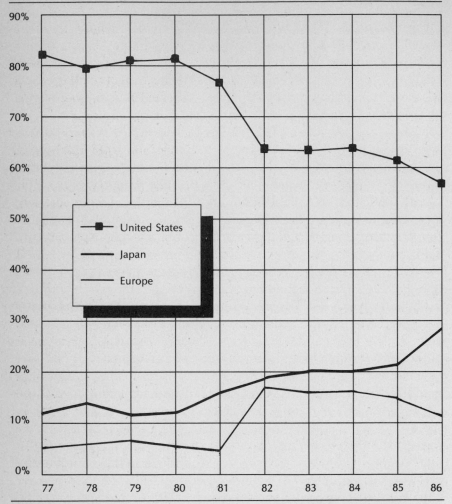

Source: Reprinted by permission of Westview Press from *The Microelectronics Race: The Impact of Government Policy on International Competition*, edited by Thomas R. Howell, William A. Noellert, Janet H. MacLaughlin, and Alan W. Wolff. Copyright © Westview Press, 1987.

as very competitive producers in the high end of the digital market. Japanese producers are capable in their labs of manufacturing a much more complicated process than most U.S. producers.[2] They are pushing the development of merged bipolar/CMOS processes (so-called Bi-CMOS), and they have taken the lead in the development of high-speed bipolar memory. Not surprisingly, the primary applications for bipolar circuits are those electronics systems markets (computer, telecom, and industrial automation) in which the Japanese economy is heavily investing.

U.S. producers remained strong in other major, newer, or niche merchant market segments that blossomed during the decade. For example, U.S. merchants continued to lead the development of field-programmable logic, developed by Signetics (now owned by Philips) and Monolithic Memories. Of 1985's $220 million field-programmable logic market, MM and its second sources claimed about 80 percent. MM's second-source arrangements are extensive, including AMD, Harris, Intel, National, TI, and start-ups Altera, Lattice, and VLSI Technology. U.S. start-ups have pushed PLD technology development, moving rapidly into CMOS processing and erasable programmable logic devices (EPLD and EEPLD). Most of the leaders in the development of CMOS E- and EEPLD are start-ups or smaller merchant companies. Altera, Solid State Scientific, and VLSI Technology are principal suppliers of EPLD. Lattice, Cypress (co-development with MM), and a host of other start ups like Si-Fab, Semi Processes, and Zytrex offer EEPLD.

Similarly, U.S. producers have led the development of new commodity semiconductor markets in digital signal processing (DSP) and telecommunications chips. As the analog world enters an era of digital networking, both DSP and telecommunications chips are high-growth markets for the future, though they accounted for only $100–150 million and $100 respectively in 1985–1986.[3] Of course, the U.S. lead here could well be temporary, given the enormous applications investment in telecom and automation being made in Japan. Given the technical leadership of NTT and the vast domestic Japanese market, it is easy to envision Japanese chip producers emerging dominant in these commodity market segments as well.

By contrast, the rapidly evolving market for semicustom circuits offered continuous opportunities for U.S. producers to fare well, though they were not without challenge. During the mid-1980s, ASICs became by far the fastest growing of IC market subsegments. Although the growth of the ASIC market was not as large as expected in predictions made in the early 1980s, it was nevertheless impressive, particularly in those years like 1985, when the overall market was dismal. In 1985 ASIC shipments increased about 70 percent over 1984, and reached about $1.8 billion, or about 11 percent of the total 1985 IC market (just about $17 billion), up from 6.4 percent of the total market in 1984.

Relative U.S. success in the mid-1980s ASIC market hinged on four primary factors. First, the major applications for application-specific circuits largely involved final markets that U.S. producers either controlled outright (defense) or in which they held substantial leadership (computers).

Aerospace/defense	25%
Computer/data processing/office	25
Telecommunications	20
Industrial control/automation	14
Instrumentation	9
Other (including consumer, automobiles)	7

Second, ASIC competitive leverage is generated less as a function of advanced process quality—that is, the smallest dimension devices with the fewest defects (or lowest "defect densities")—than of the quality of design services and of low-volume, rapid-turnaround production. Again, this is because superior design can provide distinct performance advantages, even if implemented with relatively inferior process technology, while tried and true processes can be turned around quickly. The result is unique performance with more rapid product availability, an especial set of market advantages in most electronic system markets. In short, in the ASIC market, Japan's emerging lead in process quality mattered much less, while the U.S. lead in design software and experience in semicustom design, combined with customer proximity and responsiveness, to deliver an edge over Japan in the market.

Third, and related, while Japanese producers did score notable successes in the commoditylike gate array segments of the ASIC market, where Fujitsu is by far the market leader, their sunk investment in commodity design and production techniques gave them no special advantage in the standard and macro-cell parts of the market. In this, they suffered the same problems as the entrenched U.S. merchants like Intel and TI, who attempted to enter ASIC markets. However, the overall U.S. industry performance was led by new merchant start-ups like LSI Logic and VLSI Technology. By starting with no comparable sunk investment, the start-ups were able to bring ASIC-appropriate design tools and production strategies to the competitive fray.

Fourth, particularly as the battle in electronics became more and more politicized, U.S. producers of systems products became more and more aware of the dangers of designing the microelectronics in their products with their Japanese competitors in the systems markets. Wherever competent U.S. producers were available, they were generally preferred.

Figure 7–4 indicates the relative standing in ASIC markets of the U.S. and Japanese industries by 1986. Note the difference between the gate array and other design approaches market segments. Whether the relative U.S. advantage could be sustained depended very much on the speed with which Japanese producers could develop ASIC-responsive divisions using advanced technologies that could convincingly safeguard U.S. systems producers' proprietary designs. This remains an open question.

In essence, then, Japan's dominance of commodity memory had enabled Japanese producers to push into the production of more complex commodity products and assume overall IC market leadership by the mid-1980s. They used memory dominance and financial resources to establish technical leadership in processes and manufacturing. The United States was holding its own in design, and by virtue of its diverse industry structure, the U.S. industry remained a remarkable vehicle for commercializing new product innovations. This was noticeable in ASIC markets, where venture-capital-backed new entrants led U.S. efforts into new markets.

Yet, despite the bright spots, the U.S. industry was plainly in trouble. Loss of market position and of commodity technical leadership was a double whammy from which the established U.S. industry might not recover in time to remain competitive in the 1990s. Major merchant U.S. producers therefore turned to a political adjustment strategy. Perhaps trade law and policy could accomplish what business strategies alone could not.

POLITICAL ADJUSTMENT:
TRADE AND DEFENSE

In 1985 and 1986, major merchant U.S. chip producers initiated six major legal actions under various U.S. trade-related laws, and conducted extensive, continuous lobbying of Congress, all aimed at the Japanese electronics giants. These actions coincided with mounting congressional and administration concern over ever larger, and seemingly intractable, U.S. trade deficits with Japan. By wrapping themselves in the American flag and, through legal and lobbying strategy, by forcing an identity between the industry's troubles and perceived Japanese unfair competitive tactics, the U.S. chip manufacturers were able to exercise a political clout

Figure 7–4. Rankings of Top Ten ASIC Producers.

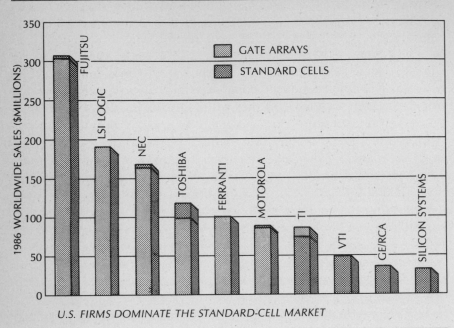

U.S. FIRMS DOMINATE THE STANDARD-CELL MARKET

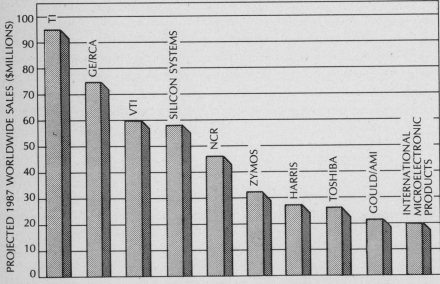

Source: Integrated Circuit Engineering.

Reprinted from *Electronics*, August 6, 1987 issue. Copyright © 1987, VNU Business Publications, Inc. All rights reserved.

they had never before achieved. If innocence ends when we recognize our own limitations and develop a successful strategy to get help in a hostile world, then the U.S. merchant semiconductor industry had finally come of age.

The industry's political-legal strategy had begun to coalesce a decade before, when it first encountered Japanese competition while seeing its own needs diverge from those of its major customers. Spinning out from the larger electronics industry associations, chip makers formed the Semiconductor Industry Association (SIA) in 1977. Headquartered in California's Silicon Valley, far from the center of political power, utterly innocent about coalition-building and lobbying, and naively believing that the merits of the case would carry the day in a Washington filled with "meritorious" causes, the SIA's efforts foundered for half a decade. With time and effort, however, a glimmer of political sophistication emerged in the SIA's activities. By the early 1980s, under the careful tutelage of the SIA's Washington trade lawyer, ex-Deputy Trade Representative Alan Wolff, the SIA had framed the industry's troubles in the only way possible if political action was to be provoked.

A series of reports, virtual legal briefs, were released which argued that a concerted effort of the Japanese government and industry had "targetted" the American chip industry for competitive defeat.[4] While denying U.S. firms fair and open opportunities to compete in the domestic Japanese market (the "market access" issue), Japanese firms were engaging in massive unfair trade practices in the U.S. market (the "dumping" issue). By dumping—that is, selling chips below fair market value (often allegedly below their cost of production), Japanese producers disrupted U.S. business practices and drove U.S. firms out of business.

With the definition and documentation of the market access and dumping issues, the SIA carefully crafted a base on which to build political support. The issues were raised in the context of ongoing U.S.-Japan negotiations in the High-Tech Working Group formed in 1984. Despite assurances from the Japanese government, however, the access and dumping issues remained unresolved. The U.S. government seemed disposed to do little, given the Reagan administration's rhetorical commitment to free trade, and the still nascent political clout of the chip makers. (Recall that the far better organized steel, textile, and automobile industries had already succeeded in winning policies that amounted to real protection from the supposedly free-trade Reagan folk.)

Then, with trade deficits mounting despite a falling dollar in 1985 and 1986, the chip makers launched an increasingly sophisticated campaign for trade relief. The SIA filed a trade petition under section 301 of the Trade Act of 1974, asking the U.S. government to negotiate increased access for U.S. firms to the Japanese market. If access was not forthcoming, the petition requested trade restrictions on Japanese imports in retaliation. The small U.S. memory producer Micron Technologies filed under U.S. antidumping laws a claim that Japanese producers were dumping 64K dRAM chips in the United States at prices below their fair market value. Micron then sued Japanese firms under U.S. antitrust law, alleging a conspiracy to monopolize the U.S. memory market. AMD, Intel, and National filed another antidumping complaint, alleging that Japanese producers were dumping high-density EPROMs on the U.S. market, and asked for an embargo on Japanese imports. TI sued nine Asian (eight Japanese and a Korean) semiconductor producers for allegedly infringing various TI patents on semiconductor memory. Not wishing to appear unresponsive with the handwriting on the wall, even the Reagan administration initiated a claim on behalf of American firms threatened by aggressive Japanese pricing tactics in the 256K dRAM market. Congressional hearings on the semiconductor trade issues and intensive lobbying completed the well-orchestrated industry campaign.

As Alan Wolff himself, among many others, has commented, the private legal routes for trade relief available in the United States have the effect of constraining the trade policy formation process.[5] In essence, the trade laws permit private parties to shape policy, most often in a way that protects profits when successful.[6] Like the textile, steel, consumer electronics, and automobile industries before them, to name but a few, the U.S. semiconductor industry's political-legal campaign successfully provoked a trade policy response. Preliminary findings in the antidumping cases began to uphold the American claims that Japanese firms were dumping, while the 301 petition and legal suits wound their way through the interminable administrative and court procedures. As increasingly negative evaluations of their chances to win on the merits filtered back to Japan, Japanese firms and the Japanese government were finally forced to the bargaining table by mid-1986. Not coincidentally, as the well-orchestrated relief campaign began to constrain administrative decisionmaking, the Reagan administration too sought a way out of the semiconductor trade issues which would minimize damage to alliance relations.[7]

After several near misses, and with the threat of a favorable ruling on the 301 petition with recommendations for strong trade sanctions hanging over the negotiations, the U.S. and Japanese governments reached a trade accord in late August of 1986. The Semiconductor Trade Agreement, running through 1991, contains essentially two major parts dealing with the dumping and market access issues.[8] On the dumping side, the agreement establishes minimum reference prices based on submitted Japanese production costs for RAM, EPROM, and several other categories of chips in which U.S. firms still retain substantial market positions. The minimum prices establish a moving price floor below which dumping would be presumed to occur; indeed, the floor prices have been repeatedly adjusted downward as Japanese production costs have fallen.

Critically, dumping was to be prohibited not only in the U.S. market, but in the Japanese and third-country markets as well. The latter was a necessary provision, if one that was to be virtually impossible to enforce, because most major chip buyers have worldwide purchasing operations. It was hoped the antidumping provisions would permit U.S. firms to stay in the process development game through a continuing presence in EPROMs and other "process-driving" products, while stabilizing prices sufficiently to enable them to return to profitability. There was even hope (some in government believed a tacit quid pro quo existed) that price stability would invite reentry by U.S. producers into RAM production. Limited reentry was in fact being planned by several U.S. producers as of late 1987.

The dumping agreement was also intended to force a shakeout among Japanese producers of RAM. Since the minimum reference prices were set on a per-firm basis, differences in production costs were reflected in substantial price variations among Japanese firms. Relatively higher cost producers like Fujitsu could not hope to compete with more efficient firms like NEC, whose permitted minimum prices substantially undercut Fujitsu's. Under MITI guidance, however, rather than accept a shakeout, the Japanese industry responded by forming a tacit production cartel and restricting supply. The resulting excess demand from customers bid up RAM prices and permitted even the less efficient Japanese producers to stay in business. Indeed, since most U.S. firms were already out of RAM production, the agreement and Japanese response mostly provided a profit windfall to Japanese producers by stabilizing the disastrous price erosion in RAMs, although new entry in the form of Korean RAM producers also occurred.

On the market access side, the agreement formally acknowledged that there was a problem which the Japanese government would try and help solve. No explicit target (domestic Japanese) market share for U.S. producers was expressly articulated in the Agreement. However, the American side came away believing that Japan had agreed to a steady increase to 20 percent through 1991 (or a rough doubling of the existing U.S. market share), while the Japanese side vehemently denied that any such numerical target existed.[9] A mere eight months later, this schism was to cause much trade distress in both countries.

It is exceedingly difficult to imagine Japanese firms agreeing, without the substantial threat of trade sanctions, to a doubling of the U.S. market share in Japan. Any substantial U.S. foothold would begin to disrupt the Japanese ability to use the closed market as a strategic mass production base from which to export. And even if no disruption of the strategic game occurred, Japanese firms would still be very reluctant to see the U.S. share double. Since U.S. firms have little position in either RAM or consumer chips in Japan, and they already sell substantial numbers of bipolar circuits, a 20 percent overall U.S. market share would imply thorough U.S. dominance of some market segments, most notably microprocessors and peripherals and probably nonvolatile memory as well. As a matter of business strategy, Japanese firms are extremely unlikely to permit U.S. dominance of such critical market segments (and remember that, as a matter of structure, they retain the ability to control U.S. sales in Japan). It is far more likely that U.S. negotiators were not dissuaded from believing that the 20 percent target existed even though, in typical negotiation fashion, it had never explicitly been agreed to by Japanese negotiators.

Eight months later, by April 1987, the U.S. share of the Japanese market had in fact shrunk, to about 8.5 percent, and there were widespread complaints of Japanese dumping in third-country markets.[10] Partly in response, and to demonstrate resolve in the face of accelerating protectionist legislation in both houses of Congress, the Reagan administration imposed tariffs on $300 million worth of Japanese televisions, computers, and power tools.[11] The sanctions and the MITI-guided production cutbacks helped to stabilize some market prices, and some firms, notably Hitachi, announced that they would abandon their assault on the politically charged EPROM market.[12] The dumping issues were thus somewhat mitigated, but even before the Administration began to limit the sanctions a scant two months later in June, the tariffs were largely regarded by all parties, foreign and domestic, as being so small as to be almost certainly ineffectual as concerned the market access problem. And since the political pressures had made Japanese firms slightly more amenable, U.S. producers were turning more and more to joint agreements with their Japanese competitors to achieve a measure of access to Japan (a subject we examine in Chapter 9).

Probably far more important than the limited working of the trade agreement were the reciprocal trade principles it implicitly codified for the first time ever. The first principle is that certain predatory business practices, like dumping, emanating from Japan should not be permitted to destroy otherwise competitive U.S. industries, even where those practices are the unintended consequence of differences in domestic policies and market structures. The second principle was that Japan would have to bear responsibility for opening its domestic market to the rest of the world's products if it expected to continue to be able to sell its products all over the world.

While the trade agreement addressed the U.S. industry's concerns with unfair Japanese business tactics, it did not address the increasingly visible and acknowledged problem of Japanese manufacturing and (potential) process superiority. These issues were raised most dramatically in February 1987 by the Defense Department in a Report of the Defense Science Board.[13] The prospect of defense dependency upon imported semiconductor technology convinced the DSB to propose that the Defense Department spend several billion dollars over five years, including support for the industry's proposed cooperative initiative, Sematech, in an attempt to ensure that leading-edge semiconductor process and manufacturing technology remained in America.

Whether the political adjustment strategy of the U.S. industry—Sematech, defense assistance, and the semiconductor trade accord—will succeed in restoring technical and market parity for the U.S. industry remains uncertain. In the U.S. efforts, both in the market and politically, there was, perhaps, the glimmer of a nascent strategy for the U.S. industry's long-term prosperity. The key components of that strategy, and the appropriate roles for the U.S. firms and the U.S. government are the subjects of Part III.

NOTES

1.   Dieter Ernst, "Programmable Automation (PA) in the Semiconductor Industry—Reflections on Current Diffusion Patterns," GERTTD-AMES Conference, Automatisation Programmable, Paris, April 2–4, 1987.

2. See Microelectronics and Computer Technology Corporation. "Japanese Government and Industry Efforts to Improve Semiconductor Manufacturing Capabilities," MCC Technical Report ILO-077-86, Austin, Tx., 1986, p. 2.

3. On the development of digital networking see Michael Borrus, Francois Bar, Patrick Cogez, Anne Brit Thoresen, Ibrahim Warde, and Aki Yoshikawa, "Telecommunications Development in Comparative Perspective: The New Telecommunications in Europe, Japan and the U.S.," BRIE Working Paper 14, 1985.

4. See Verner, Liipfert, Bernhard, and McPherson, The Effect of Government Targeting on World Semiconductor Competition," Washington, D.C., Semiconductor Industry Association, 1983.

5. Allen Wolfe, "International Competitiveness of American Industry: The Role of U.S. Trade Policy," in Bruce Scott and George C. Lodge, eds., U.S. Competitiveness in World Economy (Boston: Harvard Business School Press, 1985).

6. Michael Borrus and James Millstein, "Protecting Profits" unpublished manuscript, 1980.

7. David Yoffie, "Semiconductor Industry Association and The Trade Dispute with Japan," Harvard Business School, Boston, 1987.

8. "One Year of Experience under The U.S.-Japan Semiconductor Agreement," First Annual Report to the President by the Semiconductor Industry Association, SIA, 1987.

9. Based on conversations with U.S. Industry and Japanese industry sources and on an interview with Makoto Kuroda, MITI vice-minister, August 1986.

10. As recounted in "One Year of Experience under the U.S.-Japan Semiconductor Agreement," p. 5.

11. New York Times, April 17, 1987, p. 1.

12. Industry sources.

13. Defense Science Board to the U.S. Department of Defense, "Report of the Defense Science Board Task Force on Defense Semiconductor Dependency," (Washington, D.C.: Office of the Undersecretary of Defense for Acquisition, February 1987).

III RESTORING AUTONOMY AND GROWTH

8 THE EUROPEAN SITUATION AND THE LOGIC OF STRATEGIC ALLIANCES

Merchant U.S. chip makers dominate European component markets, holding a market share of about 50 percent. Facing the possible political limits on aggressive expansion in the U.S. market, Japanese producers have begun to eye Europe with increasing appetite. NEC, Hitachi, Fujitsu, and Toshiba all have invested in major fully integrated chip production facilities in Europe over the past half decade, with plans to increase investment in the late 1980s. Together with Japan's principal consumer electronics producers, Matsushita, Sony, Sharp, and Sanyo, they have also moved rapidly to establish production facilities for the final electronics systems that are their bread and butter products.

Preserving its position in Europe must take a top priority in any strategy to resurrect the U.S. industry's worldwide position. Restoring America's autonomy and growth requires addressing and resolving European needs and concerns. The logic of this argument is straightforward. With even fewer notable exceptions than in the United States (preeminantly Siemens and Philips), smaller European final market producers compete against Japan's integrated giants without the benefit of substantial leading-edge captive chip production. Like American systems producers, they rely on merchant chip firms for components. Unlike American systems firms, the Europeans have badly lagged behind both Japan and the United States in the application of microelectronics to products and processes in Europe. If European systems producers are to retain their market position they need to apply microelectronics more rapidly; to do so, they need secure sources of component technology. Because the Europeans compete against them in final systems markets, relying on Japanese suppliers of appropriate chip technology is a risky proposition indeed. U.S. merchants and emerging merchant European firms like SGS-Thomson and European Silicon Structures are far preferable suppliers.

In the past, U.S. producers took their European market success almost for granted, premised as it was on superior technology and superior volume manufacturing built in their home base. The attitude continues to be that Europe has little capacity to challenge the U.S. technology lead and no alternative but to rely on U.S. sources of the technology. That attitude has excluded counsel and cooperation with European governments and producers when U.S. firms and policymakers moved to confront U.S. problems through trade accords with Japan or through Sematech. Many conversations with senior U.S. merchant managers, including those leading the U.S. response to Japanese competition, reveal a disdain concerning Europe that borders on ignorance. With concerted efforts built on the strong European base in science and technology, and with the looming presence of Japanese technology in the foreground, it is clear that Europe has both the capacity and alternative to challenge entrenched U.S. supremacy in Europe. Europe is wealthy; it is a very large market, and European governments retain the decisive political will to act to preserve their position and interests. At this historical juncture, the only sensible move for U.S. merchants is not to disdain Europe but to ally with Europe in a way that preserves European options and standards of living while meeting U.S. firm needs.

The logic of alliance with Europe reveals a general strategic approach for U.S. firms, premised on a vulnerability inherent in the Japanese industry structure. Their integrated structure leaves Japan's producers competitively vulnerable to alliances between U.S. merchants and the final systems producers who compete with the Japanese firms. If the growth of Japanese competitive position in final product markets is constrained by the presence of strong competitors who are supplied by U.S. component firms, then the U.S. merchants should capture an expanding share of component sales going to final systems markets.

THE EUROPEAN DILEMMA AND COMPETITIVE CONSEQUENCES

The European position in semiconductors has been extremely weak and has declined rapidly since the late 1970s (Table 8–1), even in the domestic European market, except in certain MOS IC devices where European firms have recently concentrated both resources and technology cooperation agreements. Even in these latter market segments, the European world market position is minuscule.

The European market is dominated by U.S. producers. Of the top 25 European manufacturers, 13 are U.S. firms, 8 European, and only 4 Japanese.[2] Table 8–2 lists the major European producers. Note that only one, Philips, is large enough to enter the ranks of top ten producers worldwide.

From 1977 to 1984 European firms lost share in their home market to Japanese firms, while the U.S. share remained relatively constant, first increasing (at the European's expense) then falling back to the 1978 level (through losses to Japanese firms) over the period. (See Table 8–3.) Japanese market share gains in Europe, the world's third largest market for components accounting for about 20 percent of consumption, have strategic consequences for both U.S. merchants and the largely integrated European electronics producers who participate in merchant semiconductor markets. For the latter, the increasing reliance for components on Japanese producers who are competitors to European systems companies in final product markets, augurs increasing vulnerability in those

Table 8–1. European Firm Semiconductor (SC) Market Shares (% of value).

Market	Type	1978	1984	% Change
Worldwide	All SCs	13.9	8.6	− 38.1
	ICs	8.1	6.4	− 20.9
	MOS IC	5.2	5.6	+ 7.6
	MOS memory	0.8	3.8	+375.0
	MOS MPU	1.5	2.8	+ 86.6
Europe	All SCs	44.6	39.4	− 11.6

Note: 1984 figures are estimates.
Source: Dataquest.

Table 8–2. Major European Chip Makers.

Company	Amount
Phillips-Signetics	$1,356
Seimens (includes Litronix)	429
SGS-Thompson	806
Telefunken	219
Plessey	112
Ferranti	95
Inmos	80
Semikron	72
Matra-Harris	47

Source: Dataquest.

Note: Estimated 1986 results for the nine leading European suppliers in millions of U.S. dollars.

final markets. For U.S. producers, their strong European market position has been an integral part of their overall world leadership: Japanese gains in Europe herald intensified competition in a market that has been a bastion of U.S. strength.

A combination of domestic market structure and government policy as they have influenced firm stagies, has determined the position of European firms in international semiconductor competition. Of course, in Europe's case, those factors have combined to deliver relative weakness on world markets.[3]

Government policy, both Europewide and nationally, has been a critical variable underlying Europe's weak position, although this consequence was thoroughly unintended. The high European external tariff (currently still 17 percent ad valorem), encouraged foreign direct investment in Europe behind the tariff wall, particularly by U.S. firms during the 1960s and 1970s when U.S. leadership in semiconductor technology was unchallenged and consequently desired in Europe, and

Table 8–3. Shares of European Semiconductor Market (%).

Companies	1977	1983	1986
European	48%	40%	35%
U.S.	50	50	50
Japanese	2	10	15

Source: Dataquest.

lately by Japanese firms as well. Indeed, the setting up of local European manufacturing subsidiaries of U.S. merchants and Japanese firms was further encouraged by many European states as a condition of doing business in those countries (for example, through local content requirements).

This set of policies contrasts strongly with the Japanese strategy that completely closed the domestic Japanese market to investment by U.S. companies, thereby simultaneously reserving demand in the Japanese market for Japanese firms and forcing U.S. firms to transfer technology to Japanese companies if they wanted any return at all from the growth of the Japanese market. Consequently, U.S. firms dominate in Europe not Japan, and their lead in Europe will as likely be dislodged by Japanese as by European producers.

Also underlying the inferior position of European producers has been the fragmentation of the large Europewide market into much smaller national markets (or regional ones in the case of the Scandinavian and Benelux countries). The fragmentation of that market eliminated the potential for Europewide product specialization. The fragmentation was the result of national policies concerned to develop indigenous national component industries covering the broad range of semiconductor products. Those policies simultaneously discouraged cooperation among European firms from different countries and encouraged cooperation with U.S. producers (necessary because U.S. firms had the required technology). Paradoxically, then, as a result of national European policies, it has been multinational U.S. producers, operating in most of the major European countries, who have captured the benefits of scale of the very same Europewide market that has been denied to European producers by the very same national policies. This is, of course, an outcome with which Europe is quite familiar in other sectors, like computers.

National European policies aimed at fostering a few large, vertically integrated, national champion producers in the principal end-use final systems markets (particularly computers, telecommunications, and now consumer electronics) also exacerbated Europe's problems in microelectronics. National promotional programs of the 1960s and early 1970s were aimed largely at establishing position in final markets, and neglected the channeling of resources to semiconductor development. The contrast to Japan is again instructive. Initial Japanese promotional programs were aimed at developing position in computers and, like the European programs, failed to deliver an internationally competitive components industry. Japan succeeded only after it explicitly concentrated resources on establishing position in semiconductors through the VLSI project.

Moreover, the large, integrated national champions promoted through those European national programs, like Thomson and Siemens, were primarily interested in developing semiconductor capacities that served their internal needs—necessitating a strong focus on custom chip production for their final systems products—and only secondarily interested in serving as merchant commodity component producers for the smaller, competitive producers who comprise the bulk of European industry. As a consequence of that strategic focus, U.S. firms took up the European merchant role. With little European intercountry competition in semiconductor development among the large, integrated national champions, and with a high proportion of national demand for both components and systems reserved through state policy for those firms, there was comparatively little stimulus to technological innovation. Indeed, Europe's firms have largely been technology followers of U.S. merchant innovations.

As followers of U.S. technological innovation, Europe has been vulnerable to the strategies of U.S. merchants. Only after the technology was proven, its production refined, and costs sharply reduced through learning and scale economies in the U.S. market, did U.S. firms transfer the technology to Europe as exports or for production in their European subsidiaries. Thus, by the time component innovations appeared on the European scene, U.S. merchants had substantial advantages that European companies could not hope to overcome. Perhaps even more critical, however, the semiconductor innovations were only secondarily adapted to the needs of European final markets.

Indeed, as Table 8–4 shows, by the early 1980s European consumption of semiconductors by end-use was significantly different from the comparable U.S. consumption. This mismatch has had important consequences for Europe's position in final markets. Table 8–5 shows that by the mid-1980s, European per-capita consumption of semiconductors was disastrously far behind that of Japan and the United States and was growing far more slowly.

This low per-capita consumption means that Europe is applying microelectronics to product and production processes far more slowly and far less completely than have Japan and the United States. Europe has been much less able to provide a strong source of demand with which to leverage the growth of domestic European (and entrenched U.S.

Table 8–4.   European and U.S. Semiconductor Consumption, by End Use, 1983 (%).

End Use	European	U.S.
Telecommunications	23	20
Consumer	22	10
Industrial	22	17
Computer	20	37
Government/military	9	11
Automotive	4	5

Note: Telecom includes data communications.

Source: EACEM and BRIE estimates.

merchant) semiconductor suppliers. There are some signs that this situation could change as European plans to digitize the information network infrastructure unfold. Dynamic growth of that and related information technology markets could strengthen the position of European and U.S. chip makers to the extent they participate in the growth of those markets. The recent dramatic growth in use of personal computers in England and the resulting upsurge in demand for related chips from U.S. firms is one example.

COMPETITIVE RESPONSES AND STRATEGIC ALLIANCES

For Europe the consequences of the microelectronics dilemma have been serious. European weakness in components has meant decisive

Table 8–5.   Semiconductor Consumption per Capita ($).

Country	1978	1984
Europe Total	7	14
France		15
Germany		22
United Kingdom		20
Italy		8
United States	16	52
Japan	22	61

Source: Dataquest.

competitive vulnerabilities on final systems markets. The European position in computers is weak and sustained largely through the aid of government policies and procurement. Europe retains a position in consumer electronics mostly by virtue of policies that have limited foreign penetration of domestic European markets. Japanese firms have become directly competitive with the traditionally strong European capital goods sector by applying microelectronics to production equipment at a far more rapid pace. European sources indicate that the European test, monitoring and control equipment industry similarly lags behind the pace at which microelectronics is being applied outside of Europe. And even the historically strong European telecommunications sector has been losing its share of export markets to Japanese producers at the rate of 1 percent per year over the last 15 years.[4]

In response to these problems, European governments and firms have embarked on a series of ambitious efforts—some cooperative, others entrepreneurial, some public, still others private—designed to assure European position in the component technologies essential to Europe's future. For example, there has been a wide range of new promotional programs in Europe aimed at developing internationally competitive European semiconductor capacities. Tables 8–6 and 8–7 list these efforts at both the national and Europewide levels.

It appears that European governments have learned from their past policy failures; they are explicitly aiming at developing component know-how and fostering its application, much as did Japan with the VLSI project. Equally critical, some of the Europewide programs appear to be aimed at overcoming the "uncommon market." If they succeed in standardizing component requirements across national boundaries and in allocating national chip market shares to nonnationals, then the European strategy could successfully position a few European chip producers to play competitively in world markets.

Among the private or quasi-private European efforts, three are worthy of particular note. These are the Siemens-Philips joint attempt to become competitive in leading-edge memory chip production, the merger of SGS and Thomson's component division, and the appearance of several new entrants like European Silicon Structures, Triad, Dolphin Integration, and the ATT-Telefonica joint venture, aimed at bringing state of the art ASIC capabilities to European customers. The multibillion dollar Philips-Siemens effort to develop memory chips unveiled a prototype 1 megabit dynamic RAM (by Siemens) and 1 Mbit static RAM (from Philips) in early 1987. While still lagging behind the abilities of the

Table 8-6. Large European Development Projects.

Country	Project	Participants	Objective	Year	Funding
United Kingdom	Alvey		Commercial computing	1983–1987	
West Germany-Netherlands	Mega	2	1 Mbit sRAM/ 4 Mbit dRAM	1984–1989	$150
France	Microelectronics	Many	Semiconductors	1983–1986	
EEC	ESPRIT	Many	Commercial computing	1984–1994	$675
	EUREKA				

Table 8-7. Microelectronics Projects Receiving EUREKA Designation.

Project	Partners	Objective	Cost (Million ECU)	Duration Years
European Silicon Structures (ES 2)	BEL, UK, FRA, FRG, SWE, SWI	Design and automatic production of ICs using direct impression on silicon	94	3
Gallium arsenide	UK, FRA	Develop design and manufacturing processes for monolithic ICs for microwaves from GaAs	60	3
DIANE	FRA, SPA, UK	Nondestructive use of neutron beam for quality control in large, complex components made from new materials	15	4
DESIRE	UK, BEL	Develop an all-dry single layer photolithography technology for submicron devices	4	3
Sub 0.1-Micron Ion Projection	AUS, FRG	Increase level of integration in electronic components by reducing width of circuits capable of mass production, and by improving materials technology	5	3–5
Fast Prototyping Service for Silicon ASICs	FRA, UK	Develop compatable design and manufacturing tools for ASICs	30	5
New Design Technologies for Power Semiconductors	SWE, SWI	Develop new techniques for designing high-power semiconductors	5	2

Source: Reprinted by permission of Westview Press from The Microelectronics Race: The Impact of Government Policy on International Competition, edited by Thomas R. Howell, William A. Noellert, Janet H. MacLaughlin, and Alan W. Wolff. Copyright © Westview Press, 1987, Boulder, Colo.

Japanese, IBM, and TI in dynamic RAMs, the SRAM seems to be fully competitive. Together, the prototypes suggest a closing technical gap and a European determination to stay in the chip race whatever the cost, if only to ensure continuing competitive position in the final products that constitute the bulk of Philips and Siemens' vast sales. Similarly, the merger of SGS and Thomson creates an $800 million diversified European commodity merchant of sufficient size to become a serious player on the world market. This would be the case since the merged firm presumably has first call on the component requirements of the combined French and Italian markets.

The emerging ASIC ventures are also an exciting new development in Europe. The semicustom chip market potential emerging among the 10,000–20,000 small and medium-sized machinery and other producers in Europe who do some system design is believed to be immense, and growing very rapidly, doubling each year.[5] Along with the new entrants, Siemens, Philips, and Texas Instruments have aggressively pursued the emerging market. Rapid growth and aggressive responses give some hope that Europe's current slow application of microelectronics might be reversed in the future.

Whether or not these European efforts succeed, for U.S. merchants, the consequences of Europe's current competitive dilemma are extraordinarily serious. Europe's comparatively slow application of microelectronics means that U.S. merchants cannot rely on their entrenched position in Europe to compensate for Japanese semiconductor gains in Japan and the United States. Even if U.S. firms maintain their position in the face of Japanese encroachment in Europe, the growth that they will receive from the European market will not match Japanese gains in the other major industrialized markets. Only if Europe begins to apply microelectronics more rapidly will the European market provide a renewed and expanding base for U.S. merchants and European producers to respond to the wider Japanese challenge.

Yet, Europe's own compelling need is precisely the same: to apply microelectronics in traditional and high-technology industries at a more rapid pace in order to prevent the erosion of their position in final product markets. Critically, European producers cannot rely on Japanese semiconductor suppliers to achieve this because those Japanese producers, unlike the U.S. merchants, are competitors to those European firms in the very same systems markets where Europe needs to apply microelectronics more rapidly. Relying on Japanese components risks letting Japanese systems competitors dictate the pace and extent of microelectronics application in Europe. That will be a losing strategy for European final market producers just as it threatens to be for U.S. producers: Japanese competitors will not give timely access to the leading-edge components that give the final products of those Japanese producers performance advantages in international competition.[6]

It is, therefore, around this point that the interests and needs of U.S. merchants and European final market producers converge to mutual advantage. It is strategically necessary for both that microelectronics be applied more rapidly in Europe. It appears that only strategic alliances between U.S. merchants and European final market producers can accomplish the shared interests and aims. From Europe's perspective, U.S. merchants would have to make a commitment to supply leading-edge microelectronic components appropriate to the needs of European end-use markets. From the U.S. industry's perspective, European users would have to commit to long-term supply relations with U.S. merchants in return for leading-edge technology suitable to their needs.

The former commitment would require a change in the historical practice of U.S. merchants in Europe. They could no longer view Europe as a secondary market for the later stages of the product cycle of components developed in the United States for U.S. uses. They would have to commit time and resources to working with European final market producers to develop components, both custom and commodity, in Europe suitable to European uses. More than likely, they would have to be willing to share their R&D capacities and transfer the technology that is developed to European second sources. Without these quid pro quos, it would be difficult to receive the support of European governments. Similarly, the commitment of European producers to long-term supply relations with U.S. merchants would also require changes in traditional practice. Without the assurance of long-term supply (defined as guaranteed high-volume purchases over time, so long as cost and quality remain competitive), it is difficult to imagine U.S. firms committing the kind of resources to Europe that are necessary to assist Europe's long-term development. The logical European final product markets from which to leverage such strategic alliances include consumer electronics, telecommunications, computers, production equipment/capital goods, and test, monitoring, and control equipment. These are all sectors in which Japanese producers are aiming to increase their world market share at the expense of European producers, and in which U.S. merchant strengths in complex chips could fruitfully be brought to bear. To the extent U.S. merchants meet Europe's needs, the climate for rapid application of microelectronics in Europe will improve dramatically, and U.S. firms will be viewed as allies. And that impression will be the sine qua non of continued success for merchant U.S. producers in the European market. The obvious place to start is with cooperative R&D, given the overwhelming, rising costs of developing the next generations of process and manufacturing technologies that both need to stay competitive in electronics.

STRATEGIC ALLIANCES AND RECAPTURED INITIATIVE

Even as Japanese firms have risen to challenge U.S. leadership in semiconductors, Europe's producers have seen their international and domestic European market positions deteriorate. Europe is applying microelectronics in final product markets at a far slower pace than are the United States and Japan, and the consequence has been an erosion of Europe's position in final product markets as well as in microelectronics.

The question for Europe is whether cooperative actions will position Europe to remain a player in the application of microelectronics. It would, of course, be simple to note Europe's current problems and conclude that Europe's position will cumulatively deteriorate. Yet, the industrialized countries' pervasive application of microelectronics to the production of traditional goods and services, and the benefits to national economic development and growth that rest thereon, will only develop fully over the next decades. This provides a space for European development.

Casting Euro-pessimism aside, there are advantages to Europe's relative backwardness that have been experienced in earlier historical periods and in other industrial sectors. Indeed, Europe's most apparent weakness—mass markets for electronics that are developing more slowly than in the United States or Japan—can, with very little effort and imagination, be seen as a long-term asset.[7] In the 1960s, when the U.S. steel and auto industries faced mature markets and suffered from many of the competitiveness-sapping effects associated with stable maturity, European auto and steel production was growing at a rapid rate. A similar pattern was discernible for other consumer and industrial durables (such as washing machines, capital equipment), and particularly for intermediate inputs like chemicals.

Thus, when U.S. and Japanese markets for microelectronics begin to achieve a certain maturity, European markets are likely to be in full growth. The recent explosion in British office equipment markets, where demand has increased by over 100 percent in the last three years, gives some indication of the possibilities. Suppliers to that market will be better placed to innovate in product and process, and improve their overall competitive positions. Exploiting these advantages of backwardness can be a very successful strategy for strong producers, who can mobilize great fundamental resources—especially when they can count on a strong position in a large market that is following a well-defined trajectory developed elsewhere. Europe is wealthy, it has the political will and savvy to control the European markets in order to safeguard its position, and it has a well-developed infrastructure of science, technology, and skilled labor necessary to hold its position into the foreseeable future. By helping to address Europe's needs now, U.S. producers will be very well placed over the long term to prosper in competition with Japan, when European chip markets are in full bloom.

Yet, prospering hand-in-hand with Europe will require substantial changes in the U.S. industry's attitudes toward Europe. At a bare minimum, U.S. firms must permit European participation in efforts to define and implement successful responses to the Japanese challenge. Not only are the combined U.S. and European markets more than a match for Japan in almost all product areas, but European producers suffer the same problems vis-à-vis Japan as U.S. producers, particularly on the market access front. It would be a significant missed strategic opportunity if, from the vantage of the mid-1990s, the relatively unexamined decision to exclude Europe from counsel on the U.S.-Japan trade disputes and on Sematech had pushed Europe into embracing Japanese sources of supply and eliminating their historical ties to U.S. firms.

From the U.S. industry's perspective, the logic of strategic alliances that emerges from the European situation in microelectronics—to contain Japanese gains in final product markets, divert their attention from semiconductors, and create secure sources of demand for U.S. merchant firms—applies broadly outside of Europe. The same kinds of alliances might be struck to the same strategic advantage between merchant U.S. producers and final systems producers in the United States and elsewhere.

Selective strategic alliances with producers in Canada or newly industrializing countries that are pressed by Japanese competition would provide fertile ground for U.S. merchants. For example, Korean consumer electronics producers and computer peripherals producers represent potent threats to the long-standing dominance of Japanese firms. Indeed, recent data suggest that with the appreciation of the yen, Korean producers of televisions, terminals, printers, and audio equipment have begun to gain substantial market shares at Japanese expense.[8]

In a range of these product areas, particularly in VCRs and advanced audio equipment, Korean producers are dependent on their Japanese competitors for the components they need to compete in the higher value-added products that Japanese firms currently dominate. With Japan controlling the supply of advanced components for consumer electronics, it is not hard to predict that Korean access will be controlled sufficiently to ensure the long-term viability of a dominant Japanese market position. Indeed there is much anecdotal evidence, and much Korean concern, to the effect that access to critical technology has been systematically denied whenever a major Korean producer has begun to challenge an entrenched Japanese firm.[9]

For the U.S. merchants, an alliance with Korean firms would have the benefit of creating a renewed source of vigorous demand for consumer and other chips from U.S. producers, permitting them to reenter a market segment from which they have been largely eliminated by Japanese competition. Moreover, since the Korean producers of consumer electronics are large, diversified conglomerates with production in a wide range of areas, strategic alliances could extend into other product areas. This would have the effect of locking in increasing demand from the growth of the Korean economy for the benefit of U.S. producers.

This strategy is not, of course, without its risks. Since the price of long-term alliances with Asian producers outside of Japan could well be some kind of technology transfer from U.S. merchants to Asian producers, U.S. firms run the risk of creating long-term competitors to themselves, just as they did with Japan in the 1960s and 1970s. This danger permeates current U.S. deals with Korea, as the Table 8–8 suggests. Deals involving direct technology transfer without long-term reciprocal market access do look similar to the transfer deals with Japan that helped to create the current competitive problems for U.S. firms.

The long-term risks are, nonetheless, probably worthwhile, if only because U.S. firms would appear to have little choice. Korean and other Asian chip producers will continue to enter the market whether or not they do so in alliance with U.S. merchants. If U.S. producers can manage to refrain from competitively bidding down their "prices" for alliance formation, they can strike deals that limit the effects of technology transfer while locking in long-term, stable market arrangements in Asia. An effective device toward these ends might be an export cartel of U.S. producers, one that could discipline the tendency to provide technology

Table 8–8. Alliances between U.S. and Korean Semiconductor Companies.

Korean Company	U.S. Partner	Semiconductor Project
Goldstar	A.T.&T.	64K dynamic RAM
	LSI Logic	Semicustom chips
	Zilog	8 bit microprocessor
	Texas Instruments	64K dynamic RAM
	Advanced Micro Devices	64K dynamic RAM and 256K dynamic RAM
	Fairchild Camera and Instrument	64K static RAM
Hyundai	International CMOS Technology	1K CMOS EEPROM
	Western Design Center	8 and 16 bit microprocessors
	Texas Instruments	RAM
Samsung	Exel Microelectronics	16K EEPROM
	Micron Technology	64K and 256K dynamic RAM
	Intel	8 bit microcontrollers and microprocessors
	National Semiconductor	Semicustom chips
	Zytrex	CMOS process

Note: The structures of the alliances differ. In some cases, the Korean company is merely producing a part for the American company. In other cases the Korean company is buying technology. In some cases it is both buying the technology and producing the parts for the American company. In others there are joint ventures or equity ownership involved.

Source: Dataquest in *New York Times*, July 15, 1987, p. D-4.

in return for royalties rather than market position, which is explicitly permitted under U.S. antitrust laws.[10]

In the United States, there is an equally compelling need to apply microelectronics in areas that have so far resisted its application, but in which Japan is moving ahead; those areas could become a strong source of secure demand for U.S. merchant producers. For example, the wide range of U.S. manufacturers that have seen their competitive position erode over the last decade, including textile and apparel makers, footwear producers, producers of consumer durables and heavy capital equipment, steelmakers, and automotive component suppliers need to apply microelectronics to their products or processes to remain competitive.

For U.S. producers successfully to take advantage of this nascent market demand, they will need to build new institutional vehicles to reach more diffuse customers and longer term, closer supplier-customer relations. But such changes in structure and business practices are part and parcel of any successful strategy to restore long-term U.S. market position in chips. Longer term, stabler customer relations will be necessary with already established systems firms like the domestic computer producers, whether or not nascent market demand is ever developed and satisfied. In the next chapter we examine what changes are necessary and what is taking place.

NOTES

1. Figures extrapolated from data provided by the SIA, Dataquest, and ICE.
2. *Electronics Weekly,* January 18, 1984.
3. The information on European semiconductor development which follows, but *not* the interpretation of that information given in the text, is drawn from a number of recent studies of European microelectronics. These include Rainald von Gizycki and Ingrid Schubert, *Microelectronics: A Challenge for Europe's Industrial Survival* (Munich and Vienna: R. Oldenbourg Verlag, 1984); Organization for Economic Cooperation and Development, *Trade in High-Technology Products: The Semiconductor Industry* (Paris: OECD, 1984); Giovanni Dosi, "Semiconductors: Europe's Precarious Survival in High Technology," in Geoffrey Shepard et al., eds., *Europe's Industries: Public and Private Strategies for Change* (Ithaca, N.Y.: Cornell University Press, 1983); Rob van Tulder and Eric van Empel, "European Multinationals in the Semiconductor Industry," (IRM, University of Amsterdam, October 1984); and Maurice English, "The European Semiconductor Industry," (EEC Intelligence Unit, Brussels, June 1984).
4. Telecom figure is from A.D. Little. European Telecommunications—Strategic Issues and Opportunities for the Decade Ahead (Brussels: final report to the Commission of the European Economic Communities, November 1983), Annex B and C, at p. 13.
5. See "Chip Battle Grows in Europe," *New York Times,* May 11, 1987, p. 26.

6. It is crucial to note here that current U.S. Defense Department policy restricting the export of dual-use technologies is pushing European firms directly into the very alliances with Japanese producers that they cannot really afford. Given U.S. defense restrictions, European firms cannot be certain that dual-use technologies they need for their final systems products will be available when needed from U.S. producers. They may therefore turn to Japanese sources of dual-use technologies. In the process, U.S. firms are likely to lose critical sales opportunities in Europe. Thus, Defense Department restrictions have the disastrous unintended (and largely unexamined) consequence of simultaneously severely injuring the competitive position of U.S. firms in commercial markets and promoting Japanese gains at the expense of U.S. firms. The outcome is likely to be that defense policy undermines the industrial sectors on which defense capabilities rest.

7. I owe this formulation to BRIE's Steve Cohen; it was developed in materials prepared for the BRIE conference on "Europe in International Competition in Electronics and Telecommunications," April 22, 1985.

8. Based on conversations with U.S. industry sources.

9. Conversations with Korean producers and government officials and U.S. industry sources.

10. See, 15 U.S.C. 62, for the exception for export cartels.

9 STRUCTURE AS CONSTRAINT AND OPPORTUNITY

Were the U.S. industry to fail to secure and defend its dwindling existing positions of market strength, and fail to constrain existing Japanese final market advantages, there would be little hope for its long-term recovery. The strategy outlined in Chapter 8 is therefore necessary, but not sufficient to deal with the triad of strategic problems—market, technology, and structure—facing the U.S. industry and analyzed back in Chapter 1. What is needed is a way to solve the problems of lost technology leadership in processes and manufacturing and of structural change. If they can be solved, the U.S. industry will be in position to attack the overall market problem.

The most exploitable Japanese industry vulnerability is its relative slowness to respond to new market opportunities through innovative new product design. Conversely, new product innovation remains a distinctive U.S. industry strength. How, then, can the terms of international competition be shifted to favor the U.S. strength and exploit the Japanese vulnerability? If U.S. producers could match Japanese prowess in implementation (in processes and manufacturing), they ought to be able to win on invention. The issue is how to create a sustainable, equivalent level of manufacturing and process expertise—a common level of expertise among U.S. firms that matches Japanese prowess and can be sustained over time.

Innovative changes in structure and strategy are the keys to solving this dilemma. The loss of U.S. technological leadership in processes and manufacturing rests on the inability of the U.S. industry to match either the amount or efficiency of Japanese R&D and capital spending while maintaining design and new product leadership. That inability, in turn, stems from competitive vulnerabilities in the industry's structure and strategy, particularly from the industry's fragmentation, attendant lack of sufficient per-firm resources, and consequent willingness to sell design and product technology as a means of meeting shortfalls in resource requirements. If these structural and strategic problems can be solved, then the mechanisms will be in place for solving the technology problem as well.

Solving the technology problem is a precondition for permitting the U.S. industry to continue to capitalize on what its current structure permits U.S. firms to do well in international competition against Japanese producers—develop, commercialize, and diffuse new product innovations. Current weakness in manufacturing and processes prevents this competitive strength from coming to the fore. New product concepts can be replicated rapidly (and even improved upon) by Japanese firms that hold leadership in process technology implementation; once replicated, new products can be produced more cheaply by Japanese firms who also hold leadership in manufacturing. Because they are out-manufactured, U.S. firms cannot hold position in the market as it grows; they thereby fail to capture the returns due them as innovators. Without capturing sufficient returns, they cannot retain leadership in product innovation.

A structure that sacrifices new product innovation and rapid market diffusion for the attainment of parity in processes and manufacturing is no solution at all. That is one very important reason why simple consolidation of the fragmented U.S. industry structure into a few large, vertically integrated electronics giants, similar to the Japanese industry structure, is not an appropriate solution to the competitive difficulties facing the United States.

THE DILEMMAS OF VERTICAL INTEGRATION

Imagine a U.S. economy in which a few large, vertically integrated companies dominate chip production—say, IBM and DEC in computers, AT&T in telecommunications, Hewlett-Packard in instrumentation, GM in automobiles, GE-RCA in consumer electronics, and several defense contractors. These large companies would have the resources to stay at the forefront of semiconductor technology for their specific final product markets. They would have sufficient scale, generated partly by internal demand, to match Japanese production economies. They would also presumably have sufficiently tight ties to final product markets to match the advantages Japanese firms enjoy there. And they would have sufficient muscle in the form of widespread R&D and final market control to keep abreast, through exchanges, of Japanese technological developments in processes and manufacturing. What would be wrong with this image of the future?

The most decisive immediate loss for the U.S. economy would be in both the quantity of new semiconductor product innovations and the speed with which new innovations were diffused to users. As a matter of corporate strategy, our vertically integrated producers would have every incentive to spend to stay at the leading edge of chip development in order both to incorporate innovations into their final products and so as not to be dependent upon Japanese competitors for vital technology. One problem, however, is that our producers would also have enormous incentives to focus their chip development rather narrowly to serve their specific final product needs. With an application-specific focus on computing or automobiles or other final products, there is every likelihood that our vertically integrated world of producers would fail to replicate the synergies available to merchants—whose incentive structure is to serve simultaneously as many of those final product markets as possible (in order to amortize investments over the largest possible customer base). In all likelihood, innovation in general purpose chip technology would suffer. (Indeed, as we have seen, general product innovation is a relative weakness of the integrated Japanese industry structure.)

But even if innovation itself did not suffer, our vertically integrated producers would also face enormous incentives *not* to diffuse that technology to other U.S. users. Diffusing it would eliminate the performance edge in their products, while keeping it proprietary would tend to safeguard their final product advantages. The almost certain result would be a vast diminution in new electronics product development and application throughout the economy. In the world we are imagining, the likelihood is quite small that an Apple (or Singer, or Rolm, or Etak) could have wrested appropriate chip technology from IBM (or GE, or AT&T, or GM) in order to create the personal computer (or electronic sewing machine, PBX, or automobile map navigation system) market as rapidly and decisively as it did. It is just hard to imagine large vertically integrated companies sufficiently interested in spurring the broad application of the chip technologies they develop—except perhaps under their own control and only then very slowly as resources permit— to match the merchants demonstrated record as vehicles of diffusion.

Equally important, it is doubtful whether a few large, vertically integrated U.S. electronics producers would provide sufficient orders for the tooling, materials, and chemicals that go into the chip manufacturing process, to permit the independent U.S. suppliers of tooling and materials to continue in business. A merchant chip industry is almost certainly necessary to provide the tooling suppliers with enough customers successfully to amortize the high development and production costs of their business, while earning sufficient returns to carry on R&D for the next product generation. This is, indeed, one of the key reasons behind the support of IBM, DEC, AT&T, and Hewlett-Packard, among others, for the survival of a merchant U.S. chip industry.[1]

If an independent tooling industry did not survive, our large, vertically integrated firms would have to integrate backward even further, into production of tooling and materials sufficient to eliminate dependency on Japanese suppliers. An IBM could probably accomplish this successfully without sacrificing the spending necessary to maintain its leading position in packaging, architecture, software, and service—four other critical components of its existing competitive advantage. But it is not at all clear that a DEC or Hewlett-Packard could afford such backward integration without sacrificing existing advantages in other areas. Self-evidently, the judgment of IBM and these other firms is that a dollar spent on packaging, architecture, or software is a dollar better spent, in terms of maintaining existing market advantages, than the same dollar spent on backward integration into semiconductor manufacturing equipment and materials. This would seem to be the primary strategic reason behind the support of IBM and other integrated electronics producers for Sematech. Thus, a structure of integrated giants featuring increasing backward integration could do more harm than good to the U.S. position in final product markets.

Even if these were not sufficient disincentives for the United States to adopt a purely vertically integrated structure, there is no guarantee, and much historical experience to the contrary, that large, vertically integrated U.S. producers would remain competitive in chip development and internal application in their final product markets. They would certainly have the resources, scale, final product markets, and muscle to stay abreast of Japanese chip development, but only if they were willing to spend the dollars needed to do so rather than simply ceding the field to Japanese and European competitors, as GE has finally done in consumer electronics. The historical record of large, vertically integrated producers in the merchant world chip market is an ugly one. GE, Westinghouse, RCA, GM, Ford, Burroughs, Sperry, even Siemens, Philips, and Thomson, have generally not managed to keep abreast of the merchants' pace of chip development and sales.

More critically, outside of IBM, DEC, Hewlett-Packard, and perhaps AT&T (the jury is still out), there are not many vertically integrated U.S. producers who have successfully competed against Japanese firms in the final product markets that are their bread and butter. GE, Westinghouse, and RCA, among many others all dropped out of consumer electronics production; Unisys and Honeywell all now resell Japanese mainframe computers; Xerox's domination of the copier market has long since been lost to Canon, Ricoh, and other Japanese producers; even the massive U.S. automakers—the largest and most integrated of all the companies just mentioned—have not stopped the erosion of their market shares to Japan. There are counterexamples to be sure, particularly in chemicals and aluminum, but the failures are sufficiently numerous and persuasive to suggest that something common accounts for them.

In electronics as elsewhere, Japanese firms are vertically integrated, but only in some areas and only to some extent. Just as critical are the vertical quasi-market, quasi-ownership relations with subcontractors and suppliers that permit greater competitive discipline and faster market responsiveness than the traditional vertical integration model. Equally important are the horizontal, familial ties to other suppliers (particularly of capital) and consumers which help to stabilize supply and demand. And, of course, missing in the U.S. context too, are the widespread policies relating to shared generic R&D, capital availability, a stable fiscal and monetary environment, and domestic market protection, among others, which create the structured context within which large Japanese firms can prosper. In short, the structural and policy supports that underlie the networks and relationships through which large Japanese firms learn and prosper, simply cannot be duplicated in any simple way in the United States through vertical integration.

STRUCTURAL OPPORTUNITIES

If vertical integration would tend to sacrifice economywide innovation and diffusion while also tending to fail competitively, what model of a healthy U.S. industry can escape these ills? Remembering that the structure must safeguard U.S. advantages while overcoming weaknesses, structural change must, at a minimum, address four critical needs. First, the structure must preserve as much as possible an independent chip industry with substantial opportunity for new entry, in order to safeguard new product development and diffusion. Second, it must provide a mechanism for greater, focused cooperation in process and manufacturing development so that Japanese efficiency in production R&D can be matched at a lower per-firm cost and parity in technological leadership can be reestablished and sustained.

Third, the structure must facilitate the long-term, stabler relations with chip users (outlined in the last chapter) with suppliers and with other domestic chip firms, in order to provide a secure market base throughout the electronics industry complex on which to rebuild and sustain overall U.S. position. Fourth, and just as critical, the structure must facilitate an industrywide capability to analyze and act strategically and to ensure learning over time—the functional equivalent of an institutional memory. The aim is to ensure that long-term strategic thinking and action can take place in a context of realistic evaluation of evolving competitive strengths and weaknesses.

Preserving Independence

The structure must first safeguard the *possibility* of the survival of a relatively independent merchant chip and tooling industry, if it can be made competitive. The ultimate test of structural reorganization will be the ability to succeed in the market. We cannot know beforehand precisely what structure, if any will succeed in those terms.[2] The best bet, therefore, is to facilitate structural change without attempting to dictate any specific structure beyond the requirement that it create the possibility of the survival of independent chip producers. The industry's proposed cooperative venture, Sematech, is a facilitator of this kind, enabling a variety of industry structures to emerge.

An operative analogue is the German machine tool industry centered in Aachen.[3] Intensely competitive on a world scale, the Aachen builders have managed to retain an independent, small firm structure through a variety of facilitating mechanisms. These include widely shared research and development, training and research ties to the local university system, industrywide planning and cooperative production ventures, and local financial support, all of which are organized through the local trade association. Successfully operated for several decades, these structural facilitators now look like the natural operation of the local marketplace. They were, however, created in part through the intervention of policy and other extramarket forces. Once in place, they successfully preserved, in the face of international competition, a local industry structure that continues to serve efficiently the local, regional, and national economies. In the bargain, the preserved structure diffuses new machine tool technologies more rapidly than alternative industry structures appear to do elsewhere.

The supports that sustain the viability of smaller firms in Aachen can be considered infrastructure to the market economy that operates there. Similar supports to independent smaller firm structures operate enormously successfully in ASEAN countries like Singapore.[4] The export record of smaller Singapore-based firms suggests that structural facilitation need not sacrifice efficiency while successfully preserving the advantages of small size. From the Aachen and Singapore examples, it appears that a wide variety of market infrastructures can support a wide variety of alternative industry structures. In each case, resulting success in the market is the appropriate measure of the ultimate viability of the firms and industries involved.

Because it would simultaneously benefit independents and captives, both small and large, Sematech represents the kind of infrastructural innovation needed to preserve the possibility of the merchant's survival. Sematech, the Semiconductor Manufacturing Technology Initiative, is conceived as an industrywide consortium the aim of which is to strengthen U.S. manufacturing capacities in semiconductors. Membership is drawn from the gamut of U.S. based chip firms and electronics systems captives, that do some domestic U.S. chip manufacturing (the chip service firms that do no manufacturing and systems houses without captive production would not qualify), along with the participation of U.S. chip tooling and materials suppliers through the formal membership of a special chapter of their trade association, the Semiconductor Equipment and Materials Institute (SEMI).

The idea is to pool financial resources and technical and managerial know-how to address the common manufacturing and technical leadership problems that face all firms in the industry. By cooperating in research and the development of generic solutions to common manufacturing problems, Sematech would foster more efficient use of limited resources and create wider dissemination of advanced manufacturing technology throughout the U.S industry. Toward this end, three broad categories of activities are undertaken. The consortium conducts R&D on advanced semiconductor manufacturing techniques contributed by members and by other domestic sources including universities, national laboratories, and the SRC. Test and demonstration of the resulting techniques then occurs in an actual production environment, that is, with an appropriate product on an actual line in a factory that systematically attempts to integrate all manufacturing systems. Once demonstrated, the resulting techniques would be transferred back to member companies and other licensees for refinement and adaptation to their own products. Figures 9–1 to 9–3 show the Sematech concept, operational model, and organization.

If these goals are achieved (we will look at the prospects and details of implementation in a moment), the result would be to provide an infrastructural element to the U.S. industry which is compatible with, but by no means ensures the survival of independent chip and tooling segments. The per-firm costs of staying in the international competitive game as the technological frontier changes would be reduced through cooperative pooling of resources and know-how. Cooperation structured through Sematech would replicate the wide resource and skill base available now only to larger integrated firms like IBM and the Japanese. There would, of course, be no guarantee that the merchants would have the competitive wherewithal to make use of the available technology. Successful use would depend on a range of other variables including overall strategic market orientation, the quality of management and personnel, the innovativeness of design capabilities, and successful integration of the available technology into production, among many others. But by creating a common technology base, the resource and size advantages of Japanese firms would be neutralized as determinants of competitive position in the market. The possibility would be enhanced that nonintegrated, smaller independents might survive—and with them, continued product innovation and technology diffusion for the U.S. economy as a whole.

Raising and Equalizing the Level of Technology

Sematech would move far in the direction of creating a high level of process and manufacturing expertise between U.S. and Japanese firms.

Figure 9–1. Sematech Concept.

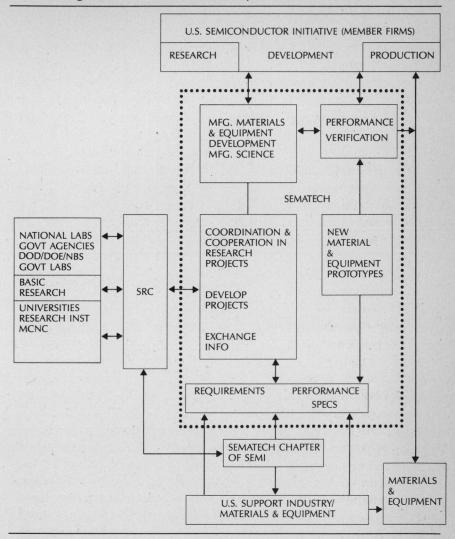

Source: Sematech.

But achieving and sustaining that playing field by matching Japanese producers on implementation involves far more than the creation of Sematech. Sematech is necessary as a vehicle to promote technological catch-up and eventually to sustain state of the art position in process and manufacturing technology. However, achieving equal or superior technology will succeed in creating a level playing field only if U.S. firms successfully adapt Sematech-developed technology into competitive

Figure 9–2. Sematech Operational Model.

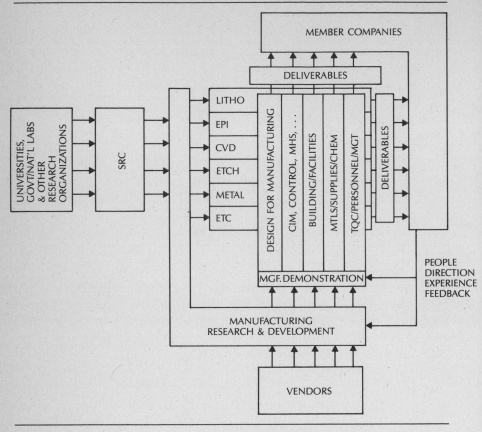

Source: Sematech.

low-cost product manufacturing in their own plants. Equally critical will be the capability and willingness of U.S. firms to invest in new production capacity in an environment of slower growth and more intense competition. These three legs of the level technology strategy—Sematech, firm implementation, and capacity investment—pose real problems.

As a vehicle to promote technology catch-up and development, Sematech's plans involve the development and integration, manufacturing demonstration, and transfer to members, of all of the key unit processes (for example, lithography, deposition, etching) required to meet specific performance goals comprising the current and next two generations of the microelectronics state of the art. Through a strategic planning process, Sematech develops detailed specifications and plans for each

Figure 9–3.   Sematech Organization Overview.

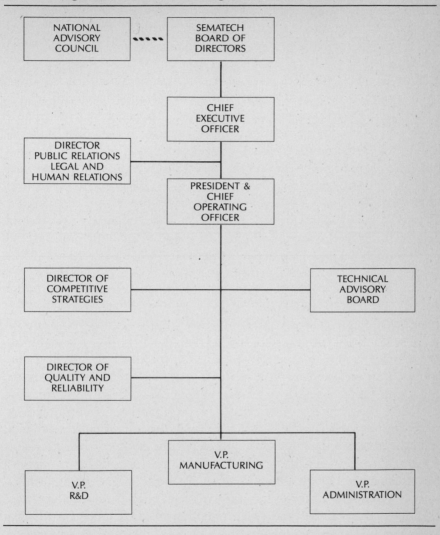

Source: Sematech.

unit process to be developed. Working under open-bid contracts with suppliers that can meet the process specifications, the necessary tooling and materials will be developed, honed, and proven in Sematech's manufacturing proving area, and then integrated and proved in the full manufacturing flow. As each unit process is demonstrated in production, it will be transferred to member companies in the form of equipment/materials/process procurement and operating specifications along with the supporting data that characterizes the operation and control of the equipment or process. In addition, member company engineers will receive hands-on training in the new processes/equipment at Sematech.

Three initial technology development phases are planned for Sematech, corresponding with the process development necessary to achieve the current and next two generation performance specifications. Phase 1, involving the development in 1988 of a Sematech capability of implementing 0.8 micron feature sizes with existing equipment on a product equivalent to a 1 Mbit sRAM, is essentially being used to assimilate employees and to develop a common technology, control, methodology and know-how base on which to build next-generation capabilities. Phase 2, begun concurrently, would attempt to regain parity with Japanese producers by developing a capability of implementing 0.5 micron features on a product equivalent to a 4 Mbit sRAM in a 1990 time frame. Phase 3 will attempt to reestablish U.S. leadership with a capability of doing 0.3–0.35 micron features on products equivalent to 16 Mbit sRAM by 1993.

Critically, a primary goal in all three phases is to develop manufacturing capabilities that are highly flexible. The aim, for manufacturing lines running multiple processes and products, is to achieve yields, production cycle times, and capacity usage levels that are competitive with the more focused factories characteristic of current Japanese practice. If achieved, such technology and manufacturing know-how would support the strategies of captive producers, traditional merchants, and the newer merchants with their explicitly flexible production and market strategies—whether these U.S. firms were focusing on commodity or application specific products. If such flexible processes for achieving the equivalent of three successive product generations can be implemented in the planned seven-year time span, the U.S. industry will have succeeded in repositioning itself at the leading edge of production technology.

While these technological goals are impressive, they will only move U.S. firms part of the way toward matching Japanese producers in implementation. As stressed in earlier chapters, Japanese production advantage is much less a product of better tooling or better technology than of better implementation. Japanese advantage obtains in the ongoing management and operation of production processes, in intimate working relations with suppliers, in highly trained and motivated equipment operators, in superior care, inspection, and cleanliness, in more rigorous control over defect-generating process variability, and in the continuous iterative tinkering that provides slow, but sure improvement. The lesson for American firms is that the greatest gee-whiz technology in the world will not substitute for competence in these areas. To the extent Sematech is viewed by U.S. firms as a technical fix, rather than as providing each firm with an opportunity to concentrate scarce resources into developing the softer factors that underlie Japanese manufacturing superiority, it will become the GM-Saturn plant of the semiconductor industry—a very expensive lesson in futility.

At a bare minimum, each U.S. firm will consequently need to undergo an audit aimed at evaluating and improving the total factor productivity of each of its manufacturing plants.[5] Moreover, such audits ought to be institutionalized on an industrywide basis, with average, best, and worst performance data provided so that firms can judge their relative standing. But the U.S. industry may need to go further. Either under the auspices of Sematech or a different industrywide approach, and probably in conjunction with U.S. government pressure, the industry will need to make a similar audit of Japanese practice. In its joint venture with Toyota in Fremont, California, GM provides an alternative (to Saturn) model to acquire the soft capabilities needed to ensure successful implementation of manufacturing technology.

Therefore, as an additional structural change, the U.S. chip industry (or a smaller coalition of U.S. firms) might consider a similar joint venture approach with one or more of the Japanese majors (or even perhaps with NTT) to acquire soft Japanese know-how. The venture should take the form of a U.S. based, export-only, CMOS memory or logic facility aimed at the domestic Japanese market.[6] An export-only facility would permit the U.S. industry to organize as an export cartel under U.S. antitrust laws so as to coordinate the participation of all willing U.S. firms. By exporting to the Japanese market, it would have a stable demand base underwritten by its Japanese partner. That would also serve to assure that the partner provided sufficient soft know-how to guarantee high-quality components for his own consumption. And in the bargain, U.S. export figures would improve while providing increased penetration of the domestic Japanese market.

Even if U.S. firms solve the implementation problems, they will still face a difficult investment environment. If Japanese firms invest more rapidly, they will simply have greater numbers of superior technical facilities on-line, and more opportunities to experiment to improve processes and manufacturing. Just as critical, given the strategic nature of chips, it is easily foreseeable that not only the Japanese, but also the Europeans, other Asians, and eventually most technically competent countries will be investing in semiconductor production capacity to ensure themselves access to the strategic technology. This implies a continuing problem of surplus capacity in an industry that will continue to grow rapidly. If it occurs, chronic surplus capacity would badly worsen the down-side of the industry's traditional business cycles, while potentially limiting available profitability during upturns. This would make continued investment at a pace that matches Japanese opportunities very difficult for the smaller and medium-sized firms that make up the U.S industry.

Surplus capacity has traditionally been a phenomenon associated with a mature industry suffering stagnating demand, as in steel. Surplus capacity in a growth industry like semiconductors is rather unusual in the world's industrial experience. There are no good blueprints for dealing with such a situation from the perspective of firm and industry strategy. However, certain premises seem reasonable which pave the way for strategy formation. First, the more flexible the available production capacity the more likely that it will be capable of being fully used at any given time. This follows logically from the assumption, based on the industry's actual historical experience, that demand for different product families cycles at different rates. If, at any given moment, demand is likely to be high for some products even when it is low for others, and if production capacity is flexible enough to switch to the products in demand, then it should be possible to maintain high utilization rates even in a situation of surplus capacity. This was, for example, the experience of firms like Cypress Semiconductor, whose production capacity and product offerings were sufficiently flexible to maintain full usage rates during the surplus capacity that obtained industrywide during 1986.

Second, production capacity needs to be highly efficient, with costs squeezed out, and with as low a capacity usage-breakeven point as possible. If a fabrication facility is going to operate at 70 percent of capacity, it needs to be profitable at that point. Third, a firm and industry production portfolio made up of high-margin, proprietary products is more likely to escape the worst consequences of surplus capacity—falling revenues and profits—even if a firm's production capacity is not fully used. This is because proprietary products by definition have fewer competitors producing them (the very reason they are normally also high-margin products), so that existing excess production capacity cannot be easily turned to compete even if it is flexible. The same logic probably applies to a heavy ASIC-orientation, at least, for ASIC design approaches other than gate arrays. The hesitation here lies in the degree to which different ASICs can functionally substitute for each other; it is possible to envision a situation in which, in order to use existing capacity, ASIC companies competitively bid down the prices of functionally fungable chips. Nonetheless, it is more likely that ASIC companies would escape this dilemma than commodity companies.

Fourth, the closer that established, long-term ties are between chipmakers and major users, the more likely that a chip producer can plan capacity investment to coincide with increasing demand, can remain a steady supplier (perhaps at a minimal premium, at least if delivering high quality) as prices get bid down during periods of surplus capacity, and thus can avoid being badly exposed to the business cycle. This will be particularly the case if close ties are to a user base in a broad variety of final markets in several major geographic locations. In that way, production capacity could be shifted among closely affiliated users in different markets and locations as variations in their own business cycles demanded. Fifth, particularly for smaller firms and new entrants, it would seem advisable to share flexible production capacity. Sharing would mitigate the risk of surplus capacity by creating a broader product base that can keep capacity fully utilized. These elements—highly flexible production of a portfolio weighted toward proprietary and ASIC products, with close ties to major users in a variety of final markets and locations, and with production capacity shared when necessary—could provide the basis of an industrywide strategy for handling surplus capacity should it become a chronic problem. The industry that best incorporates those elements into its strategy, is more likely to weather the coming competitive environment. As the premises outlined suggest, the successful industry is likely to be the one that can count on a margin of stability and diminished uncertainty in an environment of increasing volatility characterized by surplus capacity.

Cooperation for Stability and Access

Over the long run, the stability and diminished uncertainty necessary for a healthy investment environment are only likely to be provided by closer, cooperative ties between suppliers, chip producers, and users. Moreover, at least over the near term, only cooperative deals with

Japanese firms have the potential to deliver the increased access to the Japanese market necessary to justify continued rapid investment in chip production capacity (given that Japan is where the market is growing fastest). These four sets of closer, cooperative relationships—with suppliers, users, Japanese firms and other producers—can provide long-term structural solutions to the market and structure problems, which complement the other solutions examined above. They will do so, however, only if those relations are tightly managed and strategically orchestrated to mutual advantage.

Sematech ought to go some distance toward erecting better, more cooperative relations with materials and tooling suppliers. Through development alliances with selected vendors, early availability of industrywide information on process goals and needs, and the development of industry standards for automation, control systems, the interfacing of hardware, and software protocols, Sematech should provide a more coherent business environment within which suppliers can operate. But just as there is no technology fix for solving manufacturing problems, a more coherent business environment does not guarantee that chip producers will develop closer working relations with their suppliers.

U.S. chip producers will need to be as attentive to the needs and talents of their suppliers as Japanese chip firms currently are toward the few remaining U.S. tooling producers that sell successfully in Japan. Much as U.S. automobile producers are now doing with their suppliers, U.S. chip firms will need to develop closer alliances with fewer selected suppliers. They will need to provide greater financial stability by committing to long-term purchases (jointly with other producers if necessary), and perhaps by providing R&D funds. Relationships of trust must be fostered so that chip development fabrication facilities can be opened to suppliers to use in honing and integrating new equipment. Better feedback on existing problems and better responsiveness to mutual concerns will also be necessary. In short, just about everything chip producers want and need from the customers they supply, are parallel desires of their own suppliers toward them. So important is reform of existing practices, that the industry needs to develop model practice guidelines, in the way that a company like Tektronix has done with its vendors. The act of developing such guidelines with suppliers ought to educate both sides to what is needed. Early access to new technologies should be sufficient compensation for the development of closer relations, even where the resulting technology diffuses to competitors, as it must if independent tooling suppliers are to fund their next-generation efforts in the market.

As semiconductor technology migrates in the direction of greater ASIC and proprietary capabilities in order to generate strategic advantage for systems producers, major families of proprietary devices are likely to emerge built around the major systems products from companies like IBM, DEC, Hewlett-Packard, and AT&T. Indeed, in order to develop the broad array of supporting microelectronics necessary to position those dominant electronic systems in their respective market segments, it is likely that the systems firms themselves will foster closer, longer term ties with chip firms. Moreover, user-merchant ties should transcend proprietary chip families and move toward shared development and production of commodity memory chips as well. Given rising costs, staying at the leading edge in memory is too costly for most firms, whether merchant or captive, and thus is a logical opportunity for cooperation. Is is easy to envision shared memory development and production, perhaps by using a common technology base, with the partners alternating between generations of product. IBM's medium-term equity investment in Intel and long-term commitment to the 80X86 family of microprocessors, and its newly minted long-term memory development and supply plans with Texas Instruments, are examples of the kinds of relationships that are possible.[7]

Ties between chip firms themselves have been increasingly important vehicles for defraying rising R&D costs, helping to speed new product development and new technology acquisition, creating a more assured market position through second sourcing, and developing broader product families than one firm could alone. Such ties will continue to be necessary, and are likely to accelerate as the costs rise for developing the gamut of expensive technologies needed to stay in the microelectronics game. The ties between TI and Intel for the development of joint ASIC libraries suggest the degree to which strategic alliances between even traditionally cutthroat competitors will be increasingly necessary and useful. The joint construction and ownership of flexible fabrication facilities or of commodity memory facilities ought to join the list of important alliance strategies among U.S. producers.

In the development of such alliance relations, U.S. second sources ought to be preferred whenever possible for obvious reasons. And U.S. firms will need desperately to avoid acrimonious legal battles of the kind Intel has been waging against AMD. The dispute centers on licensing rights for the 80386 mpu. AMD was a highly successful and apparently innovative second source of the prior 16-bit generation, accruing revenues on sales of the mpu and related chips that Intel would apparently rather have gained for itself, and is undoubtedly determined to gain in the 32-bit generation. Whatever the monetary incentives (and they may be substantial) that particular legal fight is extraordinarily ill-timed. It distracts both companies from the business opportunities that will be the only real guarantee of survival and moves in the opposite direction from the kind of alliance relations that need to be built to ensure some measure of stability for the U.S. industry. It is quite appalling, though not altogether surprising, that two of the strongest advocates of the merchant chip industry's survival should be at each other's throat at the moment of their industry's greatest crisis.

One other category of producer alliance strategies needs careful consideration, and, if no alternatives are possible, requires even more careful implementation. This is the development of ties between U.S. and Asian producers. There are three principle problem areas. These are first, ties between U.S. and Japanese firms aimed at market access in Japan; second, ties between U.S. start-ups with good design capabilities and Asian fabricators of the U.S. designs; and third, ties between U.S. firms and Asian producers of the random access memory chips that almost all U.S. firms have abandoned.

Recent deals between U.S. and Japanese producers aimed at increasing access to the Japanese market are both risky and necessary. Notable among many others are Motorola-Toshiba, AMD-Sony, LSI Logic-Kawasaki Steel, and Harris-Fuji Electric. Before examining what an appropriate access deal might look like, it is worth repeating here the strategic reasons behind the need for increased access to the Japanese market. First, exclusion from Japan has meant the loss of the profit opportunities that finance R&D necessary for development of next-generation products. Exclusion also has meant a loss of opportunities to realize economies of scale that bring down costs and determine competitive position in world markets. These factors are very critical now that Japan is the world's largest market for chips.

Second, Japan is an advanced market, the scene of permanent innovation in chip technology and manufacturing. The only way to stay abreast of technological change in Japan is to be present in the market. But perhaps the most important reason for being in the Japanese market is that the absence of sustained foreign competition there has given Japanese companies a critical advantage in international competition. In chips today, as in steel, autos, and consumer electronics in the past, Japanese success on world markets has rested on the ability of Japanese producers to move rapidly to volume production with limited risk in a domestic market insulated from foreign competition. The strategic game being played by Japanese firms rests on competing everywhere but in Japan; if there is foreign competition at home, the game comes apart.

If it is to be enduring, access in Japan requires several things beyond the obvious one that U.S. firms must sell chips that are tailored to needs in the Japanese market. First, there must be direct access to customers rather than access mediated through a Japanese partner. Only direct access can ensure the opportunity for the U.S. producer to establish the long-term relations essential to success in Japan. Second, the aim must be establishment of direct business acccounts with Japanese customers. Only long-term business accounts provide the reciprocal obligation upon which long-term business relations can be built. Third, the expression of long-term relations must be the development of cooperative, jointly funded R&D between Japanese customers and U.S. firms aimed at developing future chip sales appropriate to the customers needs. Fourth, the U.S. firm will need to operate as a Japanese company, and will need desperately to be able to hire very good Japanese nationals. Fifth, eventually the U.S. firm will need to establish wholly owned manufacturing facilities in the Japanese market to service successfully customers there. Sixth and last, the U.S. firm needs to accomplish all of these things while safeguarding the distinctive technical product advantages that permitted it.a foothold in the first place, and that will almost certainly be required in trade for greater market access.

There are very few cases of enduring access in the chip area that were accomplished wholly without a Japanese partner. Rockwell International, a company with relatively abundant resources through its strong defense business, and early Japanese entry based on a strong chip patent position, has been able to sustain the leading position in modem chips on its own, but it is the exception. The historical record in chips and related areas suggests that a prudent approach is a deal struck between the U.S. firm and powerful Japanese firms without a strong position in the U.S. partner's business. Texas Instrument's original joint venture with Sony, Motorola with Aizu-Toko, Fuji with Xerox and Yokagawa Electric with Hewlett-Packard, were all such deals. The key in all cases was an assiduous defense of the U.S. partner's technology position on the way to meeting the other criteria outlined above.

It is this precise inability to protect the U.S. firm's technology advantage which makes current deals between Asian fabricators and U.S. startups so overwhelmingly troublesome. Over the last four years, at least

38 such deals have been struck.[8] In form and substance, they resemble the very deals struck between U.S. and Japanese firms in the 1960s and early 1970s which positioned Japanese firms to challenge the U.S. industry. Of course, the short-term reasons for the recent spate of agreements must seem compelling to the U.S. firms involved: The U.S. companies get access to state-of-the-art wafer fabrication capacity, they need not expend their own limited funds on manufacturing development, and they get a steady source of cash flow during the early years of their existence. Yet, for all of the reasons argued in earlier chapters, these short-term advantages end up being long-term liabilities. It is hard to imagine more than a few of the U.S. start-ups that have gone this route being either strategically attuned or nimble enough to prevent their Asian partners from eventually displacing them in the market once the partner has absorbed the licensed technology.

The replication of this problem is the Achilles heel of the U.S. industry. Short of government action in this area of technology investment, there appear to be only a few solutions. First, the U.S. industry ought to develop model technology licensing agreements that delineate do's and don'ts based on empirical experience. While this will not prevent such deals from being made, it might eliminate the worst terms. Second, U.S. start-ups ought to prefer European fabrication deals wherever available. Third, shared production facilities ought to be built in the U.S. by start-ups wherever possible. Several start-ups acting in concert may be better able to afford capital investment that none of them could individually. Fourth, to defend their own long-term positions, the larger U.S. merchants and captives, or consortiums among them, ought to invest in building one or more flexible fabrication facilities with a high percentage of the available capacity dedicated for those start-ups judged to have the best technology most in need of protection. Once the start-up is large enough to afford its own facility, the dedicated capacity could service newer entrants or be returned to the owner.

Similar kinds of problems confront those U.S. producers who have exited the RAM market but struck deals with Asian producers to resell Asian RAMs. Foremost among these are Motorola with Toshiba, National with NMB, and Intel with Samsung. For these U.S. firms, it is probably rational over the short term not to reinvest in a RAM market with low or no profits, even when they run the risk of creating new long-term competitors as do both National and Intel. Yet, what is rational from one firm's perspective is clearly problematic from the perspective of the U.S. electronics industry as a whole. If the U.S.

electronics industry wants domestic sources of RAMs, it is going to have to commit to long-term purchase agreements at prices that are profitable for the U.S. chip source.

The only way this will make financial sense is if U.S. systems producers view the long-term purchase commitment as part of a longer term development arrangement. One such arrangement might be that higher RAM prices are exchanged for chip technology, for a commitment to help in the design of the microelectronics for the next systems generation, or for long-term joint RAM development and production. But the very difficulty with which ideas like these are considered suggests the degree to which the U.S. industry badly lacks, but desperately needs, an institution capable of thinking strategically industrywide.

Strategic Industrywide Perspective

Almost a decade ago it was clear that Japanese producers would emerge as enduring players in the semiconductor industry, and would, as a consequence, radically alter the industry's terms of competition. Yet it has taken almost that long for U.S. firms to cooperate sufficiently to begin to devise appropriate responses. It is almost a truism that had the industry been able to coordinate its actions strategically a decade ago, an adequate response would have been far less costly and far more likely to succeed. To accomplish such strategic coordination, the U.S. chip industry needs an ongoing analytic capacity, embedded in an electronics industrywide institution, with the ability to carry on competitive analysis of foreign market and technology strategies, and with sufficient prestige to offer strategic direction on which planning can occur.

There is, of course, a substantial antitrust problem associated with industrywide strategic planning. To assure its health, the industry needs strategic coordination short of market sharing. All U.S. industries facing international competition ought to be permitted to develop industrywide competitive assessment capability, at least whenever the industry can demonstrate substantial involvement of foreign governments in assisting foreign competitors. Actual strategic coordination could be permitted thereafter only with the approval of outside auditors (perhaps the ITC) and with appropriate guarantees of quid pro quos, perhaps in the form of specified levels of future investment in production in the United States.

For the chip industry, the most logical places to embed a competitive assessment capability are in Sematech or SRC, one of the electronics industry associations, or preferably in a standing electronics panel of the National Academy of Sciences. The latter has the advantage of being outside the day-to-day competition in the industry, and thus could well develop a broader, more independent vision of the industry's competitive evolution.

While an industrywide strategic assessment, planning, and coordination institution of the kind envisioned here sounds perhaps too cumbersome and complex, there are analogues in U.S. experience. The most obvious is the strategic assessment capacity of the Department of Agriculture, run as an adjunct to the Agricultural Extension services.

TOWARD THE HIGH-TECH HOLDING COMPANY

Some horizontal consolidation of the kind already taking place in the industry (AMD's merger with Monolithic Memories, National Semiconductor's purchase of Fairchild, Thomson's merger with SGS) will continue to complement cooperative efforts like that of Sematech and others proposed here. Continuing vertical integration is also likely to take place both backward from systems firms and forward from chip makers, as the former attempt to take strategic control of the technology embedded in their systems products, and the latter maneuver to make themselves less vulnerable to slower growth and enhanced cyclicity in chip markets. Yet, for the reasons elaborated earlier, neither horizontal consolidation, vertical integration, nor Sematech by itself, will be sufficient responses. The kinds of structural and strategic changes outlined in this chapter will require additional creativity and cooperation among U.S. firms in the electronics industry complex.

Indeed, to implement the kinds of changes needed it is quite likely that additional new structural forms will come into being. As Alfred Chandler showed in his great works *Strategy and Structure,* and *The Visible Hand,* new forms of corporate organization tend to be created to solve strategic dilemmas that existing corporate structures can not adequately address.[9] In that sense, the U.S. industry's current strategic dilemma in competition with Japan is the need to retain the dynamic advantages of smaller and medium-sized merchant firms and of new entrants while simultaneously addressing both the resource constraints that plague smaller firms and the industrywide needs for greater cooperation examined above. It appears that within U.S. historical experience, the most sensible structure for dealing with that set of issues is some kind of holding company.

Indeed, as chip technology becomes application-specific, both in terms of proprietary standard products and ASICs, and production technology becomes increasingly flexible, it is possible to envision chip-firm holding companies built around common manufacturing facilities. By choosing smaller merchant firms with symmetric, complementary capabilities in terms of process specialization, chip products, and application market niches, it would be possible to construct a holding company that could be a full-line supplier. R&D resources shared among the holding company's chip firms would eliminate the problem of duplication of R&D among smaller companies. The high capital costs of staying in the technology race could be shared among firms in the form of shared flexible fabrication facilities (something suggested earlier in this chapter). Shared facilities would permit high usage of capacity. Distribution economies would also be apparent in the areas of marketing, sales, and service, which could be carried on as common activities of the parent company. The holding company should have greater access to financial resources than any of its constituent companies could alone. The holding company would also be an ideal structure within which to spin out new entrants in emerging technology areas, with the holding company retaining substantial ownership rights as lead investor.

In essence, the holding company structure would gain the advantages associated with consolidation without the disadvantages associated with integration. By permitting each chip firm within the holding company to operate autonomously with respect to nonshared resources, the dynamic advantages associated with the smaller firm environment should be retained. By coordinating efforts in finance, common R&D, common manufacturing, and marketing, the synergy should be substantial. It is also much easier to envisage a holding company of this kind having the kind of substantial and enduring ties with both tooling and materials suppliers and customers, that will be necessary to long-term success in the market. It is also possible to envision a broader high-tech holding company that would include suppliers and one or more significant customers. In the case of both types of holding companies, copying the Japanese model, some percentage of purchasing and resources might be guaranteed the constituents, but they would be required to compete in external markets for at least half their business in order to maintain market discipline.

What is suggested here is the kind of focused conglomerate structure that has been very successful for certain firms in the chemicals and financial services industries.[10] Imperial Chemicals and American Can represent two highly successful such focused, holding-company-like conglomerates. The point would be to avoid the unfocused conglomerate structure that has been so disastrous for so many U.S. companies, while also avoiding the tight vertical integration that lacks market discipline. The advantage is that such a structure is well within U.S. experience, and achievable under current laws, although it has not really been applied before to the microelectronics industry.

However, like the other structural changes suggested in this chapter, our high-tech holding company will be insufficient to resurrect the U.S. chip industry's leadership position without solutions to other problems that only the U.S. government can solve. It is to a consideration of the government's larger necessary roles that we now turn.

NOTES

1. This has been often stated by principals of those companies in various hearings and meetings concerning the proposed Sematech consortium.
2. It is possible that no amount of structural and strategic change would permit the merchants to survive. In that case, as rational a calculation of national costs and benefits as is possible would need to be made, to determine whether permanent subsidy to sustain a merchant industry is in the national interest. Short of permanent subsidy, any structural reorganization that permits the merchants to stand on their own feet is preferable from both an economic and political standpoint.
3. For the Aachen case, see *The Economist,* July 1, 1972, p. 55.
4. Conversation with Ambassador Tommy Koh; See also Peter S. J. Chen, *Singapore: Development Policies and Trends* (Singapore: Oxford University Press, 1983); Linda Lim, "Singapore's Success: the Myth of the Free-Market Economy," *Asian Survey* 6 (1983): 752–764.
5. For the total factor productivity concept, see Kim Clark, Robert Hayes, and Steven C. Wheelwright, *Dynamic Manufacturing* (New York: The Free Press, 1988).
6. Obviously, one of the Japanese majors would need some "coaxing" to participate in such a project. It is possible to envision a variety of U.S.

government bargaining chips that could be used to gain Japanese participation, ranging from general approaches like lifting the restraints on dRAM imports to firm-specific approaches like pardoning Toshiba's sale of militarily critical technology in return for its participation. It is also possible, however, to envision the participation of a firm like Matsushita without political pressure, in return for wider technology access. Finally, to spur its commitments under the U.S.-Japan Agreement on NTT procurement, NTT and some of its affiliated smaller companies would make ideal potential partners.

7.   IBM's original decision to invest in Intel was undoubtedly a way of ensuring the medium-term stability, during a very difficult chip market environment, of a supplier critical to IBM's PC business. It was also almost certainly the least cumbersome way of gaining rapid access to, and influencing the evolution of Intel's microprocessor technology, during a time in which IBM's internal commodity chip resources were directed at reasserting flagging leadership in memory production. By contrast, the recent decisions to dispose of the acquired equity stake, should probably be seen largely as an investment decision (the sales provided over $100 million in profits) rather than as an abandonment of the idea of closer ties to merchant U.S. chip makers in general or to Intel in particular. By the time of the sale, Intel was again profitable and likely to stay that way for the foreseeable future, in no small part because of technical and long-term purchasing ties to Big Blue that survived the sale of IBM's stake.

8.   The deals are recounted in Dataquest, *IC Start-ups 1987*, p. 26.

9.   Alfred Chandler, *Strategy and Structure: Chapters in the History of the Industrial Enterprise* (Cambridge: M.I.T. Press, 1962); and *The Visible Hand: The Managerial Revolution in American Business* (Cambridge: Belknap, 1977).

10.   See the discussion on focused conglomerate structures in Michael E. Porter, "From Competitive Advantage to Corporate Strategy," *Harvard Business Review,* May–June, 1987.

10 THE GOVERNMENT'S ROLE

Military strategists and national policymakers have long recognized a national security justification for government action to secure for the nation an industry or technology critical to wartime success or peacetime deterrence.[1] More recently, economists have begun to recognize that economically strategic industries also exist. These are defined in two ways:[2]

1. Industries characterized by enduring imperfect competition (sustained, for example, by scale economies and entry barriers) in which persistent direct excess returns are earned and can be captured by a nation
2. Industries that earn persistent indirect excess returns by generating "external economies" (or externalities) in the form of technological or efficiency-generating interindustry spillovers to the rest of the economy which can be captured and retained by the nation.

The latter definition is adopted here because, for nations, it is arguably the more important. The national economic gains generated by pervasive external economies are likely to be quite large relative to those generated in a single industry characterized by imperfect competition. Chapter 2 identified three kinds of pervasive externalities associated with microelectronics—linkage impacts, technological spillovers, and systemic transformations—and argued that the United States could not capture their benefits through trade or foreign direct investment. Rather, a leading-edge, domestic-based semiconductor industry is a strategic necessity for the United States if the domestic economy is to capture all of the externalities associated with microelectronics.

Even though microelectronics is a strategic industry for the United States, there might be no good reason to intervene to secure the industry's international competitive status if the industry were capable of successfully adjusting on its own. However, international competition in microelectronics has been shifted to Japanese advantage by Japanese policy and features of the domestic Japanese industry structure.

From the perspective of U.S. firms and of the U.S. industry as a whole, those foreign interventions have all of the attributes of classical market failures. The interventions have collapsed the competitive time frames facing U.S. firms and have required a scale of adjustment whose costs have overwhelmed the short-term market signals by which U.S. firms normally adjust. The overwhelming, rapid decline of the U.S. international position in microelectronics since the mid-1970s is clear testament to market failure: U.S. firms have been unable to accomplish a successful adjustment on their own.

Hence, it is both proper and necessary for the U.S. government to intervene to secure the industry's international competitive position. Obviously, the least-cost intervention is to build on top of the structural and strategic adjustments that the industry can do on its own. U.S. policy must have two components, an outward component that deals with the external effects of Japanese policy and practices, and an internal component that supports the adjustment of the U.S. industry.

THE TRADE POLICY DILEMMA

The trade debate surrounding international competition in microelectronics is typical of the debates that are likely to characterize trade conflicts throughout the remainder of this century. The central focus of trade conflicts has been on reconciling foreign industrial policies aimed at promoting a specific industrial sector, with the international impact of those policies in undermining the relative position of the competing sector in the United States. While the impact of Japanese policies has been felt before in older industrial sectors like steel and automobiles, it has been microelectronics more than any other sector that has framed the international consequences of Japanese domestic policies. This has happened for two reasons. First, semiconductors lie at the heart of an ongoing industrial transformation in which information processing and communications on the one hand, and automation on the other, are changing the character of how and what we produce, how and what we communicate. Consequently, the relative position of the advanced industrial economies will depend on differing national capacities to develop and apply microelectronics in both services and manufacturing. Second, the U.S. semiconductor industry remains a dynamic and innovative national sector, very different in character from the older industrial sectors that succumbed to Japanese competition during the 1970s. When a young, competitive U.S. industry like semiconductors, one that is central to the economy's growth, feels the impact of foreign government policies, the need for a U.S. policy response becomes obvious.

The impact of Japanese industrial "targeting" on the ability of U.S. industries to compete effectively in international markets has become a matter of great concern to U.S. policymakers. In high-technology industries like semiconductors and numerically controlled machine tools, where Japanese companies have captured substantial market share at the expense of U.S. firms, the development of a policy response to targeting is seen as the critical task for U.S. negotiators. However, Japanese government targeting of specific sectors is only a means, one set of policy tools among many, toward the more comprehensive end of *creating comparative advantage* in a range of high-technology sectors in order to ensure continued growth and international market dominance of the Japanese economy, especially in knowledge-intensive industries.[3]

The elements of targeting—establishment of industrywide goals, producer subsidies, cooperative R&D, and control over access to the domestic market in the favored sectors—should be viewed as part of a web of policy instruments that includes, among other tools, industry rationalization and export cartels, tax incentives, user-directed subsidies, learning centers, and leasing arrangements to encourage technology diffusion, and policies directed at lowering the costs of factor inputs to Japanese firms. These policies are typically directed at the competitive development of sectors that are critical because their links to other industries can affect the growth and development of the entire economy. Such strategic sectors, like semiconductors and machine tools, are thus seen as a form of industrial infrastructure, the equivalent of roads and bridges in an earlier era. So viewed, the sectoral development of an industrial infrastructure to sustain economic growth is an appropriate concern of government policy in a capitalist economy. The Japanese aim is not, as an exclusive focus on targeting suggests, to eliminate directly all competition from other nation's sectors, although that may be its effect. It is, rather, to ensure that Japanese producers become the low-cost international competitors in the critical sectors, and also across the range of industries that the critical sectors influence. In short, the aim of Japanese industrial policies is to capture the domestic benefits associated with comparative advantage by creating the domestic infrastructure that delivers lowest cost competitiveness in international markets.

Japan's systematic pursuit of comparative advantage delimits the general trade problem Japan poses for the United States, for Japanese policies have managed to avoid the full integration of Japan into the system of liberal international trade fashioned by the United States after World War II. Specifically, Japan's trade structure is unique among the advanced industrial economies, even among countries like Sweden and Germany that are dependent on the need to import raw materials: Japan tends not to import in sectors in which it exports.[4] Rather than exchanging goods within sectors as the other advanced countries do, Japan's intrasectoral trade with other nations is limited. This is true in sectors as diverse as automobiles, consumer electronics, and machine tools. Japan generally imports only those advanced components it does not yet produce, and then rapidly substitutes domestic production for imports as soon as domestic capacity comes on-line.

If the strategically critical domestic Japanese market continues to be closed to manufacturing imports while Japanese exports flood world markets, then Japan captures the benefits of open international trade without bearing the burden of competition in its own market. The full integration of Japan into international trade should therefore be defined as integration in manufactured goods; and the measure of integration should be a substantial increase in Japan's intrasectoral trade.

Quite apart from the issue of fairness, Japan's markets need to be opened fully to manufactured goods because that is the only way that our system of relatively open trade is likely to be preserved. Japan is the only industrial economy large enough to take some of the pressure off of the U.S. economy by absorbing exports from the rest of the world. As many observers have noted, the U.S. economy is no longer strong enough to be every other nation's sole export target, at least so long as the U.S. continues to carry its defense burden.[5] In that sense, Japan's closed market is every nation's concern. The U.S. absorbs about 70 percent of the manufactured exports of the developing world, Japan only about 8 percent.[6] With an economy roughly two-thirds to three-quarters as large as the U.S. economy, that is obviously a situation that must change.

Japan's unique aggregate trade structure is a product of the conscious form of domestic industrial development pursued by Japan in the past. Since the mid-1970s that formal developmental system has seemingly loosened. Formal trade barriers have been reduced; the growing competitive strength and resources of many Japanese firms have limited the government's ability to play the roles of promoter of development and gatekeeper regulating imports that characterized Japan's period of rapid growth. Nevertheless, Japan's developmental strategy persists in two critical areas. First, clear and explicit policies remain in place for the promotion of Japan's high-technology industries. Second, equally explicit policies exist to manage the problem of global excess capacity in older industries like aluminum and chemicals.

The most recent version of Japan's Structurally Depressed Industry Law permits MITI to organize recession cartels and take other actions to organize domestic markets to avert "disruptive competition" in periods of global excess capacity.[7] Such policies act to insulate Japanese firms from the impact of foreign competition in depressed industries, and preserve the domestic Japanese market for Japanese firms. Similarly, the Law for Provisional Measures for the Promotion of Designated Machine and Information Industries, and MITI's commentary interpreting it, make clear the general contours of Japan's continuing policies to promote high technology.[8] The policies are aimed at removing bottlenecks in the development of the generic technologies that underlie commercial development and production in a given sector. Elements essential to the evolution of commercial capabilities are jointly defined with Japanese industry, and their attainment jointly pursued. With generic capabilities broadly diffused to Japanese firms, strong market competition then focuses on commercial applications and on the engineering of innovative manufacturing systems that deliver low-cost goods. Joint research goals have been implemented and production equipment developed to move to the next technological generation of product and process. Public entities like NTT have undertaken development, diffused technology, and procured high volumes at premium prices thereby underwriting the move of Japanese firms to commercial production. The result of the continuing promotion is to accelerate technology development at the national level, and building on that, to enhance the international competitive position of key Japanese industries compared to the competing sectors of other nations.

The interplay of Japan's continuing interventionist policies of promotion and protection has serious implications for U.S. trade. Three points are critical. First, active promotion of high-technology sectors like semiconductors generates rapid growth and encourages private lenders to channel capital to those favored sectors. Second, continuing gatekeeper policies in areas like licensing, certification, and procurement, and the structure of demand in the key sectors (itself partly induced by past policies) reserve most of the growth of demand in the domestic Japanese market for Japanese firms. Third, recession cartels or other market arrangements provide a potential hedge against periods of drastic overcapacity and permit rapid rebounds from recession. Taken together, these three factors at once encourage excessive investment in production capacity, permit the rapid accrual of production economies in the domestic Japanese market, and lead inevitably to export drives to unload product and capture the market share necessary to justify the initial extreme investment in capacity. In sum, Japanese policy often induces the very problems in trade relations that plague *competitive* U.S. industries.

Briefly stated, Japan's formal developmental system has loosened in many ways, but its focus has also shifted toward those areas where foreign competition threatens the position of Japanese industries—high-technology sectors where Japan wants to create comparative advantage, and depressed sectors facing new foreign competitors and problems of excess capacity.[9] The Japanese economy appears to be open to high-technology foreign manufactured goods in only two areas. First, openness exists partly in sectors like aerospace where Japan still needs advanced technology from abroad; but there the market is controlled, the technology acquired, and imports rapidly displaced. Second, openness primarily exists where Japan has obtained a dominant position in international competition as in consumer electronics—that is, wherever foreign firms are unlikely to penetrate in volume and sustain an enduring presence in the domestic Japanese market. Again, this pattern suggests that Japan wants the benefits but not the burdens of international trade.

Japan's ongoing efforts to create comparative advantage pose a particularly difficult problem for any U.S. policy response under existing U.S. trade law. In general, for relief to be granted under current U.S. trade law, a showing is required that specific foreign exports are being dumped at unfair prices, are *currently* being subsidized by foreign governments, or are currently the product of a cartel organized and administered abroad. In other words, most U.S. trade law operates from a static orientation that focuses on foreign behavior—concurrent with the filing of a complaint—that represents a contemporaneous violation of U.S. law with respect to a specific product. The commercial impact of the Japanese policies that concern us here, however, are normally felt a number of years *after* the promotional programs have been completed. Where such past policies have succeeded in creating *real* competitive advantage for Japanese firms on world markets, Japanese commercial success with specific products is the result of that competitive advantage and no longer the result of ongoing Japanese policies. We have seen this clearly in semiconductors. Such real, existing competitive advantage generally does not trigger a violation under U.S. trade laws. *In short, if Japan is not caught in the act of creating advantage, its subsequent commercial success does not generally give rise to actionable claims in the United States.*

A broad interpretation of Section 301 of the Trade Act of 1974, as amended, provides a possible exception to this dilemma.[10] Section 301 permits the United States to respond to foreign government practices that are unreasonable, unjustifiable, or discriminatory and that burden or restrict U.S. commerce. Presumably, this section could cover present effects of past Japanese policies; but tracing current competitive difficulties to past policies incurs the problem of eliminating intervening variables (like innovations in manufacturing) that are not directly traceable to past policies. Moreover, it is never clear what kinds of *trade* remedies are appropriate to deal with past, foreign industrial policies. In the absence of changes in U.S. trade laws to take account of the present effects of past foreign promotional policies, compensatory domestic U.S. industrial policies aimed at the sector in question are undoubtedly the most appropriate U.S. response.

Partly as a consequence of this dilemma, current U.S. policy, with its emphasis on targeting, addresses the central issue of created comparative advantage primarily in a defensive, piecemeal way. As suggested by the semiconductor story, U.S. policy has been shaped in response to the particular concerns of respective U.S. industries that have been hurt by Japanese competition. Relief has been granted or considered in motorcycles, machine tools, and semiconductors. The need to respond to the immediate problems of producers in specific sectors is clear, but the concomitant fragmentation of U.S. policy prevents both a concise formulation of the overall problem and the development of an overall program to deal with it. The difficulty is that industrial policy is the very means by which Japan structures the growth of its domestic economy. To oppose its industrial policy would amount to declaring that Japan had no right to successfully manage the growth of its own economy. There will be definite limits to Japan's willingness to dismantle a system that has promoted such spectacular economic growth and underwritten the stability of Japanese politics since World War II.[11] Although the United States might have the leverage to accomplish a part of that goal—by selectively closing its market to Japanese producers, for example—the long-run costs of such an accomplishment, both political and economic, might well be catastrophic.

Precisely because the trade conflict in semiconductors is emblematic of the problem of created comparative advantage, and hence of future trade conflicts, the U.S. policy response here will set the tone for efforts to resolve future trade problems. How wisely, coherently, and fairly the United States responds now may very well determine whether future conflicts can be contained or will shatter our relatively open trading system into a set of protected national markets and concomitant neomercantilist conflicts. In that respect, the semiconductor sector is a fortuitous test of U.S. abilities to develop policy, because the problems are solvable and, as this book suggests, the U.S. industry retains a willingness to respond competitively to Japanese encroachments.

Instead of responding defensively in a piecemeal fashion or attacking Japanese industrial policy directly, the United States must develop an aggressive but coherent policy that seeks to preserve international openness while enhancing its own prospects for long-term growth. As mentioned previously, U.S. policy must have two related components, one domestic and one international. The approach throughout is to elaborate policies of general application, with semiconductors providing the appropriate specific examples.

U.S. TRADE AND INVESTMENT POLICY: RESURRECTING AND PROTECTING U.S. AUTONOMY

This section discusses five related policy initiatives: market access, the elimination of dumping, strategic bargaining, reciprocal investment, and technology access.

The goal of open access for foreign producers in electronic systems and component markets in Japan must be the counterpart of Japan's large-scale entry into international markets in electronics. Without open opportunities for all firms to sell in Japan, foreign firms will continue to be at a disadvantage on world markets in competition with Japanese firms. Now that Japan is a potent economic power, its domestic market strategically crucial to technology development and its economy no longer backward, Japan has the responsibility of taking affirmative steps to ameliorate the impact of past policies of exclusion. Japan should now promote the presence of foreign firms that it denied in the past.

To assist Japan in opening its markets, U.S. policy needs substantive targets, a multilateral negotiating posture and a Japanese affirmative action plan to assist foreign firms.

Japan and the United States must specify substantive targets, actual dollar values of agreed categories of goods to be purchased, with Japan meeting the purchasing targets each year. Substantive targets are necessary because the past decade of U.S.-Japan trade negotiations have revealed that anything less will fail to increase access. Japan has shown itself remarkably adept at agreeing to increased market access and failing to deliver on the promise, in part because few Japanese purchasers are willing to acquire the burden of compliance without it being shared. Only if actual numeric targets are specified will the complex political consensus needed to effect change in Japan be able equitably to specify compliance in a way that shares the resulting burden.

The numeric targets ought to be tied to the bilateral trade balance in each product area. A moving ceiling should be placed on the *value* of Japanese product permitted into the U.S. market, and the ceiling should be adjusted according to Japanese compliance with the access targets. Thus, the ceiling could be raised if Japan exceeded its purchasing commitments, or lowered in retaliation if it did not.

While moving rapidly to specify actual purchasing targets in semiconductors and perhaps a few other strategic sectors on a bilateral basis, the United States should seek a longer term solution only on a multilateral basis, perhaps under the auspices of the General Agreement on Tariffs and Trade. As argued earlier, Japan's closed market is everyone's problem, and only if most manufacturing states share in Japan's open market will pressure be removed from the U.S. market. Moreoever, a continuing bilateral approach risks further alienating U.S. allies in Europe and other parts of Asia, something that is not in the best interests of the United States for the reasons specified in Chapter 8.

Equally important, a multilateral approach creates less risk of the kind of conservative backlash in Japan which could lead to intransigence, retaliation and, at the extreme, Japan's pursuit of wholly autonomous foreign economic and security policies. The current unilateral U.S. approach has already created serious opposition to further concessions in Japan, and in the bargain has raised the active level of hostility to the U.S. No unilateral U.S. negotiation is going to be able to avoid these responses. However, a multilateral negotiation should be able to offer sufficient shared concessions to Japan to make Japan's market access concessions politically palatable at home. A more fully open Japanese market is in everyone's long-term interests, including Japan's, and a multilateral setting is likely to be the only way of driving that point home.

A critical focus of any multilateral negotiation, and of a unilateral approach if the multilateral one proves too troublesome over the short term, should be an affirmative action plan whereby the Japanese government promotes the presence of foreign firms in the Japanese market. Recent Japanese legislation to revamp standards and authorization procedures is an important first step toward affirmative action. However, a comprehensive affirmative action plan should have three more critical components.

First, Japanese policy should grant foreign firms access to domestic Japanese bank debt and bond markets, as well as to grants, loans, and guarantees from the Japan Development Bank and other public lenders, on the same terms as capital access is granted Japanese firms. So long as capital is not equally available, foreign firms will be at a disadvantage operating in Japan. Equal access to Japanese capital, however, would give the Japanese financial community a stake in the success of U.S. firms operating in Japan. Such an accelerated internationalization of the perspective of domestic Japanese finance should make Japanese financial interests an important ally in the struggle to open Japan's markets to international competition. Moreover, a policy of equal capital access would have the added benefit of partly ameliorating any cost-of-capital differential if it exists.

Second, Japanese policy should grant equal treatment to foreign and Japanese firms in tax areas like depreciation and credits, in public procurement (as through NTT), in participation in leasing programs like JECC (computers) and JAROL (robots), and in nondefense cooperative research projects. Again, specific substantive targets may need to be set. The rationale for equal treatment in these areas is straightforward: For any foreign firm to operate successfully in Japan, it must be integrated as completely as possible into the market structure of the domestic Japanese economy. Such integration, as firms like IBM have discovered, requires a major investment in resources and time before appreciable gains occur. If foreign firms are treated equally as a matter of government policy, their integration path will be smoothed. Moreover, potential Japanese customers may be more willing to deal with foreign firms when they see that their government is taking affirmative steps to help foreign firms overcome the "outsider" stigma.

Third, Japan should be encouraged to develop a package of incentives for the location and operation of foreign businesses in Japan. That package could be modeled after the incentives that export platforms like Mexico and Taiwan have long granted to foreign companies and that many U.S. states and cities now grant to foreign businesses. Tax holidays, local development grants, and the like, as well as specific solutions to problems peculiar to doing business in Japan, should all be included. For example, perhaps most central, mechanisms to place skilled Japanese workers in foreign firms would be a key piece of the overall package of incentives.

Turning to the dumping issue, as argued, dumping is the result of tendencies in the Japanese system that encourage overbuilding of capacity. The problem with current U.S. approaches to dumping is that they were framed for industries whose product lives were much longer than in high technology. The antidumping laws take too long to implement effectively and they have no real teeth (since the remedy is only to restore a fair market value). By the time the RAM dumping cases were brought and decided, most U.S. producers had long since exited the market. Such a situation is unacceptable for strategically critical industries like semiconductors. Rather than administering a complex price floor of the kind worked out in the U.S.-Japan semiconductor accord—and which drew the ire of lots of U.S. users of memory chips—it is far preferable to discourage dumping at its source, that is, to discourage the overbuilding of capacity. The only way to accomplish that is to punish dumping sharply when it occurs. Something like a complete ban on product sales in the U.S. market for one year, along with sufficient fines to cover the costs to U.S. users of switching suppliers, is necessary.

Of course, no U.S. policy initiatives of the kind suggested here will be effective unless the U.S. bargains for concessions far more strategically than it has in the recent past. There are two points to be made in this connection. First, where possible, the implementation of domestic

U.S. policies that will give an advantage to foreign firms must be bartered for concessions abroad. The best illustration of this first point is the current deregulation of the domestic telecommunications market and its opening to domestic and foreign competition. A competitive domestic telecommunications market is a worthy goal; however, to open the U.S. telecom market to foreign firms, when every major U.S. trading partner in Europe and Asia continues to exercise almost total control over its own domestic market, is simply folly. The United States, for example, could have opened its domestic telecommunications market only to U.S. firms, while reserving the right to admit firms from other nations only as they made comparable openings in their domestic markets for U.S. firms. The quid pro quo for openness here should have been openness abroad.

As a general principle, this type of strategic quid pro quo should animate U.S. policymaking. Similarly, consider the Reagan administration's decision not to take action in the early 1980s on the Houdaille Industries' petition for relief for the U.S. machine-tool sector from subsidization and cartelization of Japanese machine-tool exports to the United States.[12] The decision was taken despite a determination by the interagency executive branch group, which evaluated the petition, that Houdaille Industries had proved that substantial public subsidies were being made to the Japanese industry. There may well have been appropriate reasons not to act on the Houdaille petition, but the Reagan administration nevertheless failed to use the threat of trade sanctions on machine tools to gain concessions from Japan in other areas of trade friction.

The related second point is that in trade negotiations with Japan the United States must attempt to give priority to the needs of some U.S. sectors over others. Heretofore, as suggested earlier, negotiations have been fragmented along the lines of specific demands of U.S. sectors affected by trade, along with the demands of key domestic constituencies like agriculture that will clearly benefit from an opening of the Japanese market. There are undoubtedly potential conflicts between the demands of these various U.S. constituencies and sectors. Negotiating for concessions from Japan on oranges, beef, and tobacco almost certainly makes it more difficult to get concessions in high-technology sectors like semiconductors. Since Japan is already the largest export market for U.S. agriculture, and Japan's political stability is built on protection of rural interests, semiconductors should claim a higher priority in trade negotiations. Strategically critical sectors like microelectronics—sectors that will transform manufacturing and services in the

U.S. economy, but in which the U.S. position is threatened— should rank highest on a priority list for negotiating trade concessions. It is far less costly to negotiate to retain leadership in these sectors, which are critical to the emerging infrastructure of a high-growth domestic economy, than to attempt to restore that leadership once it is lost.

Where such strategic industries and technologies are concerned, the United States ought to adopt a new set of investment policies based on the principle of reciprocity of investment. The principle should be that U.S. technology may be purchased through the foreign acquisition of U.S. firms, only to the extent that U.S. investors have reciprocal opportunities to acquire foreign firms. The United States has acted as a technology source for Japan and many other countries in ways that have prevented the U.S. economy from recouping fully the benefits of the U.S. investment in technology development.

A rough count suggests that Japan acquired several hundred billion dollars worth of U.S. technology at a total cost of only about $9 billion over the past several decades.[13] If the United States is going to continue to provide technological public goods to the rest of the world, it is reasonable to demand equal investment opportunities in countries like Japan that have something to offer and can clearly afford to do so. In Japan's case, where it is virtually impossible for foreign firms to acquire Japanese companies, investment reciprocity would be another spur toward greater integration of the Japanese and world economies.

Quite apart from investment reciprocity, as Japanese companies assume world leadership in a wide range of technological areas, there is an increasingly critical need to ensure that U.S. firms have access to basic research and product and process technologies developed in Japan. U.S. companies must commit the time and resources and must devise strategies needed to take advantage of openings in the Japanese market, to force futher openings, and of course to justify U.S. policy initiatives in this area. Only an enduring U.S. presence in Japan will keep U.S. firms abreast of product, production, and technological developments there.

Although individual companies can barter for such access through technology exchange or similar kinds of agreements, the need remains for a broad diffusion of innovative Japanese developments to U.S. industry—particularly those developments that emerge from the programs of NTT and MITI but are not now available to U.S. firms. Formal government-to-government mechanisms should be arranged to institutionalize a diffusion-and-exchange relationship. Periodic official, government-sponsored trade missions to Japan to examine Japanese manufacturing advances and to evaluate ongoing state-sponsored research programs would be an important first step.

Indeed, in conjunction with such efforts, the United States should consider purchasing innovative Japanese technologies in order to make them available to U.S. firms (an issue to which we shall return below). The rationale for such initiatives is simply that U.S. firms should have access to developments in Japan comparable to the access that Japanese firms have to developments in the United States.

DOMESTIC DEVELOPMENT POLICIES: DEFENSE AND COMMERCIAL NEEDS

Any discussion of domestic development policies needs to start with an acknowledgement that the United States has such policies even though for ideological reasons it rarely admits they exist. As many have observed, U.S. tax policies favor consumption, particularly by homeowners and real estate investors, over production; U.S. agricultural policies are as comprehensive in support of domestic agriculture as any set of industrial policies in the world; and U.S. defense policies function as a subrosa set of domestic development policies at least where militarily vital technologies are concerned.[14] Of these, defense policy is both the most potentially comprehensive and the most alterable (since the U.S. bias toward consumption and homeowning and toward agriculture have strong political support).

Because defense spending is the only politically acceptable means of carrying on domestic development policies in the current U.S. debate, it would behoove the United States to use such policies wisely and systematically. In the past, as argued in earlier chapters, defense spending and defense procurement helped to establish an internationally competitive semiconductor industry. Unfortunately, current defense semiconductor programs like the very high speed integrated circuit program (VHSIC), tend to meet defense needs without helping, and sometimes by hurting, the commercial competitive position of the U.S. industry. [15] Indeed, a BRIE study of the commercial impacts of current defense spending found that as defense needs have been met with ever more esoteric weapons-specific technologies, the civilian impacts have been overwhelmingly negative or neutral rather than positive.[16]

Three simple rules of thumb could avoid these problems and go far toward meshing defense needs with the requirements for competitive civilian industry:

1. Meet all defense technology needs with commercially available technology whenever possible.

2. Adapt commercially available technology for defense needs whenever commercially available technology is inappropriate directly off the shelf.

3. Develop explicitly defense-specific technology *only* when 1 and 2 are unavailable.

That such a strategy is available and appropriate at least in the semiconductor area, is confirmed by the analysis of the Defense Sciences Board (DSB) of the U.S. Department of Defense (DOD). The DSB Report on Semiconductor Dependency explicitly admitted that commercial sources of chip development had outstripped defense capabilities.[17] Despite this admission, the DOD response is no more creative than to develop yet another defense-oriented program. Indeed, the DSB proposed that the Defense Department spend several billion dollars over the next five years, including contract support for Sematech, in an attempt to ensure that leading edge semiconductor process and manufacturing technology remains in America.

Will the DSB's proposed spending spree rescue the commercial competitive position of the U.S. industry? The answer depends on how DOD involvement in Sematech and in the industry's broader R&D efforts is structured.[18] Evidence from current Pentagon programs in support of chip development suggest the potential pitfalls of close DOD involvement. DOD's typical demand is for chips custom tailored to esoteric military specifications like radiation hardening. The military chips are expensive to design, tend to make inefficient use of the chip's available real estate, require many extra and costly processing steps, and often result in manufacturing techniques that are too costly for viable commercial application.

In this context, the central DSB recommendation is to provide Sematech with $200 million worth of yearly contracts for the *development* of selected production processes, equipment, materials and devices, to "satisfy certain DOD needs." The danger is that, with all good intention as the DOD-Sematech relationship evolves, such close DOD sponsorship of specific technology development objectives could distort Sematech's commercial efforts in order to "satisfy" DOD product and process needs. Even if DOD-contracted know-how might be transferable to commercial production, dual-use restrictions might well prevent its commercial sale and use. Would DOD be able to resist the temptation to restrict the diffusion of DOD-funded, Sematech-developed, x-ray lithography equipment capable of economically drawing 64 Mbit dynamic RAMs?

Given relative access to resources, and following the rules of thumb above, it is obvious that the Pentagon has the funds to adapt commercial semiconductor technology for defense uses, while the merchant chip firms do not have the cash to alter esoteric defense technology for commercial purposes. Indeed, as argued, the very logic of the DSB's analysis—increased defense-dependency on *commercially developed* foreign technology—suggests that commercial goals ought to take precedence in any program of industry support. Thus, Sematech should focus on developing commercially viable technologies, the DOD and its contractors on adapting those technologies to defense needs.

An appropriate relationship between DOD and Sematech could be modeled on past successful military procurement support to the industry's early commercial development. It could take the form of a DOD commitment to buy sets of Sematech-developed, next-generation *commercial* production tooling. The tooling sets then would be provided to DOD's contractors to alter for defense purposes.

The DOD purchase order would function as a letter of credit, virtually guaranteeing Sematech's ability to raise private capital for its needs. In turn, the discipline of private capital would serve to orient Sematech toward commercial viability. If Sematech was successful, DOD could eventually pay its purchase order at a typical price premium, thereby providing a subsidy from defense procurement to commercial development and permitting Sematech to pay off its initial private funders. In the bargain, this would permit both the chip makers and tooling producers to match Japanese pricing in the market, since neither would have to allocate development costs to product price.

The quid pro quo for any such government support would have to be widespread diffusion of the resulting technology development to all segments of the U.S. electronics industry—and, of course, a commitment to use the technology by investing in domestic U.S. production facilities. By thus making state-of-the-art production tooling widely available to U.S. merchants, indirect defense support of Sematech would negate Japanese investment advantages. In general, the U.S. government ought to consider this kind of support for any technology or industry considered to be strategic in the sense defined earlier.

COMMERCIAL DEVELOPMENT: MASS MARKETS, INVESTMENT, AND INFRASTRUCTURE

As argued in earlier chapters, the loss of the consumer electronics industry in the United States was a particularly crippling blow to the U.S. chip industry. The loss of consumer electronics removed a large source of demand for chips. Critically, it also affected relative chip production yields since consumer consumption provides Japanese producers with an extra outlet for devices that fall outside of the tight quality tolerances needed in the industrial and computer markets that dominate U.S. consumption of chips. The loss is particularly telling for, as consumer electronics goes digital, consumer requirements are beginning to converge in terms of technological sophistication with industrial and computer markets in areas like optoelectronics. Since the volumes required in production for mass consumer market demand will bring down costs much more rapidly than for the lower volume computer and industrial markets, convergence threatens the overall U.S. market position so long as the Japanese industry dominates consumer electronics markets.

Consequently, the U.S. government must seriously consider the idea of helping to resurrect a consumer electronics industry in the United States. With the exit of GE from the field, it is apparent that the costs of resurrecting a competitive market position in consumer electronics have overwhelmed private market participants. U.S. government procurement could, however, be used as a lever to help create new entry in the industry. One model for policy could look as follows.

An NAS panel would identify appropriate next-generation consumer electronics device categories, chosen for their convergence with computer, telecom, and industrial technologies, which the U.S. government requires in large quantities (for example, compact disc ROMs for the Library of Congress and for all government researchers). The government could then invite bids from specified consortiums of firms, each made up of a large systems house with a record of commercial success, coupled with one or more merchant chip firms and several new entrants in specific technology areas like flat panel displays. A competitive development process would specify price/performance targets that matched anticipated best practice of foreign consumer electronics producers in each major consumer device category chosen.[19] Procurement contracts could then be awarded to those consortiums that met the price/performance criteria. Thereafter, it would be up to the consortiums to take the technologies developed into the commercial marketplace.

In the absence of a resurrected consumer industry, or in conjunction with it, there are more modest commercial development policies that the U.S. government needs to undertake. The new competitive and cooperative strategies of U.S. semiconductor producers examined in the previous two chapters have an opportunity for success in the market only if U.S. firms can make greater capital investments in R&D and new manufacturing systems. The Japanese are in part counting on the semiconductor industry's increasingly heavy capital investment burden to eliminate the dynamic competitiveness of the merchant sector of the U.S. industry.

The industry's increasing capital intensity suggests that U.S. leadership in semiconductors and the diverse, dynamic structure of the U.S. industry can be preserved only if mechanisms are developed to make capital more available and cheaper for investment in R&D, and especially in competitive production systems and related capacity expansion. As a matter of policy, variations in capital availability and cost between the United States and Japan, variations that stem from differences in respective national financial structures and capital markets, should not be permitted to determine the outcome of market competition in semiconductors or similar strategic industries. Neither the international division of labor in this industry nor the structure of the U.S. segment should depend on national differences in finance. The stakes, in terms of long-term economic growth, are simply too high.

The merchant U.S. semiconductor companies represent a category of small and medium-sized high-technology firms that until recently have not been confronted by the well-financed competitive efforts of larger Japanese firms. The distinctive features of such U.S. firms are their extraordinarily high expenditures on R&D, and the innovativeness and consequent international competitiveness those expenditures have generated. Merchant U.S. semiconductor firms typically spend 8–15 percent of their total revenues on R&D, which is well above the all-manufacturing average. As these firms confront heavy Japanese investment in manufacturing and rapidly rising capital equipment costs, they need to make competitive expenditures in order to survive. Indeed, merchant U.S. semiconductor firms now typically spend between 15 and 20 percent of their revenues on plant and facilities. The heart of the policy problem, then, is how to channel additional capital to such R&D-intensive

industries for competitive investment in the expansion of manufacturing without forcing them to cut back on R&D expenditures (where their competitive advantage in international competition lies). One way to accomplish this is to resurrect an investment tax credit aimed at investment in domestic U.S. manufacturing, which is triggered by a high percentage of total firm revenues actually spent on R&D. Thus, firms that spend, say, 8 percent of revenues on R&D would be able to take a special tax credit for investment in manufacturing. The credit could be set at the percentage of firm expenditures actually devoted to expansion of manufacturing capacity or could be incremental, based on the average of manufacturing expenditures over the prior two years, to take account of surges in capital-intensity (or to take account of the need to respond to surges in the spending of foreign competitors). In any case, the credit should only be permitted for capital expenditures made in the United States, so that expansion occurs here rather than at offshore export platforms. Since major increases in manufacturing employment in the United States over the last decade have mostly occurred in the high-technology sectors of the economy that concern us here, credits of the kind proposed are likely to have a positive impact on employment in the United States as well.

Also worthy of some attention is a countercyclical investment tax approach. Given the Japanese efforts to spend their way into leadership in components, and the inability of U.S. firms to match those expenditures during downturns in the market, there is an additional role for U.S. policy to play in leveling that situation. This would involve countercyclical policies designed to assist U.S. firms through the next downturns. These policies should be experimental, that is, of limited duration so that they do not turn into enduring subsidy, and aimed at generating sufficient internal funds to sustain both R&D and capital spending during downturns. One example would be a tax credit for use during upturns aimed at generating an investment reserve for spending in the United States during downturns (measured, for example, by industry capacity utilization or book-to-bill ratios). Such an investment reserve would permit U.S. industry to match Japanese spending, and position them to ride the next upturn in their business cycle.

Over the longer term, domestic development policies aimed at strengthening the high-technology industrial infrastructure of the United States must be developed. Indeed, the idea of resurrecting a consumer electronics industry in the United States can be understood in this way as an attempt to strengthen the infrastructure. For a strategic sector like semiconductors, where technological advance strengthens all other industrial sectors that incorporate electronics, policies aimed at sustaining and supplementing innovation and diffusion will have a broad impact throughout the U.S. economy.

But, the problem is not simply one of lifting constraints on the expansion of U.S. semiconductor (or other strategic high-technology) producers through investment in technology development. Though such policies are necessary, they address only the production aspect of building industrial infrastructure. Policies that speed the diffusion of new technological innovations into everyday use are also of central importance. Industries that rapidly incorporate advances in semiconductor technology or that incorporate resulting downstream product and process innovations (in office or factory automation, for example) will themselves be strengthened in international competition. Innovation and its adoption must be encouraged, in the end, throughout the entire economy if it is to prosper and grow in the face of foreign government policies aimed at creating comparative advantage.

In the nineteenth century, the U.S. government ensured the construction of the railroads and thoroughfares needed to create a nationwide market economy. That infrastructure and the continental economy built on it provided the stimulus for innovations in management and manufacturing that enabled several generations of US industry to dominate global markets. Industrial infrastructure in the modern world is not, however, only roads and bridges. Funding of science education, the organization of financial systems, and the development of local and national communications networks are all crucial parts of modern industrial infrastructure that owe their genesis as much to government market-promotion policies as to market activity. Similarly, encouraging the application of microelectronics to the workplace, in order to spur electronics innovation on one side, and revitalize basic manufacturing on the other, should be viewed as a basic task of building industrial infrastructure for the U.S. economy's competitive growth in the 1990s and beyond.

The deregulation of AT&T and its concommitant privatization of Bell Laboratories has left an enormous gap in publicly available applied R&D in electronics in the United States. So long as it operated under the 1956 consent decree, Bell Labs was a national applied research and development laboratory, a national infrastructural resource of enormous dimensions. As Chapter 4 described, U.S. preeminence in high-technology industries—including semiconductors, lasers, and computers—was built in large measure on the base of research and personnel coming out of Bell Labs.

The loss of Bell Labs' role in encouraging open and dynamic competition argues for the establishment of a national applied R&D facility in electronics to replace it. Existing national military laboratories, with their focus on weapons R&D and clientele relations with a few large defense contractors, cannot substitute for an explicitly commercial national facility. As we have seen, the pace of product and process innovation coming out of Japan's NTT also argues for a comparable U.S. facility, for it augurs a gap in long-term commercial electronics development between Japan and the United States. A national applied R&D laboratory would be a basic infrastructural element bridging the gap between basic research at U.S. universities and commercial product and process development in U.S. industries, a relationship now maintained through ad hoc contractual relations between universities and firms, which carry with them potential conflicts between the respective missions of the two institutions.

Such a facility could simultaneously help to bridge the gap between foreign innovations in basic manufacturing and their refinement and adaptation to U.S. industrial production. Indeed, such a facility would be the logical place to house manufacturing innovations and other technology developed abroad and purchased by the U.S. government to ensure diffusion to U.S. firms. Such a facility would also be the logical agent to track government technology development support to strategic industries like microelectronics, to the extent state involvement is, as with Sematech, deemed to be in the public interest. The competitive market dynamics in U.S. sectors like semiconductors are such that if technological support was made cheaply available to U.S. firms, it would spur even greater competition rather than becoming a subsidy creating U.S. firm dependence on the government.

Beyond such an ambitious program, the most fundamental enhancement of the high-technology infrastructure in the United States involves education and manpower training. These issues have been broadly addressed elsewhere.[20] Federally funded training programs to develop and broadly disseminate the special skills, like IC mask design, that are necessary to diffuse microelectronics throughout U.S. industry and services, would be a crucial assist to comparative U.S. strengths in innovation and diffusion. An alternative model is the creation of an industrial equivalent to the Agricultural Extension Service, an industrial extension, to rapidly acquaint manufacturing and service sectors with the virtues of applying microelectronics.[21]

The policies suggested here are merely indicative. Indeed, they have direct analogues at the level of state policy, and many of them, like the extension idea, are more properly the reserve of state and local government. There is no a priori precise balance between state, local, and federal initiative; striking the balance is properly the subject of public debate. What is not debatable is the need for such policies: The costs and uncertainties of domestic adjustment to a microelectronics- and information-based economy overwhelm market signals and necessitate political intervention. Anything less will sacrifice a proper public role in the complex economic transformations confronting us and leave our collective fate to the few large economic institutions capable of managing the transition on their own.

NOTES

1. Rather than *industry or technology,* it is probably more accurate to use the term *technological production capability.* Technology itself has little value to either defense or the economy unless it is embodied in producable form, while any individual industry comprises a wide variety of capabilities, only some of which may be strategic.

2. See the discussion in Paul Krugman, "Strategic Sectors and International Competition," paper prepared for the conference "U.S. Trade Policies in a Changing World Economy," Institute of Public Policy Studies, University of Michigan, Ann Arbor, revised June 1985. For a more fully elaborated account of why certain industries may matter to national economic development more than others, see Giovanni Dosi, "Some Notes on Patterns of Production, Industrial Organization and International Competitiveness," paper for meeting on "Production Reorganization and Skills," BRIE, University of California, Berkeley, September 10–12, 1987.

3. The argument on "created comparative advantage" is developed in John Zysman and Laura Tyson, eds., *American Industry in International Competition* (Ithaca, N.Y.: Cornell University Press, 1983), and in Michael Borrus, Laura Tyson, and John Zysman, "Creating Advantage: How Governments Shape Trade in High Technology," BRIE Working Paper 3, 1984.

4. Michael Borrus, Stephen Cohen, Laura Tyson, and John Zysman, "The Lyrics Change but the Malady Lingers on: A Comment on Saxonhouse's 'Foreign Sales to Japan,' " BRIE publication, 1984.

5. See, for example, the discussion in Paul Kennedy, "The (Relative) Decline of America," *The Atlantic Monthly,* August 1987.

6. Henry R. Nau, "Bargaining Barriers: The United States, the NICs, and the Uruguay Round," in John Yochelson, ed., *Keeping Pace: U.S. Policies and Global Economic Change* (Cambridge, Mass.: Ballinger, forthcoming).

7.   See *The Japan Economic Journal* (February 7, 1984), p. 1.

8.   Japan Public Law no. 84, 1978; MITI Machine and Information Bureau, Trade and Industry Research Group, Commentary on Public Law 84, 1979.

9.   Chalmers Johnson, Laura Tyson, and John Zysman, *Politics and Productivity: The Real Story of Why Japan Works* (Cambridge, Mass.: Ballinger, forthcoming.)

10. Section 301 (19 U.S.C. 241), as amended by the Trade Agreement of 1979.

11. Charles Maier, "The Politics of Productivity," in Peter Katzenstein, ed., *Between Power and Plenty: Foreign Economic Policies of Advanced Industrialized States* (Madison: University of Wisconsin Press, 1978).

12. See the legal brief entitled: Houdaille Industries, Inc., Petitioner: 31 July 1982, "Petition to the President of the United States Through the Office of the United States Trade Representative for the Exercise of Presidential Discretion Authorized by Section 103 of the Revenue Act of 1971," 26 U.S.C. sect. 48(a)(7)(D).

13. Regis McKenna, Michael Borrus, Stephen Cohen, "Industrial Policy and International Competition in High Technology: Part I—Blocking Capital Formation," *California Management Review 26,* no. 2 (Winter 1984).

14. Robert B. Reich, "The Rise of Technonationalism," *The Atlantic Monthly,* May 1987.

15. Leslie Brueckner with Michael Borrus, "Assessing the Impact of the VHSIC (Very High Speed Integrated Circuit) Program" BRIE Working Paper 5, 1984.

16. Jay Stowsky, "Beating Our Plowshares into Double-Edged Swords: The Impact of Pentagon Policies on the Commercialization of Advanced Technologies" BRIE Working Paper 17, 1987.

17. Defense Science Board, "Report of the Task Force on Defense Semiconductor Dependency," Office of the Undersecretary of Defense for Acquisition, Washington, D.C., February 1987.

18. This part of the analysis is drawn from Michael Borrus and Jay Stowsky, "The Pentagon's Scenario to Bolster Chip Makers," *San Jose Mercury,* March 8, 1987.

19. Under NATO auspices it would also be appropriate to invite European participation and reserve a specified portion of procurement for European product so long as it met the required price/performance targets.

20. Barbara Baran, "Technological Innovation and Deregulation: The Transformation of the Labor Process in the Insurance Industry," BRIE Working Paper 9, 1985; Shoshonna Zuboff, *In the Age of the Smart Machine,* (New York: Basic Books, forthcoming).

21. Stephen Cohen and John Zysman, *Manufacturing Matters: The Myth of the Post-Industrial Economy* (New York: Basic Books, 1987).

INDEX

ABOUT THE AUTHOR

Michael Borrus is the deputy director of the Berkeley Roundtable on the International Economy (BRIE) and an adjunct lecturer in the School of Business Administration at the University of California, Berkeley. A member of the California State Bar, Borrus received his J.D. with honors at Harvard Law School. He has served as a consultant to the U.S. Congress' Office of Technology Assessment, the President's Commission on Industrial Competitiveness, the U.S.–Japan Trade Advisory Commission, the U.S. Trade Representative, and the State of California. His major publications include "From Public Access to Private Connections: Network Policy and National Advantage" (with François Bar), "Japan's Industrial Policy and Its Pattern of Trade," "Industrial Development Policy in Japan," and "Telecommunications Development in Comparative Perspective: The New Telecommunications in Europe, Japan and the U.S."